THE ATLAS OF CENTRAL AMERICA AND THE CARIBBEAN

Acknowledgement

The Diagram Group wishes to thank the following for their invaluable assistance in the preparation of this book.

Organizations and Institutions

American Petroleum Institute, Washington D.C.
City Business Library, London
College of Arms, London
The Daily Telegraph, London
Department of Commerce, U.S. Virgin Islands
Department of Trade and Industry, London
Economist Intelligence Unit , London
The Economist, London
Export Times, London
The Foreign and Commonwealth Office, London
Government of Puerco Rico, U.S. (Economic Development
    Administration), West Germany
The Guardian (London and Manchester)
Guildhall Library, London
Inter-American Development Bank, Washington D.C.
International Monetary Fund , Washington D.C.
International Planned Parenthood Federation, London
International Union for Conservation of Nature and Natural
    Resources, England

Kings College Library, London
Lloyds Bank PLC, London
London School of Economics Library, London
National Meteorological Library, England
Office of Population Census and Surveys, London
Panama Canal Commission, Washington D.C.
Population Reference Bureau Inc., Washington D.C.
Stockholm International Peace Research Institute, Stockholm
St. Pancras Library, London
The Times, London
UNESCO, London
United Nations Department of International, Economic and
    Social Affairs, New York
United Nations Food and Agriculture Organization, Rome
University of London Institute of Commonwealth Studies,
    London
University of London Institute of Latin American Studies, London
U.S. Bureau of the Census, Washington D.C.
World Bank, Washington D.C.

Embassies, Consulates and Tourist Boards

Antigua and Barbuda Tourist Board, London
Bahamas Tourist Office, London
Barbados High Commission, London
Belize High Commission, London
Bermuda Government Office, London
Cayman Islands High Commission, London
Costa Rican Embassy, London
Cuban Embassy, London
Dutch Consulate General, London
Embassy of the Dominican Republic, London
Embassy of El Salvador, London
Embassy of Nicaragua, London
Embassy of Panama, London
Embassy of the Republic of Haiti, London
Embassy of the United States of America, London
French Consulate General, London
French Embassy Press Office, London

French Tourist Office, London
Grenada High Commission, London
Haiti High Commission, London
High Commission for the Bahamas, London
High Commission for Commonwealth of Dominica , London
High Commission for Eastern Caribbean States, London
Honduras Embassy, London
Jamaican High Commission, London
Panama Consulate, London
Republic of Honduras Consulate General, London
Royal Netherlands Embassy, London
St. Kitts-Nevis Tourist Board, London
St. Lucia Tourist Board, London
Trinidad and Tobago High Commission, London
Turks & Caicos Islands Tourist Board, London
U.S. Virgin Islands Department of Tourism, London
Windward Islands Embassy, London

Annual publications

A Yearbook of the Commonwealth (1984)
Caribbean and Central American Handbook (1983)
The Caribbean Handbook (1984/5)
E.I.U. Quarterly Economic Review (+ Supplements) (1984/5)
Europa Yearbook (1985)
F.A.O. Statistical Review (1983)
The Geographical Digest (1985)
Hints for Exporters (1983-4, 1984-5, 1985-6)
I.M.F. Directory of Trade Statistics (1984)
Inter-American Development Bank Annual Reports (1984/5)
IUCN Directory of Neotropical Protected Areas (1982)
Latin America and Caribbean Review (1984)
Lloyds Bank Special Economic Report (1984/5)
The Military Balance (1984/5)

The South American Handbook (1984)
Statesman's Yearbook (1984/5)
Statistical Yearbook for Latin America (1983)
Statistical Abstract of Latin America (1984)
Statistical Abstract of the United States (1984)
Trade Statistics (Latin America) (1984)
U.N. Economic Survey (1982)
U.N. Statistics Yearbook (1981)
U.N. Yearbook of International Trade Statistics (1980)
UNESCO Statistical Yearbook (1984)
Whitakers Almanac (1985)
The World Almanac and Book of Facts 1985 (1984)
The World in Figures (1982)
World Population Data Sheet (1985)

Encyclopaedias and general reference

An Encyclopedia of World History (1972)
Atlas for the Eastern Caribbean (1983)
Atlas of the Living Resources of the Sea (1972)
Cambridge Encyclopedia of Latin America and the Caribbean
    (1985)
Caribbean Secondary School Atlas (1984)
Chambers Encyclopaedia (1973)

Encyclopaedia Britannica (1979)
International Petroleum Encyclopedia (1984)
Philips' Certificate Atlas for the Caribbean (1984)
The State of the World Atlas (1981)
The New State of the World Atlas (1984)
The War Atlas (1983)
The World Bank Atlas (1985)

General interest publications

Berlitz Travel Guides/Editions Berlitz (1985/6): Bahamas, Puerto
    Rico, Virgin Islands, French West Indies, Southern
    Caribbean, Jamaica
Caribbean Lands (1984)
Middle America – Its Lands and Peoples (1976)

The Caribbean, Bermuda and the Bahamas 1982/83 (1981)
The West Indies (1981)

(See Further Reading List on pages 138–141 for more extensive
coverage of general interest publications)

THE ATLAS OF CENTRAL AMERICA AND THE CARIBBEAN

THE DIAGRAM GROUP

MACMILLAN PUBLISHING COMPANY

NEW YORK

Collier Macmillan Publishers

London

The Diagram Group

Editorial director	David Lambert
Editor	Denis Kennedy
Editorial staff	Kathy Rubinstein, David Harding
Research staff	Huw Richards, Claudia Shrimplin, Reet Nelis, Payne Webber, Len Scott, Paul Melly, Ann Varley, Bill Dinning
Design director	Richard Czapnik
Design staff	Richard Hummerstone, Paula Preston, Alastair Burnside, Brian Hewson, Joe Bonello, Philip Patenall, Pavel Kostal
Bibliographer	Linda Vertrees, Head of Acquisitions Division, Chicago Public Library
Cartography	Arka, George Philip & Son Limited

Published by Professional Books Division,
Macmillan Publishing Co., Inc.,
866 Third Avenue, New York, N.Y. 10022

Library of Congress Cataloging – in – Publication Data

Diagram Group.
    The Atlas of Central America and the Caribbean

    Bibliography: p.
    Includes index.
        1. Central America -- Maps.   2. Caribbean Area -- Maps.
1. Title.
G1550. D5 1985   912'. 728   85-675595
ISBN 0-02-908020-7

Foreword

The Atlas of Central America and the Caribbean integrates maps, charts, diagrams, tables, and text to provide a unique, up-to-date reference guide to two-thirds of all Western Hemisphere countries. Many of these 30 or so nations and colonies are small and poor, but some provide valuable commodities, or financial services, or lie close to the U.S. and to major world trade routes; thus their strategic importance can be far more than their mere size or income would suggest.

Part One (Regional Profile) summarizes the natural background – land structure, seas, climate, vegetation, and wildlife – and concludes by tracing the area's prehistory and history from 12,000 years ago to the present day.

Part Two (Central America) covers North America from Guatemala through Panama: the continent's "land bridge" between North and South America. First, overview pages of integrated text, maps, diagrams, and tables cover the Central American background. Then come the profiles of individual countries arranged in geographical order, from north to south. Each profile starts with a brief introduction followed by text on salient features under subheads on history, land, people, and so on; we include up-to-date facts and figures on population, communications and transportation, and the economy. Places named in the text appear on a relief map that highlights towns, transportation systems, and features such as tourist centers and national parks. Other integral items are a panel of basic national data, a list of historical events, and a diagrammatic economic review.

Part Three (The Caribbean) embraces all islands with a Caribbean Sea frontage plus the Bahamas, Barbados, and Bermuda. We use "Caribbean" in an extended sense as a collective term of convenience. Geographers strictly define "Caribbean" lands as those facing the Caribbean Sea. Some would apply the term "West Indies" to all but Bermuda; but others restrict "West Indies" to non-Latin countries.

Many of the area's two dozen or so islands are tiny, so we give most emphasis to the larger units, especially those of particular interest to U.S. readers. Like Part Two, this part of the book starts with an overview of the region's islands and peoples, including sections on their political and financial problems and prospects. Profiles of islands follow, again arranged broadly in geographical order from north to south and west to east.

Throughout the atlas, reference is made to GNP and GDP. GNP (Gross National Product) is the amount of total domestic and foreign output claimed by the residents of a country; GDP (Gross Domestic Product) is the total final output of a country, comprising all the goods produced and services rendered within its territory by residents and non-residents alike.

There are also copious references to territories and boundaries in the text, for which the Diagram Group does not wish to imply any judgement on their relative legal status. Similarly, we accept in good faith the statistics from international sources which we have used in compiling our economic diagrams.

This atlas includes a list of the extensive sources consulted, and concludes with a detailed guide to further reading, and an index.

Contents

PART ONE
REGIONAL PROFILE

Insula hyspana

Illustration from the
first edition in 1493 of
Columbus' letter reporting
his discoveries.

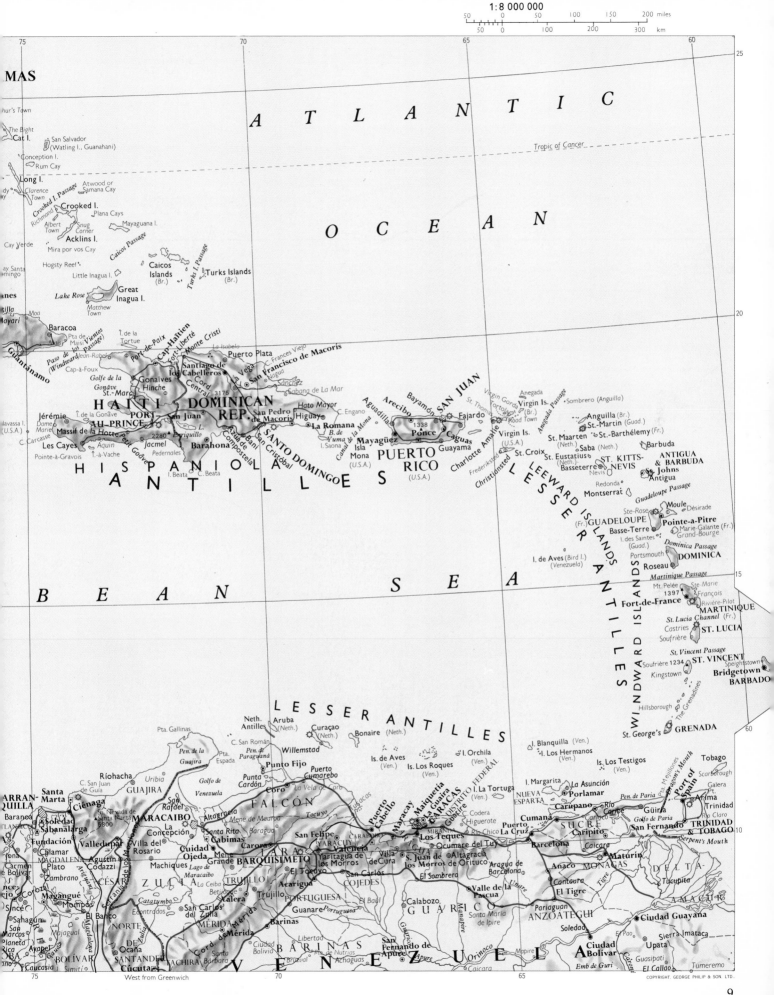

1:8 000 000

50   0   50   100   150   200 miles
50   0   100   200   300 km

25

A T L A N T I C

Arthur's Town
The Bight
Cat I.
San Salvador
(Watling I., Guanahani)
Conception I.
Rum Cay

O C E A N

Tropic of Cancer

Long I.
Clarence Town
Atwood or Samana Cay
Crooked I. Passage
Richmond
Crooked I.
Albert Town
Snug Corner
Plana Cays
Acklins I.
Mayaguana I.
Cay Verde
Mira por vos Cay
Caicos Passage
Hogsty Reef
Little Inagua I.
Caicos Islands (Br.)
Turks I. Passage
Turks Islands (Br.)

20

Lake Rose
Great Inagua I.
Matthew Town

Moa
Baracoa
Pta. de Maisí
Mayarí
î. de la Tortue
Paso de los Vientos
(Windward Passage)
Port-de-Paix
Jean-Rabel
Cap-Haïtien
Fort-Liberté
Monte Cristi
La Isabela
Puerto Plata
Cap-à-Foux
La Vega
San Francisco de Macorís
Nagua
Sánchez
Sabana de La Mar

Guantánamo
Jean-Rabel
Santiago de los Cabelleros
Cord. Central
3175
HAITI
Gonaïves
Hinche
St.-Marc
Golfe de la Gonâve
î. de la Gonâve
Jérémie
Dame Marie
PORT-AU-PRINCE
San Juan
DOMINICAN REP.
San Pedro de Macorís
Higüey
C. Engano
Hato Mayor
Aguadilla
Arecibo
Bayamón
SAN JUAN
Virgin Gorda
Anegada
Sombrero (Anguilla)
Virgin Is.
St. Thomas
Road Town
Anguilla (Br.)
St.-Martin (Guad.)

Havassa I. (U.S.A.)
Les Cayes
Massif de la Hotte
2280
Aquin
Jacmel
Petit Goâve
L.
Enriquillo
Azua
Baní
San Cristóbal
Compostela
Barahona
SANTO DOMINGO
B. de Yuma
La Romana
I. Saona
Canal de la Mona
Isla Mona (U.S.A.)
Mayagüez
Ponce
1338
Caguas
Guayama
PUERTO RICO (U.S.A.)
Fajardo
Charlotte Amalie
St. Croix
Christiansted
Frederiksted
Saba (Neth.)
St. Eustatius (Neth.)
St. Maarten (Neth.)
Basseterre
Nevis
ST. KITTS-NEVIS
St.-Barthélemy (Fr.)
Barbuda
ANTIGUA & BARBUDA
St. Johns
Antigua

Pointe-à-Gravois
î.-à-Vache
I. Beata
C. Beata

H I S P A N I O L A

A N T I L L E S

Redonda
Montserrat

Guadeloupe Passage
Ste-Rose
Moule
Désirade
GUADELOUPE (Fr.)
Basse-Terre
Pointe-à-Pitre
Marie-Galante (Fr.)
Grand-Bourg
I. des Saintes (Guad.)
Dominica Passage
Portsmouth
DOMINICA
Roseau

15

C A R I B B E A N   S E A

I. de Aves (Bird I.) (Venezuela)

Martinique Passage
Mt. Pelée
1397
Ste-Marie
François
Rivière-Pilot
Fort-de-France
MARTINIQUE (Fr.)
St. Lucia Channel
Castries
Soufrière
ST. LUCIA

St. Vincent Passage
Soufrière 1234
ST. VINCENT
Speightstown
Kingstown
Bridgetown
BARBADOS

L E S S E R   A N T I L L E S

Hillsborough
The Grenadines

60

St. George's
GRENADA

Pta. Gallinas
Neth. Antilles
Aruba (Neth.)
Curaçao (Neth.)
Bonaire (Neth.)

Tobago
Scarborough
Galera Pt.

I. Blanquilla (Ven.)
I. Los Hermanos (Ven.)
Is. Los Testigos (Ven.)

C. San Román
Pen. de la Guajira
Pta. Espada
Pen. de Paraguaná
Willemstad
Punto Fijo
Is. de Aves (Ven.)
Is. Los Roques (Ven.)
I. Orchila (Ven.)
I. La Tortuga (Ven.)
I. Margarita
La Asunción
Porlamar
NUEVA ESPARTA
Carúpano
Río Caribe
Güiria
Arima
Trinidad
Port of Spain

Ríohacha
Uribia
GUAJIRA
C. San Juan de Guía
Golfo de Venezuela
Punta Cardón
Coro
La Vela de Coro
Puerto Cabello
Maiquetía
La Guaira
CARACAS
DISTRITO FEDERAL
Higuerote
Puerto La Cruz
Cumaná
SUCRE
Carúpano
Caripito
Golfo de Paria
San Fernando
TRINIDAD & TOBAGO
Serpent's Mouth

10

BARRAN-QUILLA
Baranoa
Soledad
Sabanalarga
Santa Marta
Ciénaga
Sa. Nevada de Santa Marta
5800
San Rafael
La Concepción
Altagracia
Mene de Maura
MARACAIBO
Tocuyo
FALCÓN
Maracay
Los Teques
Ocumare del Tuy
Barcelona
ANZOATEGUI
MONAGAS
Maturín
DELTA-AMACURO
Tucupita

Fundación
Clamar
Carmen de Bolívar
Agustín Codazzi
Valledupar
Villa del Rosario
Cuidad Ojeda
Cabimas
Grande
BARQUISIMETO
Yaritagua
Valencia
Villa de Cura
S. Juan de los Morros
El Sombrero
Valle de la Pascua
El Tigre
Anaco
Contaura
Ciudad Guayana
Sierra Imataca
El Pao
Soledad

Plato
Zambrano
CÉSAR
ZULIA
Machiques
Lago de Maracaibo
La Ceiba
TRUJILLO
Acarigua
COJEDES
San Carlos
GUÁRICO
Calabozo
Santa María de Ipire
Upata
Ciudad Bolívar
Guasipati

Mompós
El Banco
Betijoque
Trujillo
Valera
PORTUGUESA
Guanare
El Baúl
Manapire
BOLÍVAR

Magangué
MAGDALENA
Mayoyal
Sahagún
Ayapel
Simití
El Banco
NORTE DE SANTANDER
Ocaña
Cúcuta
ACHIRA
San Cristóbal
MÉRIDA
Mérida
Cord. Mérida
Ciudad Bolivia
Barinas
BARINAS
Libertad
San Fernando de Apure
APURE
Achaguas
Achaguas
Brazuál
Orinoco
Caicara
Emb. de Guri
El Callao
Tumeremo

VENEZUELA

Caucasia
Simití

Structure of the Region

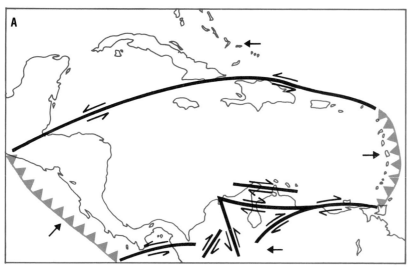

Much of mountainous Central America and the West Indies was thrust up by pressures exerted as slabs of the Earth's crust collided. The chunks involved were the Caribbean Plate flooring the Caribbean Sea, a plate bearing the Americas, and Pacific Ocean plates. Mountains were forced up around the Caribbean rim where Pacific and American plates slid over the Caribbean Plate or dived beneath it.

Geologically complex, Central America includes a mountain core of old rocks with younger intruded volcanic rocks. More than 250 volcanoes form a row that runs down much of the Pacific rim.

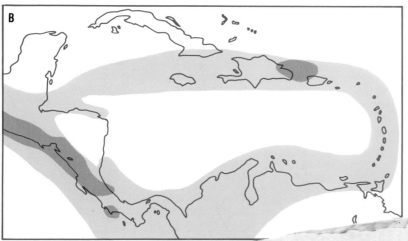

A Major plate movements
To the east and west of the Caribbean Plate are subduction zones where the neighboring plates plunge beneath it. In the north and south, conflicting lateral movement results in fault zones.

Fault zone

Subduction zone

Direction of plate movement

B Earthquake zones Because of friction between the many tectonic plate edges in the region, seismic activity is common. One of the most recent serious earthquakes struck Guatemala in 1976; more than 20,000 people were killed.

General earthquake zone

Frequent strong earthquakes

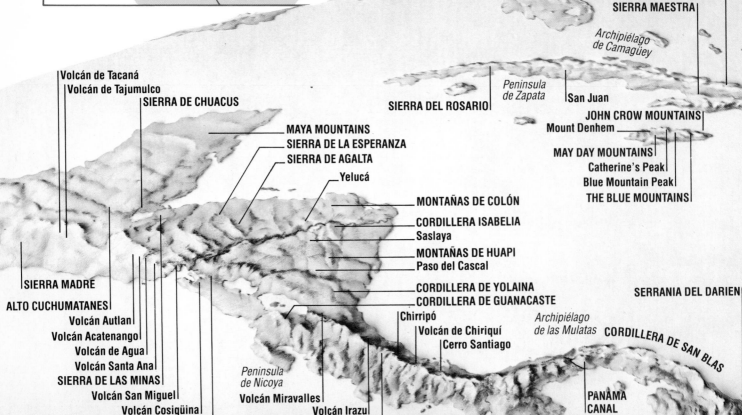

Extensions of three Central American lines of mountains crop up to form parts of the Greater Antilles, the larger West Indian islands. The Lesser Antilles to their southeast comprise an inner arc of rugged volcanic islands flanked on the northeast by an outer arc of low limestone islands crowning old drowned volcanoes. Islands off Venezuela form part of the Andes. In the Atlantic, the limy rocks of Bermuda and the Bahamas cap subsurface structures.

C Geology Continuing geological instability and consequent mountain building have resulted in a complex rock structure and numerous volcanoes. The most destructive known eruption was in 1902, when gas and lava from Mt. Pelée on Martinique killed the 30,000 inhabitants of the town of St. Pierre within seconds.

D Landform regions The varied geology is reflected in the variety of relief and landscape.

Below **Global view** of Central America and the Caribbean, showing main mountain ranges and peaks.

- Cenozoic (recent) rocks
- Mesozoic-Cenozoic rocks
- Mesozoic rocks
- Paleozoic rocks
- ▲ Volcano active since 1500 AD
- Rugged mountain ranges, hills and escarpments
- Low plains, rolling hills and intermontane basins

©DIAGRAM

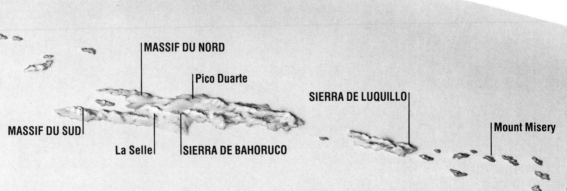

MASSIF DU NORD

Pico Duarte

SIERRA DE LUQUILLO

MASSIF DU SUD

Mount Misery

La Selle

SIERRA DE BAHORUCO

Morne Diablotin

Montagne Pelée

Gimie

Soufrière

Mount St Catherine

Mount Aripo

Part One: Regional Profile
The Sea

The Pacific Ocean lies south and west of Central America. The open Atlantic lies east and north of the West Indies. Between the West Indies and Central and South America is a vast arm of the Atlantic: the Caribbean.

Occupying some 1,050,000 square miles (2,720,000 sq.km.), the Caribbean is the world's second-largest sea – about twice the size of Alaska. It extends 1700 miles (2735km.) from west to east, and 500–800 miles (805–1287km.) from north to south. The sea floor comprises deep basins and trenches separated by submarine ridges and platforms – some bearing islands fringed by coral reefs. Average depth is 8000 feet (2400m.), but the deepest point is 25,216 feet (7686m.), in the Cayman Trench south of Cuba. This trench – a fault in the Earth's crust – continues east to become the Puerto Rico Trench, the deepest place in the Atlantic.

Trade winds push warm surface currents from the Atlantic west then north through the Caribbean. This water flows out through the Yucatán Channel to the Gulf of Mexico.

Caribbean fish and shellfish account for 2.5 per cent of the world's total catch.

A Selection of typical marine life of the Caribbean
1 Shrimp
2 Jackknife fish
3 Angel fish
4 Atlantic manta
5 Flying fish
B Bathymetry The ocean floor reflects the region's tectonic structure, deep trenches marking the edge of the Caribbean Plate.
C Major currents All the seas and oceans in the region are affected by warm currents from the equator.
D Marine life resources Crustaceans and fish that are in great demand for export abound in the shallow, warm water of the Caribbean, and fishing is an important industry for most countries.

Ocean bed features

	0–2,000 meters
	2,000–4,000
	4,000+

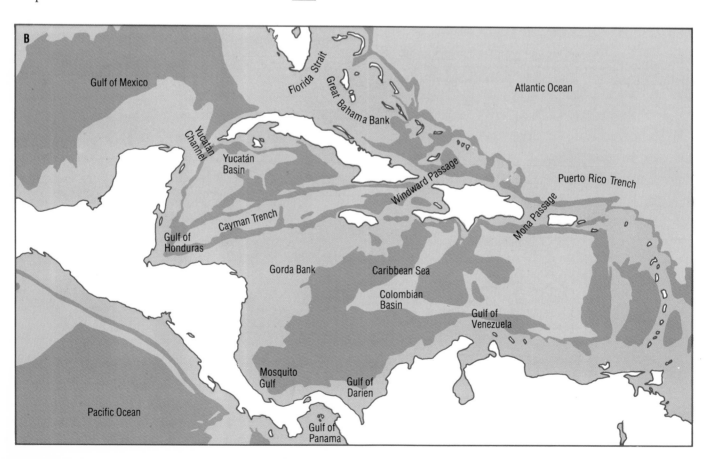

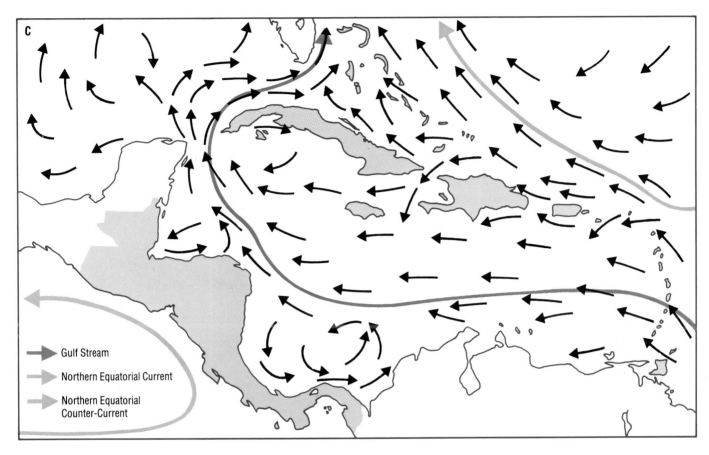

C

Gulf Stream

Northern Equatorial Current

Northern Equatorial
Counter-Current

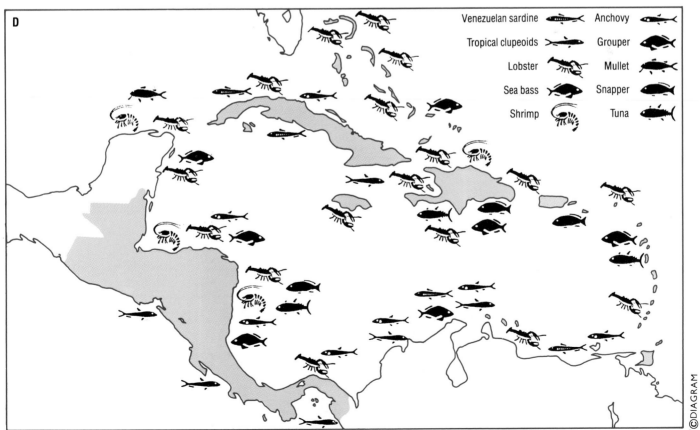

D

Venezuelan sardine		Anchovy	
Tropical clupeoids		Grouper	
Lobster		Mullet	
Sea bass		Snapper	
Shrimp		Tuna	

©DIAGRAM

Climate

Most of the region lies in the tropics, but latitude is only one factor locally affecting climate. Others include altitude and exposure to rainbearing winds.

Temperature Lowland areas are always warm. Temperature averages 80°C (27°C) on the islands and seldom falls below 75°C (24°C) even in January and February, the coolest months. But temperature drops as altitude increases – an effect most marked on the mainland. This has hot lowlands (*tierra caliente*); temperate uplands (*tierra templada*) at 2500–6000 feet (760–1830m); and "cold" highlands (*tierra fría*) prone to night frosts in the coolest months.

Rainfall Most rain falls between June and October, when the equatorial low pressure belt moves north. Rain is heavy on slopes facing rainbearing winds from the Atlantic. Pacific-facing slopes are mostly drier.

Winds The Northeast Trades predominate over the Caribbean, moderating temperature. Between July and October hurricanes bring fierce winds and rainstorms. They track west through the Lesser Antilles, then head north across the larger islands.

Climate

- Tropical wet climate: high temperatures all year, high rainfall, high humidity, no pronounced dry season
- Tropical wet and dry climate: similar to tropical wet climate, but with 4–6 month long dry season
- Tropical highland climate: mountainous areas, warm and temperate but with at least one month in the year with average temperature of less than 65°F. (18°C.), seasonal rainfall
- Semi-arid climate: areas in rain shadow of mountains, hot summers, mild winters, rainfall irregular and unreliable

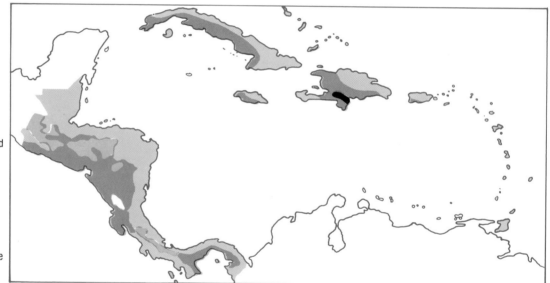

Temperature

- **Tierra caliente**
  Day 85–90°F. (29–32°C.)
  Night 70–75°F. (21–24°C.)
  No frosts
- **Tierra templada**
  Day 75–80°F. (24–27°C.)
  Night 60–70°F. (15–21°C.)
  Occasional frosts
- **Tierra fría**
  Day 75–80°F. (24–27°C.)
  Night 50–55°F. (10–13°C.)
  Frosts common
- —— Average annual temperature
- - - - Difference between average temperatures of coldest and hottest months

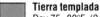

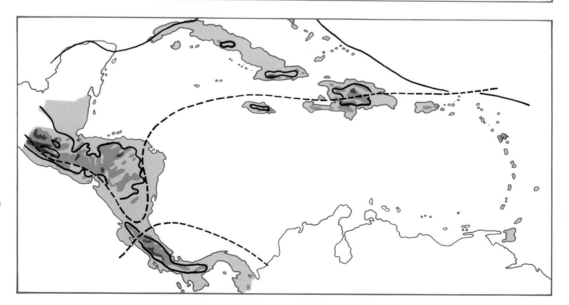

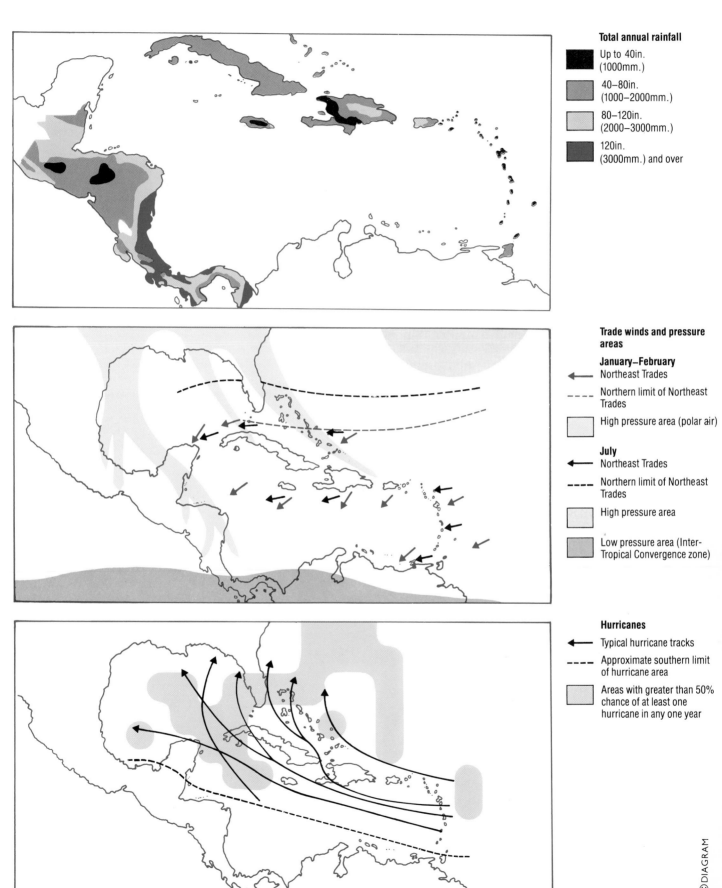

Total annual rainfall

Up to 40in.
(1000mm.)

40–80in.
(1000–2000mm.)

80–120in.
(2000–3000mm.)

120in.
(3000mm.) and over

Trade winds and pressure areas

January–February

Northeast Trades

Northern limit of Northeast Trades

High pressure area (polar air)

July

Northeast Trades

Northern limit of Northeast Trades

High pressure area

Low pressure area (Inter-Tropical Convergence zone)

Hurricanes

Typical hurricane tracks

Approximate southern limit of hurricane area

Areas with greater than 50% chance of at least one hurricane in any one year

©DIAGRAM

15

The Living World

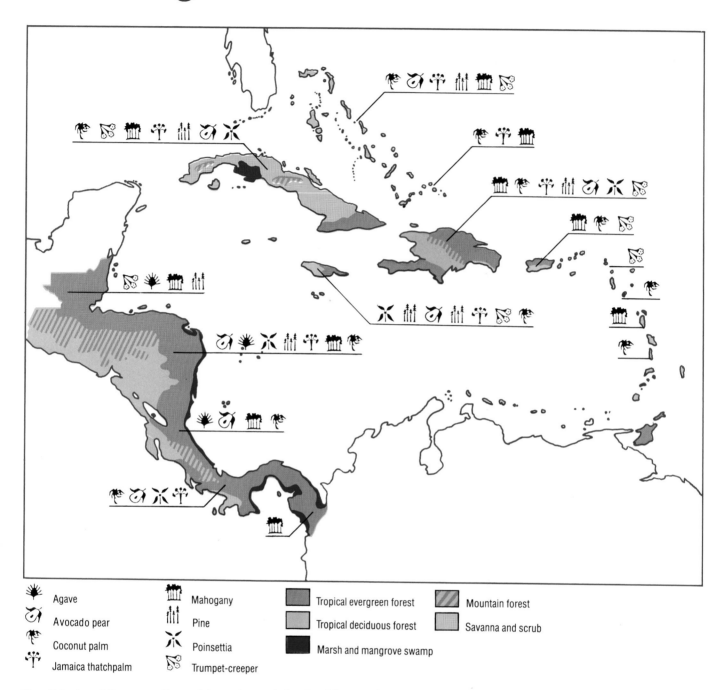

🌵	Agave	🌴	Mahogany
🍐	Avocado pear	🌿	Pine
🌴	Coconut palm	✳	Poinsettia
🌴	Jamaica thatchpalm	🌺	Trumpet-creeper

▓ Tropical evergreen forest	▨ Mountain forest
▒ Tropical deciduous forest	░ Savanna and scrub
■ Marsh and mangrove swamp	

Above Natural vegetation
The map shows the chief distribution of five major types of vegetation, but does not include isolated patches and overlaps that contribute to the five main vegetation zones referred to in the text. Symbols depict characteristic plants.

Central America and the Caribbean islands have an immensely rich variety of plants: types vary locally with rainfall, altitude, soil, and other factors. But natural plant cover has been much modified by man, and in many places, deforested soils have lost fertility and suffered from severe erosion.

Central America has five main vegetation zones. Lush tropical evergreen forest thrives in the hot, wet, Caribbean lowlands: mahogany, balsa, rosewood, and scores of other broadleaf hardwoods soar high above a lower layer formed of palms, tree ferns and

other plants. A ribbon of mangrove swamp rims much of the low Caribbean coast. The drier Pacific lowlands have evergreen and deciduous tropical forest interspersed with grass and shrubs. Cooler, higher areas inland support mixed forests of pines and evergreen and deciduous oaks, giving way to higher still needleleaf forests and grassy slopes. Scrub and cactus cover some of the driest upland areas, especially in Guatemala.

Caribbean islands have lost most of their old forest cover. Savanna predominates in Cuba, evergreen scrub in most small islands.

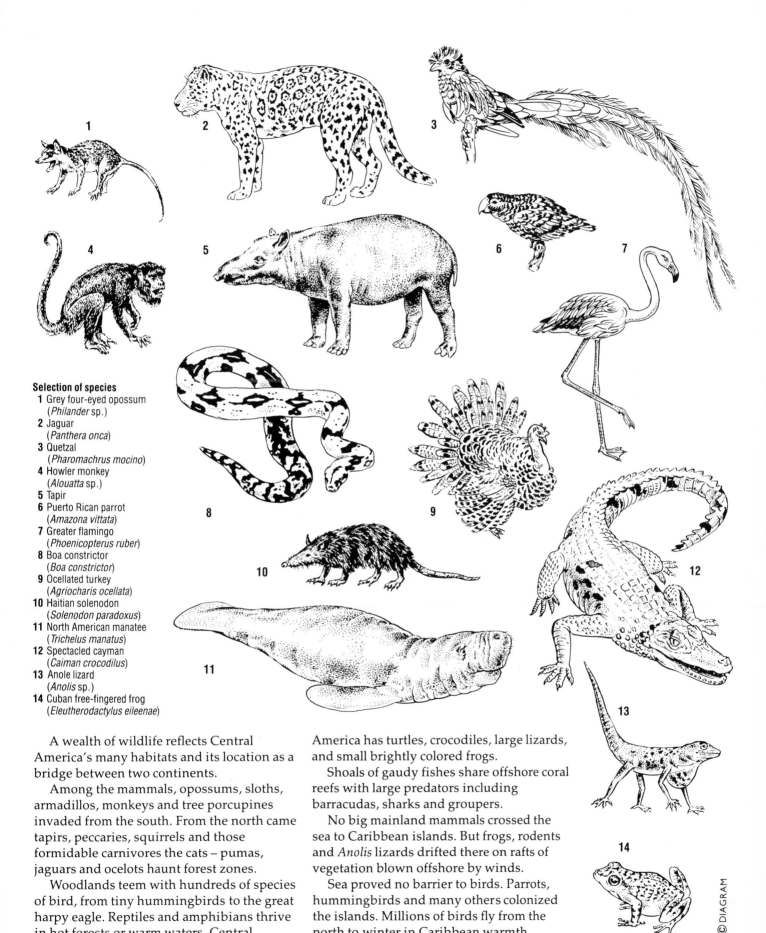

Selection of species
1 Grey four-eyed opossum
(*Philander* sp.)
2 Jaguar
(*Panthera onca*)
3 Quetzal
(*Pharomachrus mocino*)
4 Howler monkey
(*Alouatta* sp.)
5 Tapir
6 Puerto Rican parrot
(*Amazona vittata*)
7 Greater flamingo
(*Phoenicopterus ruber*)
8 Boa constrictor
(*Boa constrictor*)
9 Ocellated turkey
(*Agriocharis ocellata*)
10 Haitian solenodon
(*Solenodon paradoxus*)
11 North American manatee
(*Trichelus manatus*)
12 Spectacled cayman
(*Caiman crocodilus*)
13 Anole lizard
(*Anolis* sp.)
14 Cuban free-fingered frog
(*Eleutherodactylus eileenae*)

A wealth of wildlife reflects Central America's many habitats and its location as a bridge between two continents.

Among the mammals, opossums, sloths, armadillos, monkeys and tree porcupines invaded from the south. From the north came tapirs, peccaries, squirrels and those formidable carnivores the cats – pumas, jaguars and ocelots haunt forest zones.

Woodlands teem with hundreds of species of bird, from tiny hummingbirds to the great harpy eagle. Reptiles and amphibians thrive in hot forests or warm waters. Central America has turtles, crocodiles, large lizards, and small brightly colored frogs.

Shoals of gaudy fishes share offshore coral reefs with large predators including barracudas, sharks and groupers.

No big mainland mammals crossed the sea to Caribbean islands. But frogs, rodents and *Anolis* lizards drifted there on rafts of vegetation blown offshore by winds.

Sea proved no barrier to birds. Parrots, hummingbirds and many others colonized the islands. Millions of birds fly from the north to winter in Caribbean warmth.

© DIAGRAM

Early Times

Between 10,000 B.C. and A.D. 1500 the region supported a rich variety of Stone Age cultures.

Paleo-Indian hunter-gatherers arrived in Central America from the north over 12,000 years ago. By 1500 B.C. Indians in Guatemala were growing corn and building villages. As a bridge between North and South America, Central America learnt much from the high civilizations of Mexico and Peru. Culture reached a peak between A.D. 300 and 900 as Maya Indians built great ceremonial centers in the lowland forests of Guatemala, Belize, and Honduras. They raised stone temple-pyramids, developed hieroglyphic writing and a calendar, worshiped ancestors and gods, and practiced human sacrifice. But soil exhaustion forced the Maya to desert old centers by A.D. 900. Nahua-speaking Indians developed later cultures in the southern highlands, and by trade and war, Mexico's Nahua-speaking Aztec Empire made its presence felt south to Costa Rica in the 15th and early 16th centuries.

Peaceful, farming Arawak Indians peopled the Caribbean islands. But by A.D. 1500 they had lost the eastern islands to invading warlike Carib Indians.

Spanish discovery began in the late 1400s. In four voyages, Christopher Columbus criss-crossed the Caribbean. His discoveries included the Bahamas, Cuba, and Hispaniola (1492); Dominica, Puerto Rico, and Jamaica (1493); Trinidad (1498), and the coast from Honduras south to Panama (1502). By 1513 Vasco Núñez de Balboa had crossed Panama to the Pacific.

Settlement and conquest followed. In the 1520s Spanish conquistadores struck east from Mexico to Guatemala, Honduras, and El Salvador. Others moved northwest from Panama as far as Nicaragua.

By the mid 1520s newly founded Spanish cities stood in Cuba, Hispaniola, Puerto Rico, Guatemala, Panama, and elsewhere. From such centers, Spanish colonists and rule extended through the region. War, disease, and slavery were now swiftly wiping out the Caribbean island Indians. So Spain imported slaves from Africa as labor for the islands' farms and mines. Meanwhile, the Spanish monarchy set up a system of provincial government to run its sprawling New World empire.

Above Pre-Columbian artefacts of different cultures
1 Maya figure of the maize god, from Copan in Honduras.
2 Arawak carving of a spirit, from the West Indies.
3 Jaguar-shaped grindstone, from Costa Rica.
4 Copper-gold alloy pendant featuring a bat and condor, from Panama.

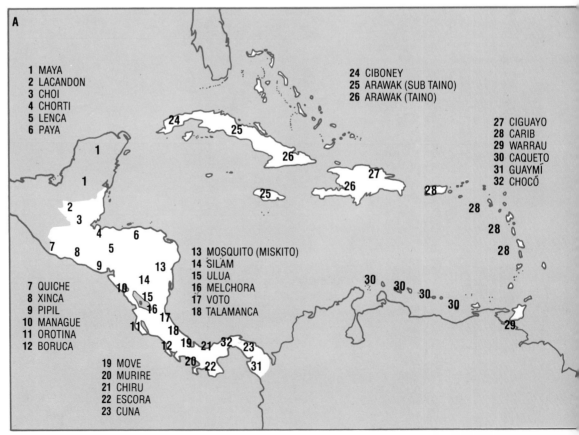

A

1	MAYA
2	LACANDON
3	CHOI
4	CHORTI
5	LENCA
6	PAYA

7	QUICHE
8	XINCA
9	PIPIL
10	MANAGUE
11	OROTINA
12	BORUCA

13	MOSQUITO (MISKITO)
14	SILAM
15	ULUA
16	MELCHORA
17	VOTO
18	TALAMANCA

19	MOVE
20	MURIRE
21	CHIRU
22	ESCORA
23	CUNA

24	CIBONEY
25	ARAWAK (SUB TAINO)
26	ARAWAK (TAINO)

27	CIGUAYO
28	CARIB
29	WARRAU
30	CAQUETO
31	GUAYMÍ
32	CHOCÓ

18

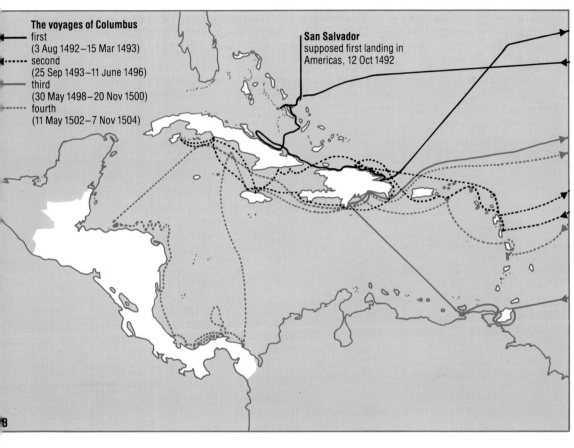

San Salvador
supposed first landing in
Americas, 12 Oct 1492

B

**A General distribution of
early Indian tribes**
Of the many tribes that
populated the region before
the Spanish conquest,
few survive today in
significant numbers: the
Mosquito, Lenca, Sumo,
Boruca, Bribri, Cuna,
Guaymí, and Chocó.

B The voyages of Columbus
Although he discovered
America in 1492, he did not
reach the mainland of Central
America until his fourth
voyage, of 1502-4.

C

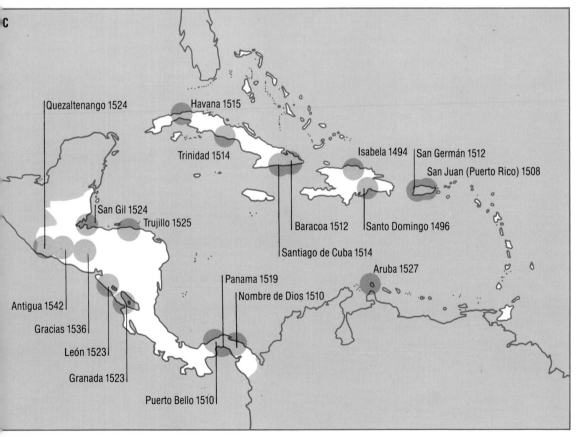

Quezaltenango 1524

Havana 1515

Trinidad 1514

Isabela 1494

San Germán 1512

San Juan (Puerto Rico) 1508

San Gil 1524

Trujillo 1525

Baracoa 1512

Santo Domingo 1496

Santiago de Cuba 1514

Aruba 1527

Antigua 1542

Panama 1519

Nombre de Dios 1510

Gracias 1536

León 1523

Granada 1523

Puerto Bello 1510

C Settlements up to 1550
Within 60 years of
Columbus's first journey,
Spain had colonized most of
Central America and the
Caribbean, establishing
settlements throughout the
region.

©DIAGRAM

19

1600-1800 (Colonial Development)

This period saw the Spanish stamp their rule and culture on the region. But Spain faced increasing competition from three northwest European powers.

The Spanish crown ruled through agents known as viceroys, captains general, and high courts called *audiencias*. For long, the region fell within two major units. The Viceroyalty of New Spain included Caribbean islands and America north of Panama. Panama lay in the Viceroyalty of Peru. Big subdivisions came under captains general wielding almost independent power.

The Spanish enriched their New World lands with Old World food plants and animals, beasts of burden, the wheel, printing, and Spanish art and architecture. Missionaries spread Roman Catholic faith and ethics. But economic greed brought overexploitation of the Indians and African slaves forced to work on cotton, fruit, and sugar-cane plantations; and in gold and silver mines.

Spain's monopoly of New World wealth soon attracted competition. By 1600 English and French freebooters were attacking

Patterns of ownership
These maps show the changes in patterns of possession among the four major territorial powers during the periods 1525–1650, 1650–1763, and 1763–1830.

SPAIN

A Possessions 1525–1650

1 Caicos Is.	8 Trinidad
2 Grand Cayman	9 Aruba
3 Little Cayman	10 Panama
4 Bahama Is. (except	
Eleuthera I.)	11 Santiago
5 Captaincy-General of	
Havana	12 Española
6 Captaincy-General of	
Guatemala	
7 San Juan Bautista	

B Possessions 1650–1763

1 Captaincy-General of Cuba	
2 Captaincy-General of	
Guatemala	
3 Captaincy-General of Santo	
Domingo	5 Panama
4 Puerto Rico	6 Trinidad

C Possessions 1763–1830

1 Puerto Rico	2 Cuba

UNITED KINGDOM

D Possessions 1525–1650

1 Montserrat	6 Antigua
2 St. Vincent	7 Nevis
3 Barbados	8 Anguilla
4 Mosquito Coast	9 Barbuda
5 Eleuthera I.	10 Belize

E Possessions 1650–1763

1 Bahama Is.	11 Nevis
2 Montserrat	12 Barbuda
3 Dominica	13 Antigua
4 St. Vincent	14 Virgin Is.
5 Barbados	15 Anguilla
6 Grand Cayman	16 Santiago
7 Little Cayman	17 Belize
8 St. Eustatius	18 Caicos Is.
9 St. Christopher	19 Grenada
10 Mosquito Coast	

F Possessions 1763–1830

1 Montserrat	13 Nevis
2 Dominica	14 Barbuda
3 St. Lucia	15 Antigua
4 Barbados	16 Jamaica
5 St. Vincent	17 Virgin Is.
6 Bahama Is.	18 Anguilla
7 Caicos Is.	19 Grenada
8 Grand Cayman	20 Tobago
9 Little Cayman	21 Trinidad
10 St. Christopher	
11 Mosquito Coast	
12 British Honduras	

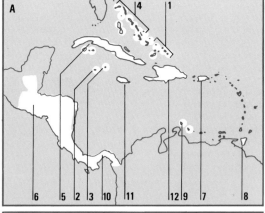

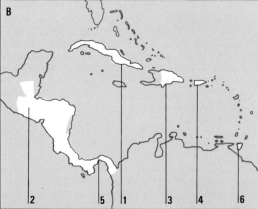

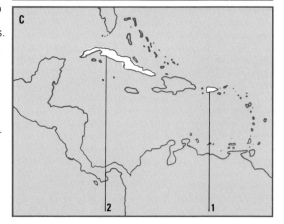

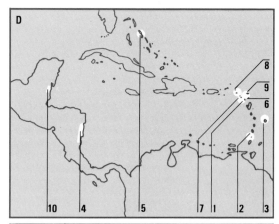

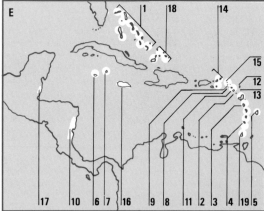

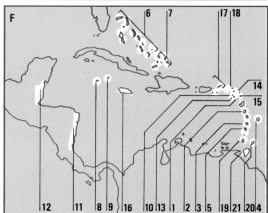

Spanish treasure-fleets en route for Spain, and destroying colonial towns.

By the 1650s attacks had vastly weakened Spanish power. Spain could no longer stop the English, French, and Dutch moving in on Caribbean islands, some claimed but never colonized by Spain. By mid century, the English held Bermuda, the Bahamas, Barbados, Nevis, and Antigua. The Dutch had taken Curaçao. Even old-established Spanish settlements lay open to seizure. In the later 1600s, England seized Jamaica, and Western Hispaniola (now Haiti) fell to France. In the 1700s sea supremacy won Britain Belize and Trinidad. By 1800, though, Spain still held Cuba, Puerto Rico, Mexico and all Central America except Belize.

The Caribbean's new colonists at first produced tobacco, grown by European labor. They soon found it paid to switch to sugar cane cut by African slaves. This encouraged a three-way trade. Merchants shipped sugar north to England or New England. From there rum or manufactured cloth moved south to West Africa, where slaves were bought and ferried west to the Americas.

FRANCE
A Possessions 1525–1650
1 I. de la Tortue
2 St. Martin (St. Maarten) (with Netherlands)
3 St. Barthélemy
4 St. Christopher
5 Guadeloupe
6 Marie Galante
7 Dominica
8 Martinique
9 St. Lucia
10 Grenada
B Possessions 1650–1763
1 I. de la Tortue
2 Saint-Domingue
3 St. Martin (St. Maarten) (with Netherlands)
4 St. Barthélemy
5 Guadeloupe
6 Marie Galante
7 Martinique
8 St. Lucia
9 Tobago
C Possessions 1763–1830
1 St. Martin (St. Maarten) (with Netherlands)
2 Guadeloupe
3 Marie Galante
4 Martinique

NETHERLANDS
D Possessions 1525–1650
1 Virgin Is.
2 St. Maarten (St. Martin) (with France)
3 Saba
4 St. Eustatius
5 Tobago
6 Bonaire
7 Curaçao
E Possessions 1650–1763
1 St. Maarten (St. Martin) (with France)
2 Saba
3 Bonaire
4 Curaçao
5 Aruba
F Possessions 1763–1830
1 St. Maarten (St. Martin) (with France)
2 Saba
3 St. Eustatius
4 Bonaire
5 Curaçao
6 Aruba

©DIAGRAM

1800-1985 (Independence and Conflict)

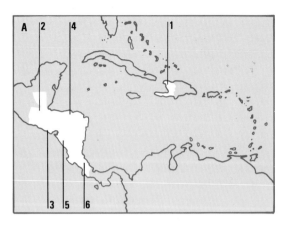

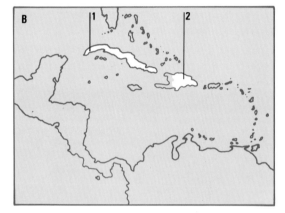

Gaining independence
These maps show when today's Central American and Caribbean states gained their independence.

A 1800–1850
1 Haiti (1804)
2 Guatemala (1838)*
3 El Salvador (1838)*
4 Honduras (1838)*
5 Nicaragua (1838)*
6 Costa Rica (1838)*
* From 1823–38, these countries formed the independent Provincas Unidas del Centro de América (United Provinces of Central America).

B 1850–1900
1 Cuba (1898)
2 Dominican Republic (1865)

C 1900–1950
1 Panama (1903)

D 1950–
1 Belize (1981)
2 Panama Canal Zone (1979)*
3 The Bahamas (1973)
4 Jamaica (1962)
5 St. Kitts-Nevis (1983)
6 Antigua and Barbuda (1981)
7 Dominica (1978)
8 St. Lucia (1979)
9 St. Vincent and the Grenadines (1979)
10 Barbados (1966)
11 Grenada (1974)
12 Trinidad and Tobago (1962)
* Date on which sovereignty reverted to Panama. The Zone will continue to be administered by the U.S. until 2000.

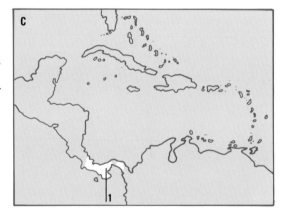

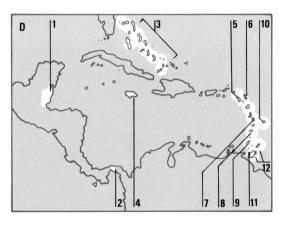

In 1800 European powers controlled the region. By 1985 most of it had independence, if not complete stability or wealth.

Central America won freedom after the Napoleonic Wars had weakened autocratic Spanish rule. In 1821 Mexico revolted and proclaimed a short-lived empire, briefly joined by Guatemala, Honduras, El Salvador, Nicaragua, and Costa Rica. In 1823 the five broke away to form the United Provinces of Central America, which lasted until 1838. Meanwhile Panama joined newly independent Great Colombia but left Colombia in 1903. The Dominican Republic finally shook off Spain in 1865. As a result of the Spanish American War in 1898, Cuba won its freedom and Puerto Rico was ceded to the U.S. Spanish rule was dead.

France had lost Haiti to a slave revolt as early as 1804. British rule waned later. Between 1962 and 1983 Britain freely granted independence to 10 West Indian countries and Belize. By the mid 1980s only small island groups were still in British, French, or Dutch control.

After independence many states developed vulnerable cash-crop economies where land ownership was concentrated in few hands. Social injustices contributed to military coups and spells of autocratic rule, while territorial disputes caused local wars. By 1980 civil wars had spawned two large, influential Marxist states: Cuba, which came under Fidel Castro's control in 1959, and Nicaragua, where revolution swept the Sandinistas to power in 1979.

Meanwhile many small-scale international wars broke out in this century, mainly in Central America. In 1907 Nicaragua fought Honduras and backed a revolt in El Salvador in a doomed attempt to forge a Central American Union. In 1921 Panama and Costa Rica clashed over a boundary dispute, and the collapse of the new Federation of Central America in 1922 led to years of frontier troubles. In 1957 Nicaragua and Honduras grappled in a brief border war. In 1969 El Salvador bombed and invaded Honduras in the so-called Soccer War, sparked off by soccer rivalry. In 1978 Costa Rican police fought Nicaraguan forces in another boundary squabble. In the 1980s Nicaraguan rebels based in Honduras and Costa Rica made hit-and-run attacks on Nicaragua, provoking counter strikes.

International fighting has affected the Caribbean much less than Central America. But in 1937 many Haitian immigrants were killed in the Dominican Republic. In 1961 U.S.-based Cuban rebels invaded Cuba's Bay of Pigs, only to suffer heavy defeat; and the 1960s saw unsuccessful landings in Haiti by small Haitian rebel forces.

From time to time, in both regions, the U.S. has threatened force or actually sent in troops, chiefly to restore order or protect U.S. lives and property from civil war or other disturbance. In the 1920s frequent U.S. intervention in Central America provoked strong anti-U.S. feeling in Latin America, countered in the 1930s by President Franklin D. Roosevelt's noninterventionist Good Neighbor Policy. But in 1962 the U.S. forced Russia to remove nuclear missiles based in Cuba, and later involvements have included cash aid for Nicaraguan rebels and a brief U.S. invasion of Grenada. (For details of these see pages 32–33 and 72–73.)

Most international disputes have ended peacefully with arbitration or mutual agreement. Some settlements involved land claimed by both local governments and the U.S. In 1979 the U.S. ended a long-standing Panamanian grievance by formally handing Panama sovereignty of the Canal Zone in return for a share in running it until the year A.D. 2000. The U.S. also gave up claims to several tiny disputed west Caribbean islands. Thus in 1971 the U.S. handed Honduras the Swan Islands (Islas del Cisne); and in a 1981 treaty with Colombia, renounced Quita Sueño Bank, Roncador Cay, and Serrana Bank – all uninhabited and largely under water.

Even so, by the 1980s there were still areas whose disputed ownership remained a source of potential conflict. In Central America, the El Salvador-Honduras and Costa Rica-Nicaragua borders are not yet finally agreed, and Guatemala presses a long-standing claim on Belize. In the Caribbean region, Colombia, Honduras, and Nicaragua lay rival claims to certain western islets, and Venezuela may seek Aruba, Curaçao, and Bonaire if all three gain independence from the Netherlands. Lastly, Cuba unsuccessfully demands the return of the Guantánamo naval base, ceded to the U.S. by Cuba in 1901.

Current dependencies
These maps show the current dependencies of the present major territorial powers

A United Kingdom
1 Cayman Is. (British Crown Colony)
2 Turks and Caicos Is. (British Crown Colony)
3 British Virgin Is. (British Crown Colony)
4 Anguilla (British colony administered under the Anguilla constitution order)
5 Montserrat (self-governing British colony)

B France
1 Guadeloupe, St. Barthélemy, and St. Martin (overseas departments of the French Republic)
2 Martinique (overseas department of the French Republic)

C Netherlands
1 St. Eustatius
2 St. Maarten
3 Saba
4 Bonaire
5 Curaçao
6 Aruba
All form an autonomous part of the Kingdom of the Netherlands. Full independence is under discussion.

D U.S.
1 Puerto Rico (in commonwealth association with U.S.)
2 U.S. Virgin Is. (self-governing American colony)

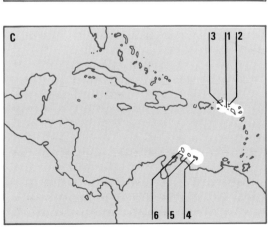

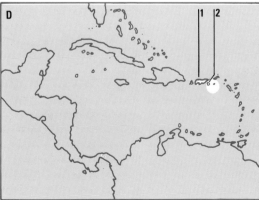

PART TWO
CENTRAL AMERICA

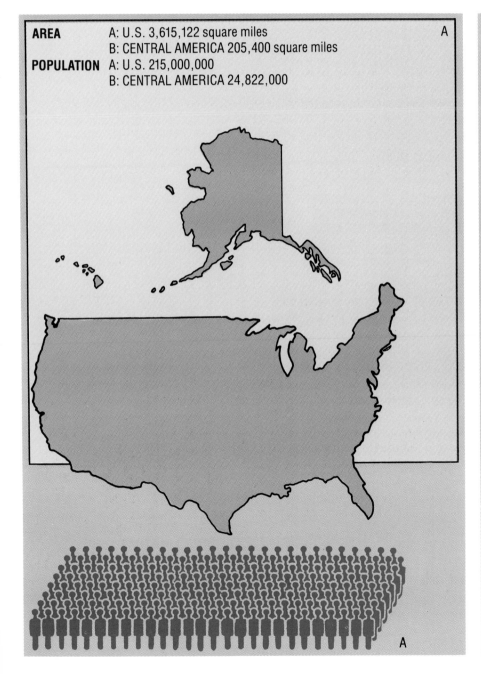

AREA
A: U.S. 3,615,122 square miles
B: CENTRAL AMERICA 205,400 square miles

POPULATION
A: U.S. 215,000,000
B: CENTRAL AMERICA 24,822,000

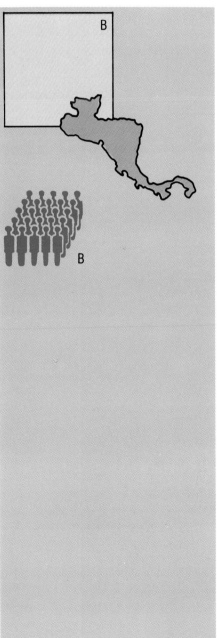

The People 1 (Lands and Peoples)

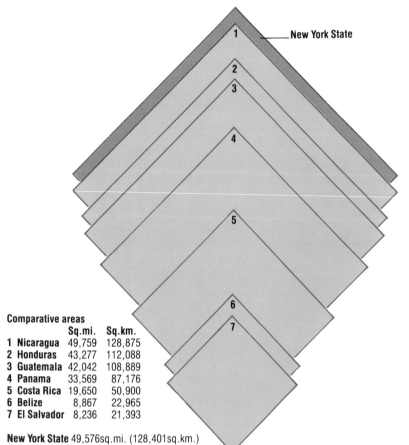

New York State

Comparative areas

	Sq.mi.	Sq.km.
1 Nicaragua	49,759	128,875
2 Honduras	43,277	112,088
3 Guatemala	42,042	108,889
4 Panama	33,569	87,176
5 Costa Rica	19,650	50,900
6 Belize	8,867	22,965
7 El Salvador	8,236	21,393

New York State 49,576sq.mi. (128,401sq.km.)

Countries Central America comprises a land corridor 1150 miles (1850km.) long and 50–250 miles (80–400km.) wide, trending southeast between Mexico and Colombia. To its northeast is the Caribbean Sea; to its southwest, the Pacific Ocean.

From north to south its seven nations are the parliamentary state of Belize, and the six republics of Guatemala, Honduras, El Salvador, Nicaragua, Costa Rica, and Panama. They occupy about 210,000 square miles (543,900 sq.km.) – less than Texas. Nicaragua, the largest country, is a bit bigger than New York State; El Salvador, the smallest, is about the size of Massachusetts.

Population In 1985 Central America contained an estimated 25.26 million people. This was roughly equal to the population of California, and less than one-third that of Mexico. Two countries – El Salvador and Guatemala – held more than half the total. Guatemala had the largest population, about eight million. This was more than that of Nicaragua, Costa Rica, Panama, and Belize combined. Belize's population was the smallest at about 160,000.

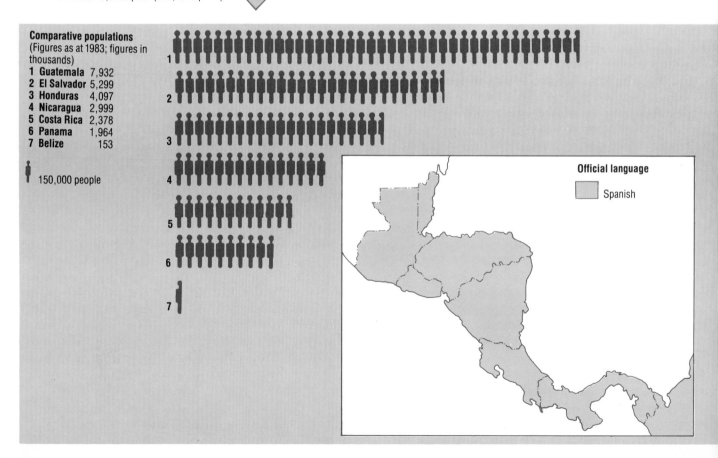

Comparative populations
(Figures as at 1983; figures in thousands)

1 Guatemala	7,932
2 El Salvador	5,299
3 Honduras	4,097
4 Nicaragua	2,999
5 Costa Rica	2,378
6 Panama	1,964
7 Belize	153

150,000 people

Official language

Spanish

Population density and distribution All Central American countries except Nicaragua and Belize have a higher population density than the U.S.

By far the most densely peopled nation is El Salvador. In the early 1980s its 570 people per square mile (220 per sq.km.) approximated to the concentrations in West Germany and the United Kingdom. In the U.S., only New Jersey, three New England States, and Washington D.C. were more thickly populated.

By far Central America's most thinly peopled country is Belize. In the early 1980s its 16.7 people per square mile (6.5 per sq.km.) made Belize more unpopulated than all U.S. states but eight. Cold, drought, or rugged terrain restrict settlement.

Most people live in the pleasant upland climate of the mountains that parallel the Pacific coast. Before 1950 the huge majority lived on the land; but industrial growth, land reform, social welfare, and other factors hugely boosted urban growth. By the mid 1980s in most countries more than 40 per cent lived in cities or towns.

Ethnic groups Most people in Central America are Mestizos (of mixed White-Indian ancestry). They derive from mixed marriages between Spanish settlers and aboriginal Indians. The populations of El Salvador and Honduras have the highest recorded Mestizo component, about 90 per cent.

Costa Rica is the only country where Whites (of Spanish origin) form the majority. Elsewhere Whites make up 1–20 per cent.

Guatemala is the only country where reputedly most people are Indians. Some sources suggest that 50–60 per cent of all Guatemalans are Indians. Elsewhere, Indians form a shrinking percentage of the total population.

In Belize most people are Negro or part Negro. Negroes and Mulattoes (those of mixed White-Negro ancestry) are common on other Caribbean coasts, and in Panama.

Languages Spanish is the official language everywhere except Belize where the chief language is English. Much English or English dialect is spoken elsewhere on the Caribbean coast and in Panama. The two main groups of Indian languages are Mayan in northern Central America, and Chibchan in the south.

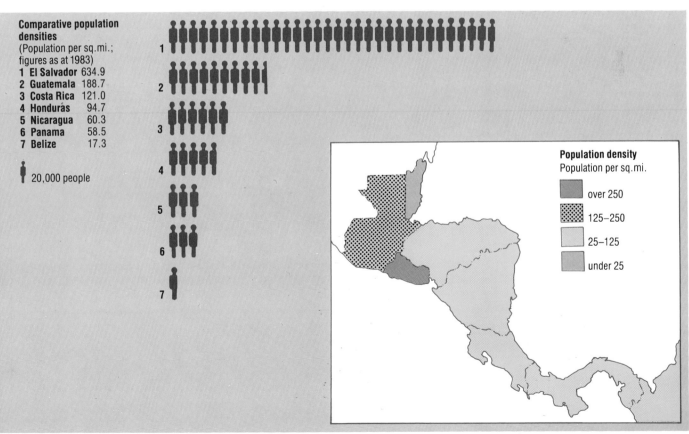

Comparative population densities
(Population per sq.mi.; figures as at 1983)
1 El Salvador 634.9
2 Guatemala 188.7
3 Costa Rica 121.0
4 Honduras 94.7
5 Nicaragua 60.3
6 Panama 58.5
7 Belize 17.3

20,000 people

Population density
Population per sq.mi.
over 250
125–250
25–125
under 25

©DIAGRAM

The People 2 (Population Trends)

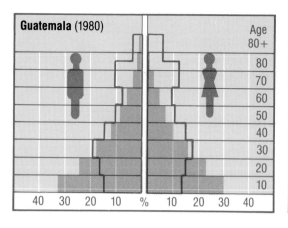

Guatemala (1980)

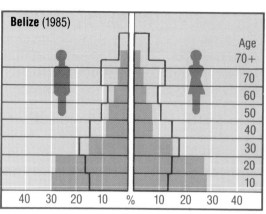

Belize (1985)

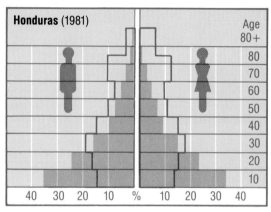

Honduras (1981)

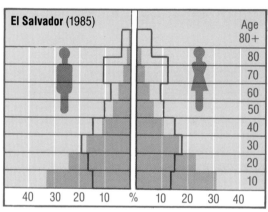

El Salvador (1985)

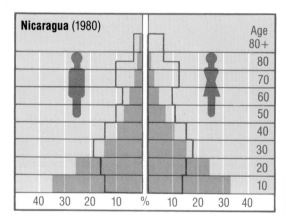

Nicaragua (1980)

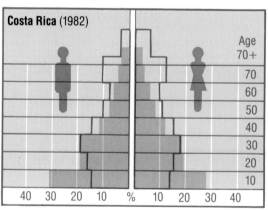

Costa Rica (1982)

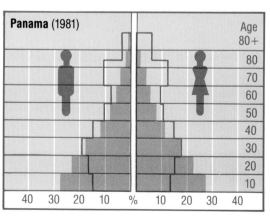

Panama (1981)

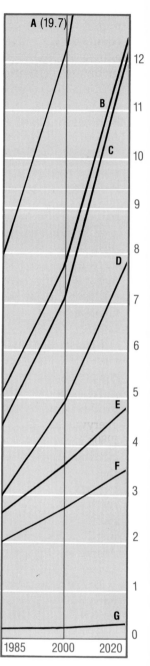

Population pyramids
Pyramids show composition by age and sex of the populations in Central America's seven nations. Each stage represents a 10-year age group. The lowest stage is the youngest group. The wider a stage, the higher the percentage of the population in that age group. The left side of each pyramid consists of males; the right side, of females. The solid areas in the pyramids represent the population figures for the particular country; the outlined areas those for the U.S. by comparison.

Growth to A.D. 2020
Lines on the diagram above show the projected growth in population of each Central American state between A.D. 1985 and A.D. 2020. Numbers represent millions of individuals.
- **A** Guatemala
- **B** El Salvador
- **C** Honduras
- **D** Nicaragua
- **E** Costa Rica
- **F** Panama
- **G** Belize

Statistics for Central America show population features found in developing countries. These theoretically pass through a three-stage sequence of development, involving social progress and fertility.

In the first stage, a country has poor social conditions, high birth and death rates, and little population growth. No Central American nation fits this description.

In the second stage, improving social conditions bring a drop in death rate while birth rate stays high, and population grows fast. This is what we find in almost every part of Central America. Take annual death rates first. Between the early 1970s and mid 1980s one estimate shows the death rate to have decreased in six of the region's seven nations. In Honduras and Nicaragua it fell from 17 to 10 deaths per 1000, while Guatemala's death rate almost halved from 15 to 8.

Birth rates stayed high. In Guatemala, Honduras, and Nicaragua, the birth rate remained over 40 per 1000.

A high birth rate and reduced death rate produced rapid growth in population almost everywhere. Between the mid 1970s and mid 1980s, Central America's population leaped by nearly 40 per cent. Demographers predicted that the rapid increase would continue well beyond the year 2000. At estimated rates of increase, the populations of Guatemala, Honduras, and Nicaragua could double in just 20 years, and by A.D. 2020 each Central American country might hold at least twice as many people as it had in 1985.

Belize, Costa Rica, El Salvador, and Panama showed signs of slowing population growth. But all had far to go to reach the third stage of development: where birth rate falls till births and deaths are equal once again, and population stabilizes. Central American populations were still growing at 2.1 to 3.5 per cent a year in 1985, compared with less than 1 per cent in the U.S. Accordingly their population pyramids had very different profiles from that of the U.S. Central America's booming birth rate and low living standards gave broad-based pyramids tapering upward sharply through the older age groups. Belize had roughly twice as many people aged under 10 as in the 20–29 bracket; in Honduras and Nicaragua one-third of all males were aged under 10. Nowhere in Central America was more than 4 per cent of the population aged more than 64.

Contrast this with the U.S., with its low birth rate, high living standards, and aging population. The U.S. population profile of the 1980s looked more like a stack of plates than a pyramid.

Of course, Central America's overall growth conceals shrinkages. Scores of thousands have died in civil strife. Indian minorities have dwindled. There has been emigration, too – more than 130,000 people moved to the U.S. in the 1970s alone.

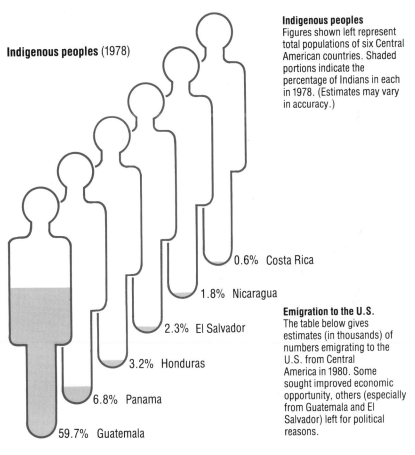

Indigenous peoples (1978)

0.6% Costa Rica
1.8% Nicaragua
2.3% El Salvador
3.2% Honduras
6.8% Panama
59.7% Guatemala

Indigenous peoples
Figures shown left represent total populations of six Central American countries. Shaded portions indicate the percentage of Indians in each in 1978. (Estimates may vary in accuracy.)

Emigration to the U.S.
The table below gives estimates (in thousands) of numbers emigrating to the U.S. from Central America in 1980. Some sought improved economic opportunity, others (especially from Guatemala and El Salvador) left for political reasons.

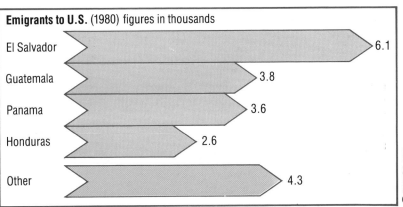

Emigrants to U.S. (1980) figures in thousands

El Salvador — 6.1
Guatemala — 3.8
Panama — 3.6
Honduras — 2.6
Other — 4.3

©DIAGRAM

Land Use and Economy

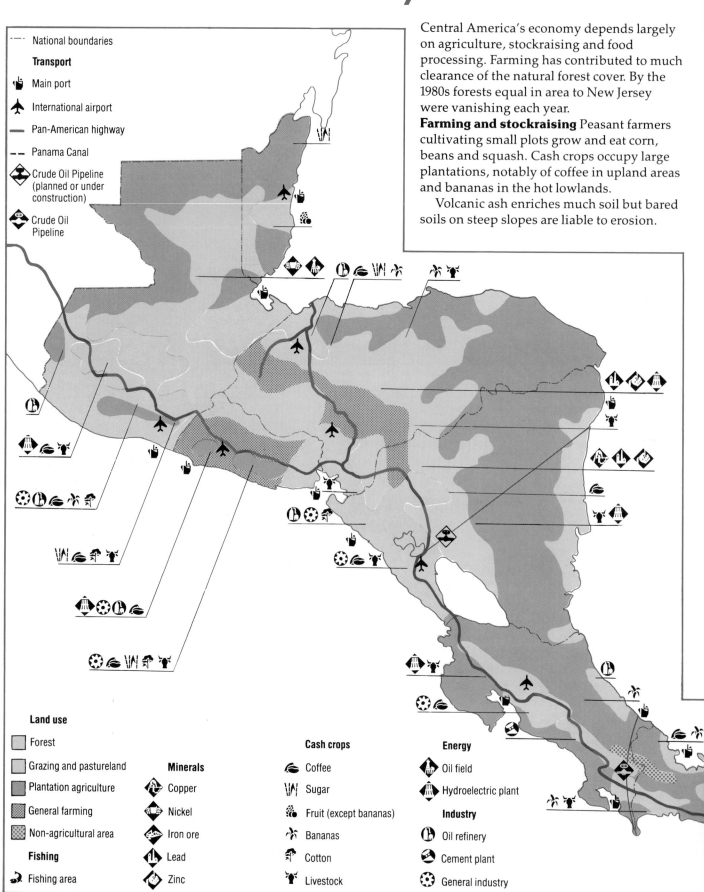

Central America's economy depends largely on agriculture, stockraising and food processing. Farming has contributed to much clearance of the natural forest cover. By the 1980s forests equal in area to New Jersey were vanishing each year.

Farming and stockraising Peasant farmers cultivating small plots grow and eat corn, beans and squash. Cash crops occupy large plantations, notably of coffee in upland areas and bananas in the hot lowlands.

Volcanic ash enriches much soil but bared soils on steep slopes are liable to erosion.

Transport

- 👆 Main port
- ✈ International airport
- — Pan-American highway
- – – Panama Canal
- ◈ Crude Oil Pipeline (planned or under construction)
- ◈ Crude Oil Pipeline
- – · – National boundaries

Land use

- Forest
- Grazing and pastureland
- Plantation agriculture
- General farming
- Non-agricultural area

Fishing

- 🐟 Fishing area

Minerals

- ⛏ Copper
- Nickel
- Iron ore
- Lead
- Zinc

Cash crops

- ☕ Coffee
- Sugar
- Fruit (except bananas)
- Bananas
- Cotton
- Livestock

Energy

- Oil field
- Hydroelectric plant

Industry

- Oil refinery
- Cement plant
- General industry

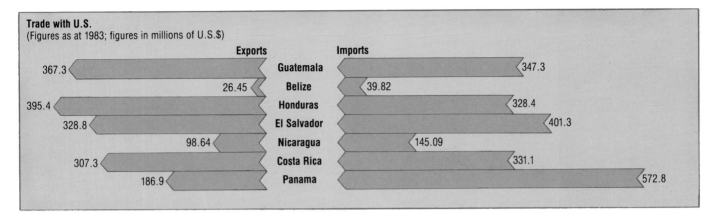

Trade with U.S.
(Figures as at 1983; figures in millions of U.S.$)

	Exports	Imports
Guatemala	367.3	347.3
Belize	26.45	39.82
Honduras	395.4	328.4
El Salvador	328.8	401.3
Nicaragua	98.64	145.09
Costa Rica	307.3	331.1
Panama	186.9	572.8

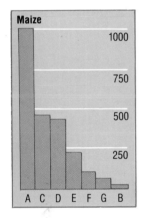

Maize

1000 / 750 / 500 / 250

A C D E F G B

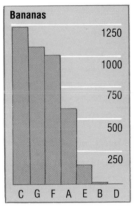

Bananas

1250 / 1000 / 750 / 500 / 250

C G F A E B D

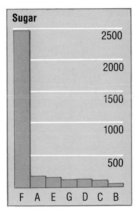

Sugar

2500 / 2000 / 1500 / 1000 / 500

F A E G D C B

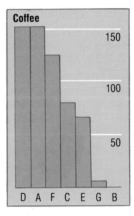

Coffee

150 / 100 / 50

D A F C E G B

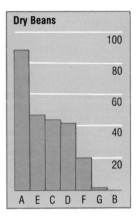

Dry Beans

100 / 80 / 60 / 40 / 20

A E C D F G B

Rainfall is mostly adequate for crops but Pacific plantations benefit from irrigation. Beef-cattle raising is important in highland and Pacific lowland areas.

Forestry Forest resources remain large. Commercially valuable trees include such tropical hardwoods as mahogany and rosewood. Pines are the most productive softwoods. Much wood is burned for fuel.

Fisheries Shrimps are the chief commercial harvest for several nations. Lobsters, anchovies, tuna and snappers come from Caribbean waters. The Pacific catch includes members of the herring family.

Minerals Gold and silver mining go back to Pre-Columbian times. Zinc, lead, copper and other minerals are extracted. But resources are mostly small or undeveloped.

Energy Fuelwood and imported oil provide most energy supplies. But hydroelectric output is increasing.

Manufacturing This includes processing sugar, coffee, meat and other foods, and making consumer goods such as clothing. There are also cement and fertilizer factories, and oil refineries.

Trade and transportation Tropical food and other crops dominate Central America's export trade. Coffee, bananas, sugar, and cotton are major export items. Other exports include meat, cattle and shrimps. The chief imports include machinery, transportation equipment, chemicals, and fuel oil.

Roads and railroads connect ports with manufacturing towns and plantations. The Pan American Highway runs down Central America's western side. Several roads, and railroads and the Panama Canal link the Caribbean and Pacific coasts.

Crop production
The diagrams above compare the production by country of the five principal crops of the region. Figures are as at 1983 and are in thousands of tons produced.
A Guatemala
B Belize
C Honduras
D El Salvador
E Nicaragua
F Costa Rica
G Panama

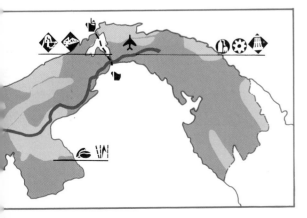

©DIAGRAM

Current Political Situation

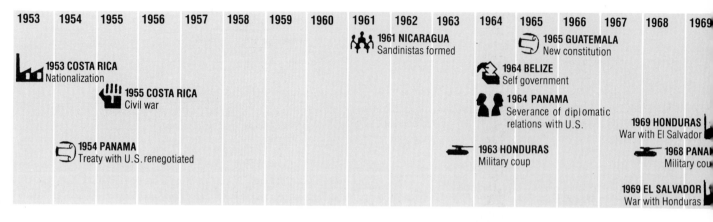

| 1953 | 1954 | 1955 | 1956 | 1957 | 1958 | 1959 | 1960 | 1961 | 1962 | 1963 | 1964 | 1965 | 1966 | 1967 | 1968 | 1969 |

1961 NICARAGUA
Sandinistas formed

1965 GUATEMALA
New constitution

1953 COSTA RICA
Nationalization

1964 BELIZE
Self government

1955 COSTA RICA
Civil war

1964 PANAMA
Severance of diplomatic relations with U.S.

1969 HONDURAS
War with El Salvador

1954 PANAMA
Treaty with U.S. renegotiated

1963 HONDURAS
Military coup

1968 PANAM
Military cou

1969 EL SALVADOR
War with Honduras

In the 1980s revolution and guerrilla warfare brought turmoil to parts of Central America, with implications for the rest of the region, and the U.S. as well. Yet there were also hopeful signs of some new political stability.

Political unrest had its roots in social injustices that date back to exploitation of the peasant masses in colonial times. By the early 1900s, North American and European demand for tropical cash crops made a minority of big landowners richer than ever, at the expense of peasant laborers. The wealthy few clung to political and economic power with the backing of the armed forces. Troops harshly smothered efforts to make governments more democratic. But pressure for reform increased with the emergence of an underprivileged but educated middle class. By the late 1970s, hardships deepened by a worldwide economic slump left some Central American countries rife with discontent and ripe for revolution.

By the 1980s civil strife was nothing new to Guatemala. Here, right-wing governments run by army officers had been battling leftist guerrillas since the 1950s. In the mid 1980s international human rights groups reckoned that 100,000 citizens had disappeared or been murdered; up to a million people – mostly Indians – had fled their homes or been moved to "model" villages under army control.

Meanwhile Guatemala's southeastern neighbor El Salvador was having its own troubles. Five guerrilla groups under the collective lead of the Farabundo Marti National Liberation Front (FMLN) ambushed troops, blew up bridges, and controlled large tracts of countryside. By the early 1980s some 35,000 people had perished

in the fighting, most of them civilians killed by trigger-happy troops and right-wing death squads. This contradicted the government's declared objective of reforms.

But the major flashpoint was Nicaragua. In 1978–79 leftist Sandinista guerrillas led a popular revolt that threw out General Anastasio Somoza Debayle's repressive regime at an estimated cost of 30,000 lives. The U.S. looked on uneasily as Sandinistas took control of government and started forging ties with Cuba.

This had several political and military results. It helped to force the Sandinistas to make concessions to their political opponents, and it lost them much international support. Also U.S. military aid strengthened El Salvador's army enough to weaken the guerrillas' hold on rural areas.

By 1985 much of Central America was looking politically healthier than at any time for decades. In 1984 elections for a Constituent Assembly pointed Guatemala toward democratic government after many years of military rule. In El Salvador the Farabundo Marti National Liberation Front (FMLN) showed new willingness to negotiate with the government, and by early 1985 democratically held elections had produced a reformist Christian-Democrat President (José Napoléon Duarte) and Assembly. Meanwhile in 1981 Honduras had elected its first civilian president for almost a decade.

Outside these "hot-spot" countries, the young nation of Belize had kept its parliamentary democracy. Politically stable Costa Rica (with no armed forces since the 1940s) remained a democratic model for the region. Lastly, in Panama, popular elections (albeit with disputed results) assured

1975 BELIZE British troops arrive

1975 HONDURAS Military coup

1978 NICARAGUA Uprisings against Somoza

1979 NICARAGUA Somoza leaves

1981 BELIZE Independence

1980 HONDURAS Peace with El Salvador

1979 PANAMA Canal sovereignty from U.S.

1979 EL SALVADOR Civilian/military coup

1982 GUATEMALA Military coup

1985 NICARAGUA Attacks rebels in Honduras

1983 GUATEMALA Military coup

1984 GUATEMALA Elections for democratic government

1982 HONDURAS Civilian government

1982 EL SALVADOR Government formed

1985 EL SALVADOR Democratic elections

continuity of rule by the political party founded by General Omar Torrijos, who had held power from 1968 to 1981.

Nicaragua's problems spilled over to its neighbors Costa Rica and Honduras. Just inside their borders, anti-Sandinista Nicaraguans known as Contras set up bases from which they harassed Sandinista forces. The Contras comprised assorted disaffected elements who ranged from former members of Somoza's National Guard to persecuted Mosquito (Miskito) Indians.

Cash, arms, and training to support this operation came from the CIA. The U.S. government of the mid 1980s seemed to have good reasons to distrust, and wish to see dislodged, the Sandinista government of Nicaragua. Washington saw events developing like this: leftists had usurped a revolt aimed at removing social injustice in Nicaragua. They were receiving military aid from Cuba and East European countries and they seemed ready to make Nicaragua a center for spreading Communism through the rest of Central America. Disputed reports claimed that Nicaragua had already started large-scale arms smuggling to leftist rebels in El Salvador. Pessimists in the U.S. foresaw communists toppling shaky governments all through the region, one by one. Hostile states would then fill the region to the south of the U.S. In any major East-West war, two-thirds of the U.S. foreign trade and half its NATO supplies would be at risk on passing through the Panama Canal and Caribbean.

Thus Central America and the Caribbean assumed a strategic importance unparalleled since the Cuban missile crisis of the 1960s.

The U.S. government accordingly took action. By the mid 1980s it had a twofold anti-left policy in Central America, based on military pressure and negotiation. Military pressure included covertly backing Contras against Sandinistas; holding huge military exercises in Honduras and off Nicaragua's coasts; and helping El Salvador's military drive against guerrillas. Negotiation included holding talks with and exerting economic pressure on the Sandinistas; encouraging government and guerrillas to hold talks in El Salvador; and giving qualified support for mediation efforts by the Contadora countries (Colombia, Venezuela, Mexico, and Panama).

Government Finances

In the 1980s almost all Central American governments faced acute financial problems. Aid from the U.S., International Monetary Fund (IMF), and other sources propped up economies hit by high interest rates and low prices for exported cash crops. But some nations found it ever harder to repay capital and interest on loans secured abroad.

Belize's problems stemmed largely from the fall in the price of sugar. Financial help came in IMF loans, British capital aid, and U.S. aid granted under the Caribbean Basin Initiative. But loss of export earnings and increased borrowing forced Belize's government to cut back spending and raise taxation.

In Guatemala the government kept military spending at a rate the IMF declared to be excessive. Accordingly the IMF withheld part of a loan conditional upon austerity reforms. That was one blow to the economy. Another was the virtual collapse of CACM (the Central American Common Market). Belonging to that group had helped boost Guatemala's economic growth from 1961 to 1980. By the early 1980s

unemployment raged, and all sectors of the economy were in decline or slowing in growth.

Besides trade-balance problems, El Salvador faced high costs incurred by civil war. One consequence was high inflation. But by 1983 price controls had maybe halved the inflation rate, imports had been kept in check, and export earnings had increased. Meanwhile, President Duarte's humane reforms encouraged the U.S. to release financial aid.

Honduras faced the familiar difficulties of low commodity prices, high interest rates, and government unwillingness to meet tough terms demanded in exchange for IMF loans. Austerity measures had already increased unemployment to 25 per cent before the IMF pressed for higher taxation, and large cuts in public spending, or devaluation of the currency.

Nicaragua's embattled Sandinista government spent hugely on defense, and suffered from U.S. economic sanctions. By the mid 1980s investment dropped, inflation leaped, and the external debt was rising fast, although Nicaragua still benefited from

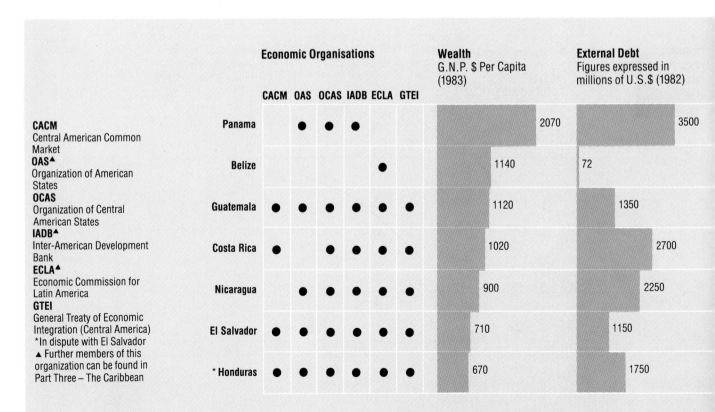

		Economic Organisations						Wealth G.N.P. $ Per Capita (1983)	External Debt Figures expressed in millions of U.S.$ (1982)
		CACM	OAS	OCAS	IADB	ECLA	GTEI		
CACM Central American Common Market	**Panama**		●	●	●			2070	3500
OAS▲ Organization of American States	**Belize**					●		1140	72
OCAS Organization of Central American States	**Guatemala**	●	●	●	●	●	●	1120	1350
IADB▲ Inter-American Development Bank	**Costa Rica**	●		●	●	●	●	1020	2700
ECLA▲ Economic Commission for Latin America	**Nicaragua**		●	●	●	●	●	900	2250
GTEI General Treaty of Economic Integration (Central America) *In dispute with El Salvador ▲ Further members of this organization can be found in Part Three – The Caribbean	**El Salvador**	●	●	●	●	●	●	710	1150
	***Honduras**	●	●	●	●	●	●	670	1750

generous debt-rescheduling arrangements dating from the first year of the revolution. The nation's leaders increasingly favored central planning as a solution to their country's problems.

Costa Rica differed from some neighbors by agreeing in 1984 to a painful package of reforms suggested by the IMF The main points included resuming external-debt payments; cutting the balance-of-payments and public-sector deficits; maintaining wage restraint; and keeping down capital spending. Costa Rica asked for and got assurances of added U.S. aid, and aid from Mexico.

While most of Central America struggled to balance its financial books, Panama was making real economic progress. In 1983 Panama agreed with the World Bank to lift some foreign trade restrictions and abolish price controls on domestic goods. Panama also agreed with the IMF on limiting the public-sector deficit. By the mid 1980s, Panama still had debt problems, but they were less than any neighbor's, and inflation was the lowest in Central America.

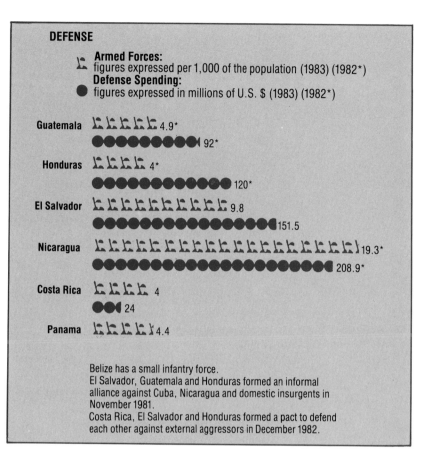

DEFENSE

Armed Forces:
figures expressed per 1,000 of the population (1983) (1982*)
Defense Spending:
figures expressed in millions of U.S. $ (1983) (1982*)

Guatemala 4.9* / 92*
Honduras 4* / 120*
El Salvador 9.8 / 151.5
Nicaragua 19.3* / 208.9*
Costa Rica 4 / 24
Panama 4.4

Belize has a small infantry force.
El Salvador, Guatemala and Honduras formed an informal alliance against Cuba, Nicaragua and domestic insurgents in November 1981.
Costa Rica, El Salvador and Honduras formed a pact to defend each other against external aggressors in December 1982.

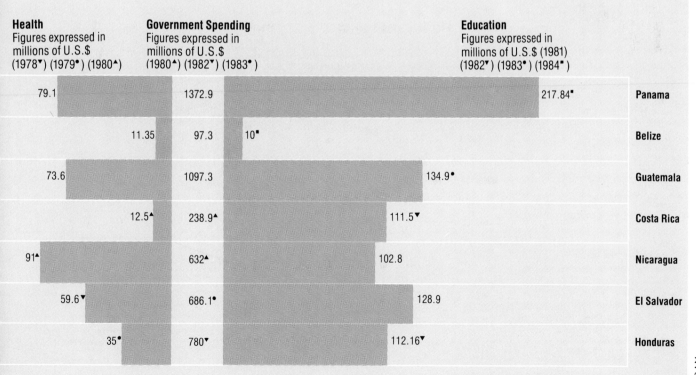

Health
Figures expressed in millions of U.S.$
(1978▼) (1979●) (1980▲)

Government Spending
Figures expressed in millions of U.S.$
(1980▲) (1982▼) (1983●)

Education
Figures expressed in millions of U.S.$ (1981)
(1982▼) (1983●) (1984■)

Health	Government Spending	Education	Country
79.1	1372.9	217.84■	Panama
11.35	97.3	10■	Belize
73.6	1097.3	134.9●	Guatemala
12.5▲	238.9▲	111.5▼	Costa Rica
91▲	632▲	102.8	Nicaragua
59.6▼	686.1●	128.9	El Salvador
35●	780▼	112.16▼	Honduras

Guatemala

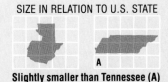

SIZE IN RELATION TO U.S. STATE

A

Slightly smaller than Tennessee (A)

OFFICIAL NAME
República de Guatemala

Above **Flag of Guatemala**
State: Vertical divisions of pale
blue, white, pale blue, with a
central coat of arms (also
shown left), including the
quetzal, the national bird.
Civil: As above, but with no
coat of arms.

AREA	**42,042** square miles (108,889sq.km.)
POPULATION	**7,932,000** (1983 preliminary figure)
POPULATION DENSITY	**188.7** per square mile (1983)
CURRENCY	**Quetzal** (1 quetzal = 100 centavos)
PRINCIPAL RELIGION	**Roman Catholic**
OFFICIAL LANGUAGE	**Spanish**
CAPITAL	**Guatemala City**
ADMINISTRATIVE DIVISIONS	**22 departments**

The third-largest Central American nation, occupying an area about the size of Tennessee, Guatemala has the most people. It is the westernmost nation of Central America, bounded west and north by Mexico; east by Belize and the Caribbean Sea; southeast by Honduras and El Salvador; and south by the Pacific Ocean. The nation's name may come from *Quauhtemallan*, an Indian word that means "land of trees".
History More than 1500 years ago, Maya Indians built Tikal and other imposing temple complexes in the lowland forests of the north. But these had been in long decline by 1524 when the Spanish conquistador Pedro de Alvarado crushed the local Indians. In 1527 newly founded Guatemala City became the capital of a Spanish colonial unit comprising much of Central America. Spanish settlers mostly occupied the lower uplands, leaving the hot, humid lowlands and chilly upper highlands to the Indians. In 1821 the Spanish colonies of Central America declared independence. But Guatemala became a separate republic only in 1839

Since then the country has experienced a

HISTORICAL REVIEW

1524	Spanish conquest.		leads to the overthrow of the military junta.
1821	Independence from Spain declared.		
1823	Creation of Central American Federation.	**1945**	Juan José Arévalo elected President.
1838	Dissolution of Central American Federation.	**1965**	New constitution.
		1970	State of siege imposed.
1839	Guatemala became a separate independent republic.	**1972**	Severe drought and international monetary crisis.
1856	Dallas-Clarendon Treaty between England and U.S. British relinquish rights over Central America.	**1976**	Severe earthquakes left 23,000 dead.
		1980–81	Growth of guerrilla movement.
		1982	Coup staged by military officers. General Efrain Rios Montt assumes Presidency.
1871	Beginning of "Liberal Era" under Presidency of Justo Rufino Barrios.	**1983**	General Oscar Humberto Mejia Victore led successful coup against Rios Montt.
1944	October Revolution and Indian uprising		

number of dictatorships and periods of military rule. In the 1870s the reformist president Justo Rufino Barrios stimulated coffee growing and road building. He also opened Guatemala to foreign investment. All this laid a basis for future economic growth. The U.S.-based United Fruit Company (now United Brands) gained its first concession in 1906. It went on to build much of Guatemala's railroad system, largely routed to take farm produce to the ports.

But Guatemala has always lagged economically, despite periods of economic growth, as in the 1970s. Earthquakes are one recurrent hazard: the 1976 earthquake killed some 20,000 people. Since then Guatemala has suffered heavily from armed internal conflict and a worldwide economic slump. By the mid 1980s, government attempts to crush leftist guerrillas had forced more than half a million Indians from their villages; many fled to Mexico as refugees. Meanwhile income from tourism and exported commodities fell off and the national debt increased.

Land Guatemala has three main regions: the Pacific coastal lowlands, highlands in the south and center, and the northern plains of Petén.

The fertile Pacific coastal lowland forms a southern rim about 25 miles (40km.) wide. Lagoons and sand bars lie along the gently curving coast.

Highlands take up nearly two-thirds of the country. The main mountain range is a southeast extension of Mexico's Sierra Madre. This range runs parallel with the Pacific coast. It rises about 40 miles (64km.) inland to a general level of 3500–8000 feet (1066–2438m.). But there are many high volcanic peaks, some active. At 13,845 feet (4220m.), Tajumulco in the southwest is the highest peak in Central America. Between volcanic peaks lie basins mostly filled with rich volcanic ash. Severe earthquakes often shake this mountain region.

From the northern side of the main mountain range, sharp ridges and deep valleys trend eastward parallel to one another. Here, Guatemala's longest river, the Motagua, flows east to the Gulf of Honduras. Here, too, the Polochic river drains into Lake Izabal, the republic's largest lake.

The plains of Petén – a great, thinly populated limestone lowland – take up most of northern Guatemala. A narrow, fertile coastal plain rims the short Caribbean coast.

Climate The cooling effects of seas and highlands give this tropical nation a variety of local climates. Coasts are hot and humid, with year-round temperatures of about 80°F (27°C). Upland areas inland are cooler. At Guatemala City, nearly 5000 feet (1524m.) above sea level, the average annual temperature is only 64.4°F (18°C), like perpetual spring. December and January are the coolest months.

The main rainy season lasts from May to November. Onshore winds bring heavy summer rain to the Pacific coast. But this stays dry all winter. Caribbean-facing slopes may get rain almost all the year. Annual rainfall varies from 80 inches (2032mm.) on high plateaus to half that in parts of the east.

Vegetation and animals Forest covers more than half of Guatemala. Evergreen tropical forest takes up much of the northern lowlands, with mangroves on the swampy Caribbean coast. The rather dry Pacific lowland supports savanna grasses and trees that shed their leaves in winter drought. In the highlands, lowland trees give way to

General Justo Rufino Barrios, known as "The Reformer" (1873).
(stamp issued 1924)

©DIAGRAM

Guatemala

CLIMATE
Average monthly rainfall and temperature for Guatemala City

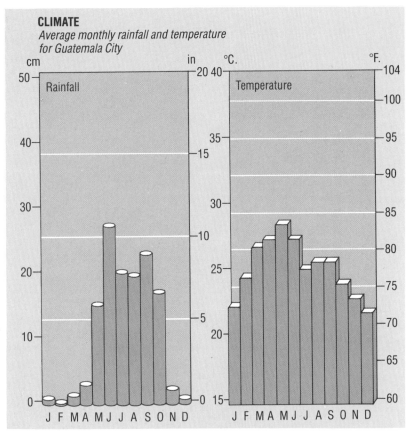

ECONOMIC REVIEW

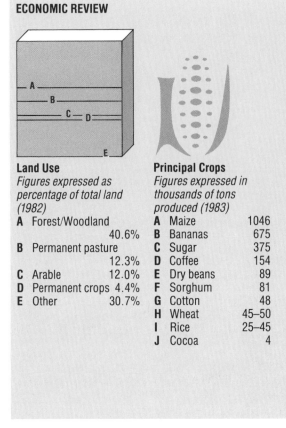

Land Use
Figures expressed as percentage of total land (1982)

A	Forest/Woodland	40.6%
B	Permanent pasture	12.3%
C	Arable	12.0%
D	Permanent crops	4.4%
E	Other	30.7%

Principal Crops
Figures expressed in thousands of tons produced (1983)

A	Maize	1046
B	Bananas	675
C	Sugar	375
D	Coffee	154
E	Dry beans	89
F	Sorghum	81
G	Cotton	48
H	Wheat	45–50
I	Rice	25–45
J	Cocoa	4

pines and evergreen oaks, among others. Only mountain grasses thrive on high peaks.

Guatemala's forests conceal wild mammals such as monkeys, deer, and peccaries; jaguars, pumas, and tapirs are scarcer. Crocodiles inhabit the Polochic river. Bird life is varied, plentiful and colorful: the splendid plumage of the quetzal inspired Guatemala's emblem.

People More than four in five of all Guatemalans are Indian or of mixed blood. The government recognizes two main groups: Indians and Ladinos. Ladinos are mostly of Spanish-Indian extraction, but they include Indians who have adopted European dress and speak Spanish. There are few Whites or Negroes.

The official language is Spanish, but there are also about 20 Indian dialects, most of Maya origin. Many Indians speak one of these and Spanish.

There is no official religion, but nearly nine-tenths of the population is Roman Catholic. There are a few Protestants and even fewer Jews.

Most of Guatemala's nearly 8 million inhabitants live in the relatively cool, fertile

A depiction of the rainy season in the nineteenth century.

uplands where most cities stand. About 1.5 million live in or near Guatemala City, the capital. Other, much smaller, centers include Antigua, Mazatenango, and Puerto Barrios. But more than two-thirds of the population lives in the countryside.

Social conditions Most people work on the land, but almost half work only part time or are unemployed.

The first six years of education are in theory compulsory and free, but many children get no schooling. Illiteracy is widespread but has recently been reduced. Guatemala has four universities.

The government runs three dozen hospitals where patients receive free medical aid. But lack of medical facilities, poor sanitation, and malnutrition remain problems among the rural and urban poor. Life expectancy was about 60 years in the mid-1980s. But a high birth rate means that the population is increasing at the rapid annual rate of about 3 per cent.

Government Elections held in 1984 marked at least a nominal end to years of military rule. Voting at elections is compulsory for all literate citizens aged over 18. Every

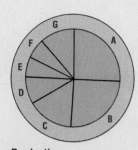

GDP
9298.2 million U.S.$
(1983)

Production
Goods and services expressed as percentage of GDP (1983)

A Commerce 25.8%
B Agriculture/Forestry/ Fishing 25.2%
C Manufacturing 15.7%
D Finance 8.9%
E Transport/ Communication 6.6%
F Government 6.1%
G Construction 3.1%
H Other 8.6%

Exports
Figures expressed as percentage of total (1983)

A Coffee 29.6%
B Sugar 10.7%
C Bananas 5.8%
D Cotton 4.2%
E Other 49.7%

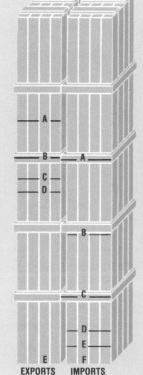

EXPORTS   IMPORTS

Total World Trade
Figures expressed in millions of U.S.$ (1983)

Exports World 1220.3
U.S. 367.3
Imports World 1054.4
U.S. 347.3

Imports
Figures expressed as percentage of total (1983)

A Raw materials 40.9%
B Fuel and oil 22.6%
C Non durable consumer goods 16.7%
D Capital goods 10.2%
E Building materials 5.3%
F Durable consumer goods 4.3%

EXPORTS   IMPORTS

four years they choose a President with executive powers, and a Congress of 55 representatives, with legislative powers. A Supreme Court of Justice is responsible for the country's tribunals. Guatemala is divided into 22 departments with governors appointed by the President.

Communications and transportation
Guatemala has three television channels, dozens of radio stations, and several newspapers, most based in Guatemala City.

There are more than 11,800 miles (18,000km.) of roads, including part of the Pan-American Highway. But most roads are dirt tracks. Railroads link Guatemala City with Mexico, El Salvador, and the Caribbean. Guatemala City has the only international airport, but others serve domestic flights. Puerto Barrios on the Caribbean and San José on the Pacific are the main seaports.

Economy Guatemala's economic output is worth more than that of any other state in Central America. But the per capita gross domestic product is one-tenth that of the U.S.

Agriculture takes up one-quarter of the land and accounts for one-quarter of the national income. Guatemala is one of the world's chief coffee growers and also produces bananas, cotton, sugar, and beef for export. Corn (maize), wheat, rice, and beans are grown for home consumption. Shrimping is the main commercial fishing.

There are zinc, lead, nickel, oil, and other deposits. But by the mid 1980s an anticipated oil boom began to seem wishful thinking. Also, faulty work hindered construction of big hydroelectric projects aimed to give Guatemala self-sufficiency in electricity by the year 2000.

Factories process sugar, flour, hides, and meat; and make cement, fertilizer, and household products.

The main exports are coffee, cotton, sugar, meat, and bananas. In peaceful times much income comes from tourists, many of them drawn to the Maya ruins of Petén. Machinery, transportation equipment, fuel oil, and chemicals are among the main imports.

Guatemala's chief trading partner is the U.S. Others include Central American states, Venezuela, Japan, and West Germany.

Maize (American corn) – the principal crop in Guatemala.

©DIAGRAM

39

Belize

SIZE IN RELATION TO U.S. STATE

Slightly smaller than New Hampshire (A)

OFFICIAL NAME
Belize (formerly British Honduras)

Above **Flag of Belize**
Blue edged top and bottom with a narrow red band. A white disk in the center bears the arms of Belize (also shown left).

AREA	**8,867** square miles (22,965sq.km.)
POPULATION	**153,000** (1983 preliminary figure)
POPULATION DENSITY	**17.3** per square mile (1983)
CURRENCY	**Belizean dollar** (Bz. $1 = 100 cents)
PRINCIPAL RELIGION	**Roman Catholic**
OFFICIAL LANGUAGE	**Spanish**
CAPITAL	**Belmopan**
ADMINISTRATIVE DIVISIONS	**6 districts**

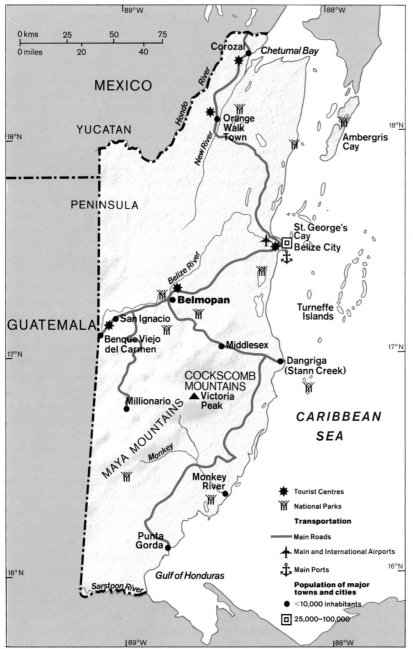

Belize is the youngest state in Central America, gaining independence in 1981. With fewer than 200,000 people, Belize has by far the smallest population in the region. It is also the area's second-smallest nation – somewhat smaller than New Hampshire. Belize lies on the Gulf of Honduras, extending farther north than any other Central American state. The border with Guatemala forms its short southern and long western boundaries. Mexico lies to the north. To the east a long coast faces the Caribbean. Belize gets its name from a Maya word for "muddy water".

History Jungle ruins date from the Maya Indian civilization that existed from about A.D. 300 to 900. Christopher Columbus reached the Gulf of Honduras in 1502, without visiting the coast. English settlers arrived in 1638. They began cutting logwood trees, then used in dye manufacture. This broke a Spanish monopoly and sparked off conflict. The Spanish launched many attacks from nearby settlements but under the 1763 Treaty of Paris, Spain recognized British settlers' rights. Nevertheless, attacks continued until 1798, when British naval support helped settlers and their African slaves decisively to defeat a Spanish force at the Battle of St. George's Cay.

From then on, the British government increased its control over the settlement, but Guatemala claimed much of it, after shaking off Spanish rule in 1821. In 1859 Guatemala and Great Britain signed an agreement, never ratified by Guatemala, but in 1862 Britain declared the settlement of British Honduras a colony. The name was changed to Belize in 1973.

Belize gained independence in 1981, after delays due to Guatemala's opposition. Only

HISTORICAL REVIEW

1638	British woodcutters established the Bay Settlement which was subject to continual Spanish attack.
1786	British government appointed a Superintendent for the region.
1798	Spanish forced to retreat after initiating a sea battle at St. George's Cay.
1821	Guatemala declared its independence from Spain and claimed sovereignty over Belize.
1859	Anglo-Guatemalan Convention according to which Guatemala recognized the boundaries of Belize.
1862	Region recognized as a British colony called British Honduras. Superintendent replaced by Lieutenant Governor.
1884	British Honduras became an independent colony. Full Governor appointed.
1954	First general election won by the People's United Party.
1964	Colony granted full internal self government.
1975-77	British troops sent to protect Belize from threatened Guatemalan invasion.
1981	Belize gained independence.

the combined support of the United Kingdom, U.S., and United Nations made independence possible. After 1981 a British military force stayed on to deter Guatemalan intervention.

Heavily dependent on sugar-cane exports, Belize suffered from low world sugar prices in the early 1980s. But it has profited from increased output of cattle and bananas, and a growing tourist industry.

Land Belize forms the southeast chunk of the Yucatán Peninsula. It is up to 174 miles (280km.) long from north to south, and 68 miles (109km.) across at its widest. Its main regions are the northern lowlands, southern uplands, and the coast. Much of the northern lowlands, which lie less than 200 feet (61m.) above sea level, are swampy. The southern uplands comprise hills and valleys of the Maya Mountains, an eroded plateau, and its northeast extension the Cockscomb Mountains. These have the country's highest point: Victoria Peak, 3681 feet (1122m.). The Hondo, New, Belize, Sarstoon, and other rivers (some navigable) drain into the Caribbean. Behind the low and swampy coast are lagoons. The world's second-largest barrier reef lies 10–40 miles (16–64km.) offshore. There are also many small, low islands known as cays.

Climate This is subtropical, with onshore trade winds. The mean temperature at Belize City on the coast ranges from 74°F (23°C) in December to 85°F (29°C) in July. Inland, days are hotter and nights cooler. Annual rainfall ranges from 170 inches (4318mm.) in the south to 50 inches (1270mm.) in the north. February to May is the dry season; there can be drastic seasonal variations, even droughts. Hurricanes sometimes sweep in from the Caribbean.

Vegetation and animals About half the total area is forested. Trees include mahogany, ironwood, Spanish cedar, oak, and pine. Mangroves fringe the coast, while swamp forest hugs rivers. Tall, evergreen trees thrive mostly in the south; parklike savanna covers much of the coastal plain.

This range of habitats supports a wealth of animals. Mammals include deer, tapirs, jaguars, pumas, and the aquatic coastal manatee. The keel-billed toucan, the national bird, is one of many species. Reptiles include crocodiles and turtles. Freshwater and marine fishes abound.

People Belize's population is very mixed racially. Most people are Negro or part Negro, especially along the coast. Smaller groups include Mestizos of Maya-Spanish ancestry, descendants of Europeans, and even Arabs and Chinese.

The official language is English, but in parts of the north and west most speak Spanish. Indian tongues persist in the south. About 62 per cent of the people are Roman Catholics. Most of the rest belong to one of many Protestant groups. There are a few Bahais.

Most of the population of about 153,000 lives on or near the coast, where nearly one-third of all citizens inhabit the chief town and old capital Belize City. Only some 3000 inhabit the new inland capital, Belmopan, a floodproof site to which the government moved in 1970 after a severe hurricane badly damaged Belize City. Other towns include Orange Walk, Dangriga (formerly Stann Creek), and Corozal, each with fewer than 10,000 people. National population density is low at 18 per square mile (7 per sq. km.) and large tracts of the interior remain almost empty.

Queen Victoria of England, who also ruled Belize (then British Honduras).
(stamp issued 1865)

©DIAGRAM

41

Belize

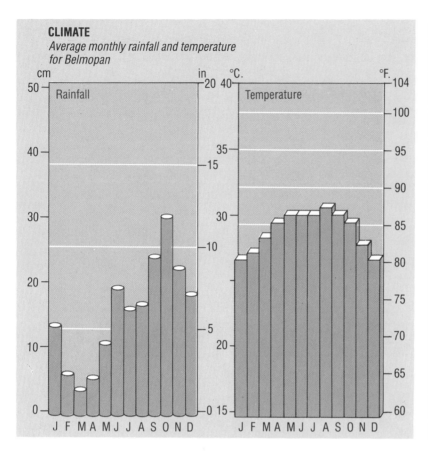

CLIMATE
Average monthly rainfall and temperature for Belmopan

Rainfall

Temperature

J F M A M J J A S O N D

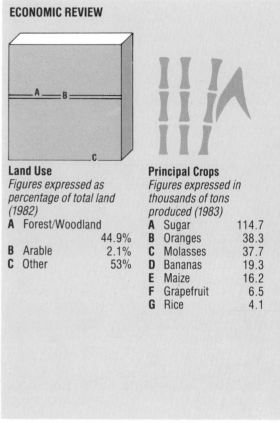

ECONOMIC REVIEW

Land Use
Figures expressed as percentage of total land (1982)

A Forest/Woodland
　　　　44.9%
B Arable　　2.1%
C Other　　53%

Principal Crops
Figures expressed in thousands of tons produced (1983)

A	Sugar	114.7
B	Oranges	38.3
C	Molasses	37.7
D	Bananas	19.3
E	Maize	16.2
F	Grapefruit	6.5
G	Rice	4.1

Social conditions About 30 per cent of the labor force works on the land. Average income is about one-ninth that in the U.S.

Education is compulsory between ages 6 and 14. The literacy rate of over 93 per cent is the highest in Central America. Belize has post-secondary institutions of learning but no university.

There are no free medical services but each district has a government hospital. In 1982 life expectancy was about 65 years. Fewer than 4 per cent of people were aged 65 or over in 1985 and a relatively young population helps to explain an overall death rate half that of the U.S. Infant mortality fell from 51 to 21 per 1000 births between 1970 and 1980. The low death rate and a high birth rate produce a high annual population increase of over 2.5 per cent.

Government Belize is a parliamentary democracy based on the British system. The head of state is the British monarch (as head of the Commonwealth) represented by a Governor General. Executive power rests with a Prime Minister and Cabinet drawn from the 18-member House of Representatives. This is elected at not more than five-year intervals by citizens aged over 18. There is also an appointed eight-member Senate. Belize has six administrative districts. Its law is based on the English legal system.

Communications and transportation Belize has several weekly newspapers, one radio station, 11 cinemas, and no television.

There are 930 miles (1500km.) of surfaced roads, but no national railroads. Small boats ply rivers and sail to the cays. Belize City has the main port, and stands near the only international airport.

Economy The value of this small nation's economic output is tiny compared with that of any other state in Central America. But government and international development agencies work to promote economic growth.

Agriculture takes up only 5 per cent of the land but accounts for more than one-fifth of the gross domestic product. Sugar cane is by far the largest crop, followed by corn (maize), citrus fruits and bananas. Forestry and fisheries contribute less than one-tenth of the gross domestic product. Lobsters are the main catch, and shrimp farms have been started. Rosewood, cedar, and mahogany are

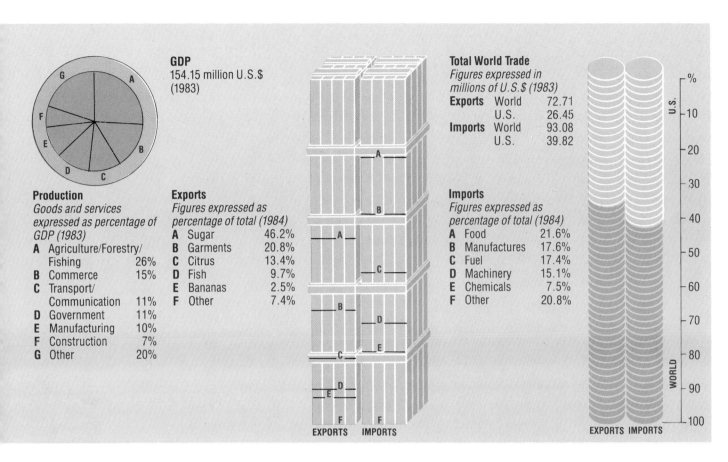

GDP
154.15 million U.S.$
(1983)

Total World Trade
*Figures expressed in
millions of U.S.$ (1983)*

Exports	World	72.71
	U.S.	26.45
Imports	World	93.08
	U.S.	39.82

Production
*Goods and services
expressed as percentage of
GDP (1983)*

A	Agriculture/Forestry/ Fishing	26%
B	Commerce	15%
C	Transport/ Communication	11%
D	Government	11%
E	Manufacturing	10%
F	Construction	7%
G	Other	20%

Exports
*Figures expressed as
percentage of total (1984)*

A	Sugar	46.2%
B	Garments	20.8%
C	Citrus	13.4%
D	Fish	9.7%
E	Bananas	2.5%
F	Other	7.4%

Imports
*Figures expressed as
percentage of total (1984)*

A	Food	21.6%
B	Manufactures	17.6%
C	Fuel	17.4%
D	Machinery	15.1%
E	Chemicals	7.5%
F	Other	20.8%

EXPORTS IMPORTS

EXPORTS IMPORTS

important timber trees, but fast-growing pines and tropical hardwoods are becoming significant.

Mining is insignificant, and manufacturing is small-scale and limited to processing farm products, producing flour and fertilizers, and making consumer goods such as beer and cigarettes.

Sugar accounts for more than half the value of all foreign exchange earnings. Other exports include citrus fruits, bananas, mangoes, lobsters, timber, and clothing. Imports include machinery, transportation equipment, manufactured goods, food, and oil. Belize's main trading partners are the U.S. and United Kingdom.

An 18th-century illustration of "The Culture of Sugar".

©DIAGRAM

43

Honduras

OFFICIAL NAME
República de Honduras

Above **Flag of Honduras**
Equal horizontal bands of
blue, white, and blue with
a central group of five blue
stars. The design comes
from that of the former
United Provinces of Central
America.

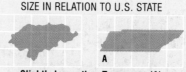

SIZE IN RELATION TO U.S. STATE

A

Slightly larger than Tennessee (A)

AREA	**43,277** square miles (112,088sq.km.)
POPULATION	**4,097,000** (1983 preliminary figure)
POPULATION DENSITY	**94.7** per square mile (1983)
CURRENCY	**Lempira** (1 lempira = 100 centavos)
PRINCIPAL RELIGION	**Roman Catholic**
OFFICIAL LANGUAGE	**Spanish**
CAPITAL	**Tegucigalpa**
ADMINISTRATIVE DIVISIONS	**18 departments**

Honduras is Central America's most central, most mountainous, and second-largest state – a little larger than Tennessee. A land of forests and plantations, it takes its name from *Las Honduras* ("The Deeps"), an early Spanish term for the Gulf of Honduras. This forms part of the country's long Caribbean border to the north. To the west is Guatemala; to the southwest, El Salvador. A short stretch of Pacific coast and a long border with Nicaragua rim the south.

History Maya Indian culture flourished in the area about AD 300–900. Christopher Columbus discovered Honduras in 1502, and in 1539 it became part of Spain's Captaincy General of Guatemala. Silver prospectors later moved in. For a while, English settlers and Mosquito (Miskito) Indians controlled the north's forested Mosquito Coast.

Honduras broke free from Spain in 1821, and was one of the United Provinces of Central America from 1825 to 1838. The five stars on its flag represent the federation's five members. Since leaving the federation in 1838, the republic has suffered civil strife and wars with neighbors. Its strong economic

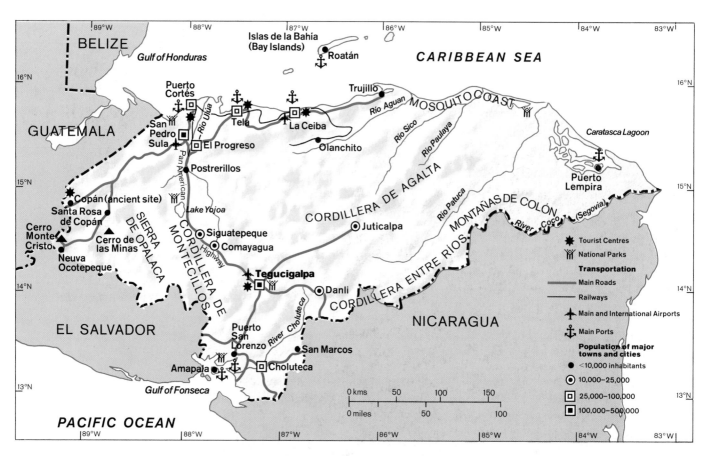

1502	Discovery of the region by Christopher Columbus.		**1969**	War between Honduras and El Salvador over a border dispute. Honduras defeated.
1539	The region became part of Spain's Captaincy General of Guatemala.		**1974**	Country devastated by hurricanes and floods. 5,000 people killed.
1821	Independence from Spain declared.		**1975**	General Lopez Arellano ousted by the armed forces.
1823-38	Honduras a member of the United Provinces of Central America Federation until the organization disintegrated as a result of internal strife.		**1980**	Treaty signed in Peru settling the border dispute between El Salvador and Honduras.
1963	Power seized by General Oswaldo Lopez Arellano.		**1982**	Elected civilian government took power.
1965	New constitution introduced. General Lopez Arellano elected President.			

links with the U.S. date from the late 1800s, when the American-based United Fruit Company (now United Brands) developed railroads and other facilities for banana plantations on the Caribbean coast.

In the mid 1980s the U.S. saw Honduras as playing a vital role in a campaign against El Salvador's leftist guerrillas and Nicaragua's leftist regime. Regional conflict and depressed commodity prices kept out investment and contributed to a drop in already low living standards.

Land Wedge-shaped Honduras is about 400 miles (644km.) from west to east, and 180 miles (290km.) from south to north. Unlike its neighbors, Honduras lacks active volcanoes, but dissected uplands occupy more than three-quarters of the land. Saw-toothed ranges approach the northern coast at an angle. In the northwest, one range continues submerged out to sea, to reappear as the Islas de la Bahía (Bay Islands) chain. Much of the northern coast is rimmed by a lowland of rich clay and loam soils. The northeast's swampy lowlands, with Caratasca Lagoon, comprise part of the so-called Mosquito Coast. Rivers draining north form fertile alluvial valleys, notably the Ulúa river valley in the northwest.

Nearly two-thirds of Honduras is highland covered in old lava and volcanic ash. The highest peak is Cerro de las Minas at 9347 feet (2849m.), in the west.

In the south, narrow lowlands edge the Gulf of Fonseca which forms the country's Pacific coastline. This gulf contains an archipelago of nearly 300 tiny islands.

Climate Coastal lowlands are hot and humid, but the upland interior is cooler and much drier. Average temperatures vary from about 86°F (30°C) on the coast to 58°F (14°C) at

about 7000 feet (2133m.). Temperatures mostly stay much the same all the year, though nights are much cooler than days at high inland places, and Tegucigalpa, the capital, has an annual temperature range of 11°F (6°C). The northeast is the wettest part: here, onshore winds bring up to 110 inches (2794mm.) of rain a year. But some inland valleys get a mere 40 inches (1016mm.). There are only two seasons: rainy from May through November, and dry from December through April.

Vegetation and animals Tropical or mountain forests cover more than two-fifths of the country. Mangroves rim swampy lowland coasts. Pacific plains and slopes support savanna grasses and trees that shed leaves in the seasonal drought. Deciduous woods and grassland clothe high inland valley slopes. High, rainy mountainsides have much oak and pine forest. The hot, humid northern lowland supports evergreen tropical rain forest of mahogany, balsa, Spanish cedar, rosewood, and many more species, with areas of palm and pine.

Honduran woodlands teem with insects, birds, and reptiles, while waterfowl abound on coasts. Lizards, snakes, crocodiles, and turtles are plentiful in lowland areas; hill forests are the homes of such large mammals as bears, jaguars, and pumas.

People The population is 90 per cent Mestizo (Spanish-Indian) with tiny percentages of Indians, Negroes, and Whites. There is no official religion but most people are Roman Catholics. Spanish is the official language; Indian dialects survive.

With over four million people, Honduras is the third-most-populous state in Central America. About 70 per cent of the people live in scattered rural settlements, concentrated

President Francisco Morazán (native of Honduras), elected head of the Central American Federation (1830). *(stamp issued 1878)*

Honduras

CLIMATE
Average monthly rainfall and temperature for Tegucigalpa

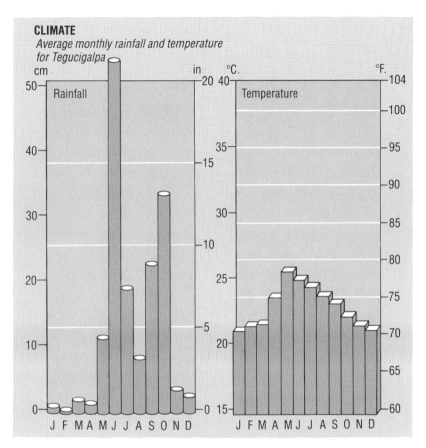

ECONOMIC REVIEW

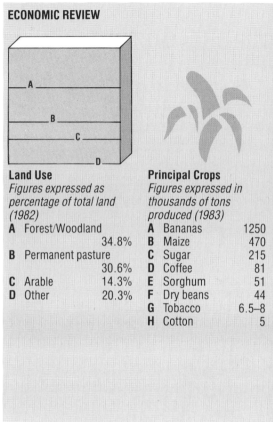

Land Use
Figures expressed as percentage of total land (1982)
A	Forest/Woodland	34.8%
B	Permanent pasture	30.6%
C	Arable	14.3%
D	Other	20.3%

Principal Crops
Figures expressed in thousands of tons produced (1983)
A	Bananas	1250
B	Maize	470
C	Sugar	215
D	Coffee	81
E	Sorghum	51
F	Dry beans	44
G	Tobacco	6.5–8
H	Cotton	5

John Hawkins' account of the treacherous Spanish attack on his fleet in the harbor of San Juan de Ulúa (1568).

in the west, where most towns are. About 20 per cent of Hondurans live in cities, mainly in Tegucigalpa (the capital), San Pedro Sula (the largest industrial city), and the chief port.

Social conditions More than half the working population consists of peasants or farm laborers; only some 12 per cent works in industry. Incomes average less than one-tenth those in the U.S., and there is only a small middle class, so living standards are generally low. But government reforms have included raising minimum wages, distributing land, and launching a literacy campaign.

Children in theory have six years of compulsory education, but many rural areas have no school. In the mid 1980s only 55–60 per cent of the population was literate. The chief center of higher education is the National University in Tegucigalpa.

The Honduran birth rate is among the highest in the world. Population was increasing at 3.5 per cent a year in the early 1980s, despite an infant mortality rate over 10 times higher than in the U.S., and population growth seems set to soar.

Average life expectancy in the mid 1980s was 60 years. This was more than 12 years less than in the U.S. Health-care services are limited, and largely absent outside towns.

Government A Constituent Assembly elected in 1980 revised the Constitution, and in 1982 Honduras formally returned to civilian government as a democratic republic after almost a decade of military rule. All men and women aged over 18 may vote in elections. Deputies in Congress, the single-house legislature, are elected by a proportional vote. Executive power belongs to a President elected by direct popular vote every four years. Presidents may not stand for re-election. Judicial power rests with a Supreme Court elected by Congress. For local government the country is divided into 18 departments.

Communications and transportation There are five daily newspapers, three television channels, more than 100 radio stations, and direct telephone links with the U.S.

The 9300 miles (15,000km.) of roads are mainly unpaved. Surfaced routes include the Pan-American Highway, between El

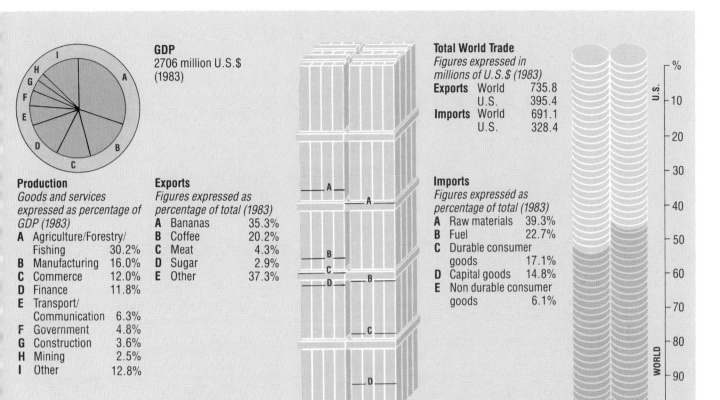

GDP
2706 million U.S.$
(1983)

Production
Goods and services
expressed as percentage of
GDP (1983)

A	Agriculture/Forestry/	
	Fishing	30.2%
B	Manufacturing	16.0%
C	Commerce	12.0%
D	Finance	11.8%
E	Transport/	
	Communication	6.3%
F	Government	4.8%
G	Construction	3.6%
H	Mining	2.5%
I	Other	12.8%

Exports
Figures expressed as
percentage of total (1983)

A	Bananas	35.3%
B	Coffee	20.2%
C	Meat	4.3%
D	Sugar	2.9%
E	Other	37.3%

Total World Trade
Figures expressed in
millions of U.S.$ (1983)

Exports	World	735.8
	U.S.	395.4
Imports	World	691.1
	U.S.	328.4

Imports
Figures expressed as
percentage of total (1983)

A	Raw materials	39.3%
B	Fuel	22.7%
C	Durable consumer	
	goods	17.1%
D	Capital goods	14.8%
E	Non durable consumer	
	goods	6.1%

EXPORTS   IMPORTS

EXPORTS   IMPORTS

Salvador and Nicaragua. Most roads are in the west and northwest; railroads serve only north coast plantations. Air travel is the main way of reaching much of the country. There are international airports at Tegucigalpa, La Ceiba, and San Pedro Sula. The chief Caribbean ports are La Ceiba, Puerto Cortés, and Tela. On the Pacific, Puerto San Lorenzo has replaced Amapala.

Economy The country's economic output is comparable with that of most other Central American states, although there was no economic growth in the mid 1980s when world recession hit commodity prices and export income fell.

Agriculture dominates the economy, though only 10 per cent of land is cultivated (mostly in the west and north). About 25 per cent is pasture. The main crops are corn (maize), bananas, coffee, sorghum, rice, beans, cotton, and tobacco. Honduras is a major world producer of bananas, grown on northern plantations. By the early 1980s there were some 2.4 million cattle and over 700,000 pigs. Cattle ranching is expanding.

Honduras has huge resources of pine, mahogany, and cedar. But fire and pest damage have limited exploitation.

Commercial fishing depends largely on shrimps and lobsters.

Lead and zinc mining contribute to the economy. The considerable mineral resources include silver, gold, tin, coal, and mercury. Plans to develop hydroelectric power are designed to boost the country's very low electricity output.

Growth in small-scale manufacturing for export is helping to cut dependence on cash crops. Factories process foods and produce textiles, clothing, shoes, furniture, cement, pharmaceuticals, radios, and other goods.

The chief exports by value are coffee, bananas, meat, wood, lead, and zinc. Tourism is becoming a significant revenue earner: visitors are drawn by the warm climate, beaches, colonial architecture, and Maya ruins at Copán.

Major imports are machinery, transportation equipment, basic manufactured goods, chemicals, oil, and foods.

The U.S. is Honduras's main trading partner. Others include West Germany, Japan, Guatemala, Costa Rica, and Venezuela.

A "date-marker" in the old Maya city of Copán,

El Salvador

OFFICIAL NAME
República de El Salvador

Above **Flag of El Salvador**
Equal horizontal bands of
blue, white, and blue. One
version bears in the center the
arms of El Salvador. Another
version bears the national motto
"God, Union, Liberty".

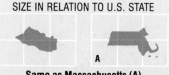

SIZE IN RELATION TO U.S. STATE

A

Same as Massachusetts (A)

AREA	**8236** square miles (21,393 sq.km.)
POPULATION	**5,229,096** (1983 official estimate)
POPULATION DENSITY	**634.9** per square mile (1983)
CURRENCY	**Salvadorean colón** (1 colón = 100 centavos)
PRINCIPAL RELIGION	**Roman Catholic**
OFFICIAL LANGUAGE	**Spanish**
CAPITAL	**San Salvador**
ADMINISTRATIVE DIVISIONS	**14 departments**

The republic of El Salvador is the most densely peopled, most industrialized, and smallest state in Central America – the size of Massachusetts. It is also the only Central American state with no Caribbean coast. The Pacific forms its long southern border. Other boundaries are formed by Guatemala to the northwest and Honduras to the north and east. El Salvador's name commemorates a Spanish victory over local Indian tribes on the eve of the Roman Catholic festival of San Salvador ("Holy Savior").

History Three groups of Indians inhabited the region in the 15th century. The Pipil, the major group, called it Cuscatlán ("Land of the Jewel"). Spaniards led by Pedro de Alvarado invaded from Guatemala in 1524. In 1525 they founded the present capital, San Salvador, and the region became part of Spain's Captaincy General of Guatemala. The country won independence from Spain in 1821. After union with Mexico, and then with other Central American states, El Salvador became formally independent in 1841. Revolutions and wars hindered the country in the later 1800s. After 1900, strong dictators

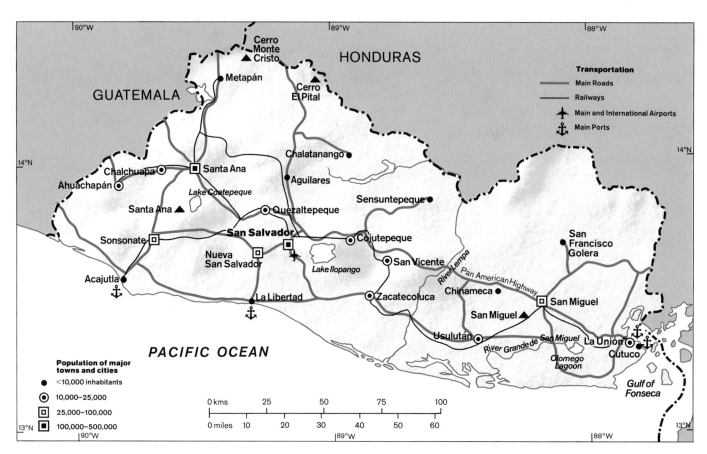

brought stability that helped economic progress. But by the mid 1980s El Salvador suffered overpopulation, labor unrest, and savage civil war. Inflation rose and economic output fell.

Land El Salvador is roughly rectangular: 160 miles (257km.) from west to east, and 60 miles (97km.) from south to north. Four regions run the length of the country. From south to north they are the Pacific lowlands, southern mountains, plateau, and northern mountains.

Pacific lowlands and coastal hills take up 12 per cent of the land. Lagoons fringe parts of the coast. The southern mountain chain takes up nearly one-third of El Salvador. Some of its more than 20 volcanoes are active; Santa Ana is its highest peak at 7812 feet (2381m.). Ilopango, the nation's largest lake, lies in an extinct volcanic crater. Volcanic ash and lava give this region the country's richest soils, but the area is prone to earthquakes. More than two-fifths of El Salvador is plateau, averaging 2000 feet (600m.), but deeply pierced by valleys of the rivers Lempa and San Miguel. The northern mountains occupy 15 per cent of the land, and include the country's highest peak, Cerro El Pital at 8956 feet (2730m.).

Climate Temperature varies with altitude. The coast is hot and humid, and the high inland areas are cooler. San Salvador at 2290 feet (698m) has an annual average temperature of 73°F (23°C), with a range of only 5.4°F (3°C). The hottest months are April and May; the coolest, December through February. The rainy season lasts from May to November. Annual rainfall averages 72 inches (1830mm.). The plateau and deep valleys have less than this; the higher mountains more.

Vegetation and animals Tropical grassland and deciduous broadleaf trees thrive on the Pacific lowlands and slopes. Natural vegetation on the mountains includes the remains of pine and oak forests, with temperate grassland higher up. Subtropical grasses and deciduous trees and bushes grow on the plateau and in the valleys. Only 10 per cent of the land is forested.

El Salvador lacks the variety of wildlife found in nearby countries where less land is cultivated, and rodents are the most numerous mammals. However, the country abounds with insects from bees and butterflies to malarial mosquitoes; birds include blue jays and royal herons; and crocodiles and turtles feature among the reptiles. Anchovies, groupers, grunts, mullet, sharks, snappers, and other fishes swim offshore.

People Nine-tenths of the population is Mestizo (of mixed Spanish-Indian descent). Most of the rest is Indian. Whites account for only one per cent.

The official language is Spanish. Indian dialects have mostly died out, but Nahua survives with government help.

Three-quarters of the population is Roman Catholic.

The fast-growing population passed the five million mark in the early 1980s. The density of about 635 per square mile (244 per sq. km.) was far higher than that of any other Central American country. Most people live on the rich volcanic soils of the southern mountains. Here are the large cities of Santa Ana (pop. 205,000 in 1980), San Miguel (pop. 158,000) and the capital San Salvador (pop. between 375,000 and one million: emigration has made estimates unreliable).

José Matias Delgado, a fighter for El Salvador's independence (1811). *(stamp issued 1932)*

©DIAGRAM

El Salvador

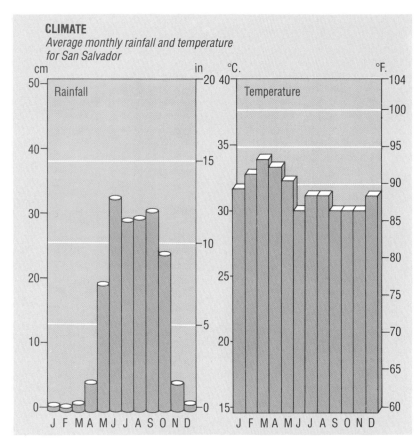

CLIMATE
Average monthly rainfall and temperature for San Salvador

Rainfall

Temperature

J F M A M J J A S O N D

J F M A M J J A S O N D

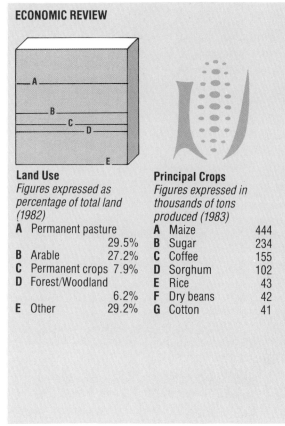

ECONOMIC REVIEW

Land Use
Figures expressed as percentage of total land (1982)

A Permanent pasture 29.5%
B Arable 27.2%
C Permanent crops 7.9%
D Forest/Woodland 6.2%
E Other 29.2%

Principal Crops
Figures expressed in thousands of tons produced (1983)

A	Maize	444
B	Sugar	234
C	Coffee	155
D	Sorghum	102
E	Rice	43
F	Dry beans	42
G	Cotton	41

Social conditions More than one-third of the labor force works on the land and about one-fifth in industry. Annual per capita income is low (U.S. $470 in 1983) and inflation has eroded buying power. Low earnings, overpopulation, and civil war have triggered much emigration to nearby states.

Education is free and compulsory from the age of 7 to 15, but the literacy rate is low: 50 per cent in towns and only 30 per cent outside them. Centers of higher education include the University of El Salvador.

There are a number of hospitals, but most doctors work only in towns.

The Social Security Institute administers sickness, old age and death benefits for workers affiliated to it.

Life expectancy in the early 1980s was 57 for men and 60 for women. Infant mortality was more than five times higher than in the U.S. The very high birth rate had begun to fall, and annual population increase dropped to a still high 2.1 per cent by 1985.

Government A new Constitution came into force in 1983. Executive power rests with a President (elected for a non-renewable five years) and his appointed ministers and under-secretaries. The Legislative Assembly of 52 members is chosen by universal suffrage for a three-year term. Judicial power rests with a Supreme Court elected by the Assembly, and with subordinate courts. El Salvador is divided into 14 departments with governors appointed by the President.

Communications and transportation In the mid 1980s there were five television channels, more than 50 radio stations, and six daily newspapers.

The Pan-American Highway crosses the country. There are more than 6200 miles (10,000km.) of roads, nearly half of them all-weather. Railroads run the length of the land. They link San Salvador with other inland cities, the Pacific ports Acajutla and La Unión Cutuco, and Guatemala.

Economy Labor unrest, civil war, and a worldwide recession cut the value of El Salvador's economic output by 28 per cent in five years; the fall stopped in 1983.

Nearly one-third of El Salvador is cultivated, and more than one-quarter is pasture. Agriculture accounts for about one-quarter of the gross domestic product. The most important crop has long been coffee,

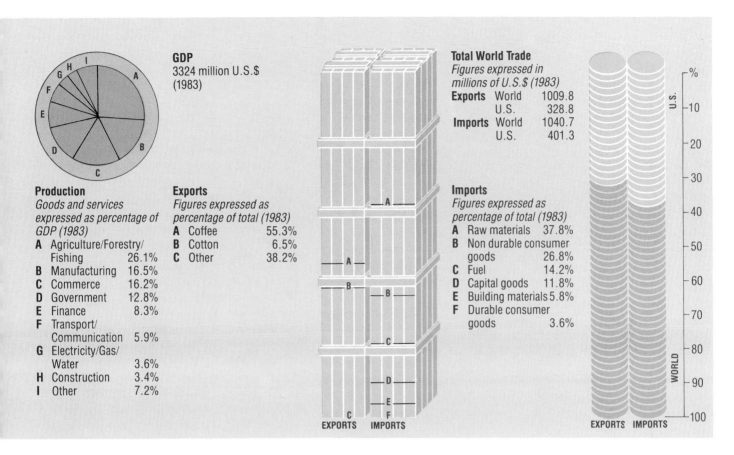

GDP
3324 million U.S.$
(1983)

Production
*Goods and services
expressed as percentage of
GDP (1983)*

A	Agriculture/Forestry/Fishing	26.1%
B	Manufacturing	16.5%
C	Commerce	16.2%
D	Government	12.8%
E	Finance	8.3%
F	Transport/Communication	5.9%
G	Electricity/Gas/Water	3.6%
H	Construction	3.4%
I	Other	7.2%

Exports
*Figures expressed as
percentage of total (1983)*

A	Coffee	55.3%
B	Cotton	6.5%
C	Other	38.2%

Total World Trade
*Figures expressed in
millions of U.S.$ (1983)*

Exports	World	1009.8
	U.S.	328.8
Imports	World	1040.7
	U.S.	401.3

Imports
*Figures expressed as
percentage of total (1983)*

A	Raw materials	37.8%
B	Non durable consumer goods	26.8%
C	Fuel	14.2%
D	Capital goods	11.8%
E	Building materials	5.8%
F	Durable consumer goods	3.6%

EXPORTS IMPORTS

EXPORTS IMPORTS

grown on the southern mountains' volcanic soils. Other leading crops are cotton, corn (maize), and sugar cane. El Salvador has more than a million cattle, five million chickens, and 350,000 pigs. Forest products include cedar, mahogany, and walnut. Shrimps are the main fishery resource.

There is some gold and silver mining, and mineral resources include copper, iron, and lead. El Salvador is developing its considerable hydroelectric power potential.

Manufacturing accounts for some 15 per cent of the gross national product. Items include shoes, textiles, clothing, fertilizers, chemicals and pharmaceuticals, cement, and leather goods. Civil unrest and lack of investment have badly hit production.

Trade, tourism, and transportation account for nearly one-third of the gross domestic product. More than half the total value of exports comes from coffee. Other exports include cotton and textiles. The main imports are manufactured goods, chemical products, fuel oil, machinery, tools, and transportation equipment. El Salvador's main trading partners include the U.S. Guatemala, West Germany, and Japan.

An 18th-century illustration of "The Culture of Cotton".

©DIAGRAM

Nicaragua

OFFICIAL NAME
República de Nicaragua

Above **Flag of Nicaragua**
State: Equal horizontal
divisions of blue, white, and
blue with a coat of arms in
the center. (The coat of
arms is also shown left.)
Civil: As above but with no
coat of arms.

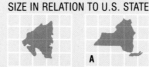

SIZE IN RELATION TO U.S. STATE

A

Slightly larger than New York State (A)

AREA	**49,759** square miles (128,875 sq. km.)
POPULATION	**2,999,000** (1983 preliminary figure)
POPULATION DENSITY	**60.3** per square mile
CURRENCY	**Córdoba** (1 córdoba = 100 centavos)
PRINCIPAL RELIGION	**Roman Catholic**
OFFICIAL LANGUAGE	**Spanish**
CAPITAL	**Managua**
ADMINISTRATIVE DIVISIONS	**16 departments**

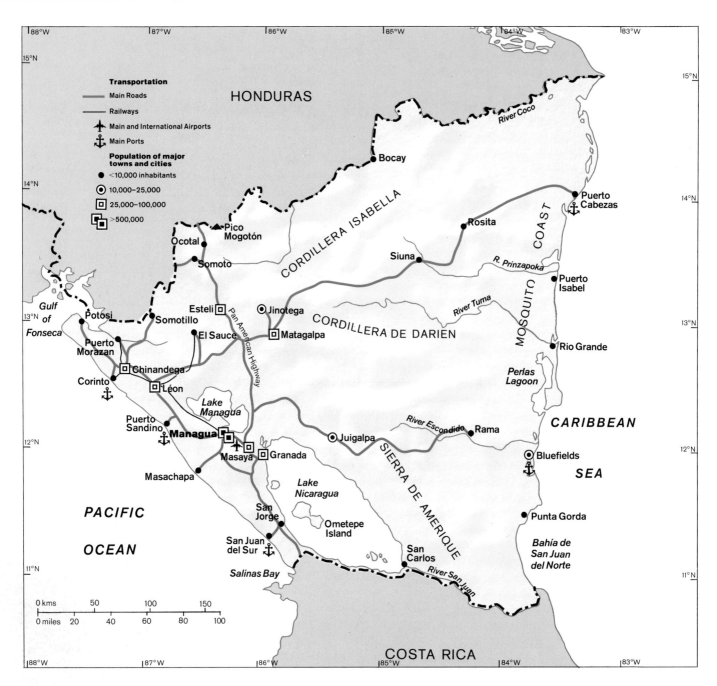

Tradition has it that Nicaragua takes its name from Nicarao, an Indian chief living in the region when the Spanish subdued it in the early 1500s. Nicaragua is Central America's largest nation – a little larger than New York.

Nicaragua straddles mid Central America, with the Pacific Ocean to the southwest, the Caribbean Sea to the east, Honduras to the north and northwest, and Costa Rica to the southeast.

History Indian tribes were living in the region when Christopher Columbus discovered it in 1502. The Spanish conquest began from Panama in the 1520s. In 1570 the area came under Spanish jurisdiction based in Guatemala. Later, the British claimed a protectorate over the Mosquito (Caribbean) Coast.

After Central American states broke with Spain in 1821, Nicaragua joined Mexico in 1822. Then came civil war. From 1826 to 1838 Nicaragua was in the Central American Federation. Liberal-Conservative friction allowed U.S. adventurer William Walker briefly to step in as President (1856–57). In the early 1900s, fresh turmoil was followed by repeated U.S. military intervention. From 1937 to 1979 Nicaragua was run mostly by the autocratic Somoza family, who wielded power with help from the National Guard. Guerrilla opposition by the Marxist Sandinist Liberation Front culminated in wider civil war (1978–79).

Land Nicaragua resembles a triangle with sides formed by Honduras, the Caribbean, and a line produced by the Pacific coast and Costa Rican border. Inside this triangle a smaller, central triangle of mountainous land juts south from Honduras almost down to Costa Rica. This area consists of short, steep mountain ranges with fertile valleys between. Pico Mogotón at 6913 feet (2107m) is the country's highest mountain. East of the central mountains lies one of the broadest Caribbean lowlands in Central America. Nicaragua's Mosquito (Caribbean) coast is 336 miles (541km) of deltas, sandbars, and lagoons, with offshore reefs and islands. Southwest of the mountains is Lake Nicaragua, Central America's largest lake. This lake and Lake Managua lie in a lowland running northwest to the Pacific. West of the lowland, about 40 volcanoes (some active) form a line that parallels the Pacific coast. Volcanic ash covers large areas, producing fertile soil. The low Pacific coast runs from the Gulf of Fonseca in the northwest to Salinas Bay in the southwest.

Climate Lowlands are hot and humid, with average annual temperatures of 81°F (27°C) on the Pacific coast and 79°F (26°C) on the Caribbean coast. Northern mountains have lower, more springlike, temperatures, with an annual average of about 64°F (18°C).

The Caribbean side has one of the highest rainfalls in Central America, with up to 150 inches (3810mm) a year. The Pacific side averages half that amount, and has a more marked dry season (December–April).

Prevailing winds blow from the northeast.

Vegetation and animals Tropical forest covers almost half the land. Trees include *lignum vitae*, mahogany, and quebracho. Mangroves rim the swampy east coast. Much of the west is savanna grassland with forest lining rivers.

Forest mammals include deer, peccaries, rodents, monkeys, jaguars, and pumas. The hot lowlands teem with insects, and tropical reptiles including snakes and crocodiles. Land and water birds abound. A variety of fishes inhabit lagoons, lakes, and rivers.

President José Santos Zelaya, architect of a period of modernization and national development.
(*stamp issued 1903–4*)

©DIAGRAM

53

Nicaragua

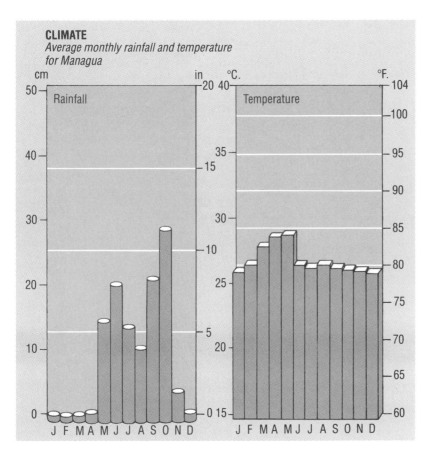

CLIMATE
Average monthly rainfall and temperature for Managua

Rainfall

Temperature

J F M A M J J A S O N D

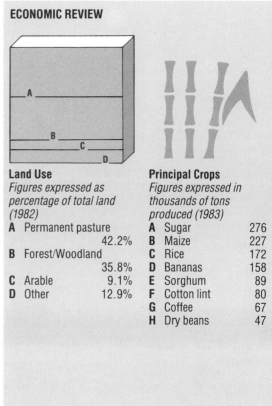

ECONOMIC REVIEW

Land Use
Figures expressed as percentage of total land (1982)
A Permanent pasture 42.2%
B Forest/Woodland 35.8%
C Arable 9.1%
D Other 12.9%

Principal Crops
Figures expressed in thousands of tons produced (1983)
A Sugar 276
B Maize 227
C Rice 172
D Bananas 158
E Sorghum 89
F Cotton lint 80
G Coffee 67
H Dry beans 47

People Most citizens are Mestizos (Spanish-Indian), with White, Negro, and Indian minorities. The majority is Roman Catholic, but there are various Protestant groups. Spanish is the chief language. English is spoken on the Caribbean coast.

About half the population of about three million is rural. Most people live on the volcanic mountains and lowlands of the west.

Social conditions About half the working population is involved in farming. Industry occupies 15–20 per cent. Incomes average less than one-tenth those in the U.S.

Inadequate health, welfare, and education services have been improved by the Sandinista government. Education is free and compulsory. By the early 1980s a literacy campaign had raised the literacy level to 88 per cent (it had been 58 per cent in 1971). Centers of higher education include universities at Managua and León.

The Nicaraguan birth rate is one of the highest anywhere.

Average life expectancy in the mid 1970s was about 53 years, compared with more than 70 in the U.S. Infant mortality is more than three times higher than in the U.S.

Government Elections held in 1984 replaced a post-revolutionary Junta of Reconstruction with a President and National Assembly, chosen for six years by an electorate comprising all aged over 16. The President had executive power, the Assembly legislative power. Both had a say in electing the Supreme Court, the main judicial authority. For local government the country was divided into 16 departments run by seven authorities.

Communications and transportation In the mid 1980s there were several daily newspapers, many radio stations, two television stations in Managua, and automatic telephone links between major cities.

The road system has been greatly extended but most of the 11,000 miles (18,000km) of roads are unsurfaced. Paved roads link the main centers. These routes include the Pan-American Highway, crossing the nation from Honduras to Costa Rica. A 252-mile (405km) single-track railroad runs along most of the Pacific side of the country. There is an international airport

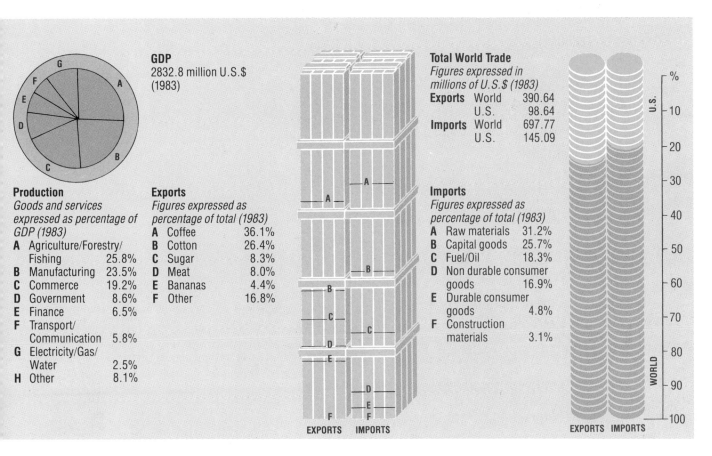

GDP
2832.8 million U.S.$
(1983)

Production
Goods and services expressed as percentage of GDP (1983)
A Agriculture/Forestry/
Fishing   25.8%
B Manufacturing   23.5%
C Commerce   19.2%
D Government   8.6%
E Finance   6.5%
F Transport/
Communication   5.8%
G Electricity/Gas/
Water   2.5%
H Other   8.1%

Exports
Figures expressed as percentage of total (1983)
A Coffee   36.1%
B Cotton   26.4%
C Sugar   8.3%
D Meat   8.0%
E Bananas   4.4%
F Other   16.8%

Total World Trade
Figures expressed in millions of U.S.$ (1983)
Exports World   390.64
         U.S.   98.64
Imports World   697.77
         U.S.   145.09

Imports
Figures expressed as percentage of total (1983)
A Raw materials   31.2%
B Capital goods   25.7%
C Fuel/Oil   18.3%
D Non durable consumer
goods   16.9%
E Durable consumer
goods   4.8%
F Construction
materials   3.1%

EXPORTS   IMPORTS

EXPORTS   IMPORTS

at Managua. Puerto Cabezas and Bluefields are the two chief Caribbean ports. The three major Pacific ports are Corinto, Puerto Sandino, and San Juan del Sur.

Economy Nicaragua's economic output is worth less than that of any other Central American state except Belize. Civil war, low commodity prices, and U.S.economic pressure have all hit the economy since the mid 1970s.

Agriculture probably accounts for about one-quarter of the entire gross domestic product. Cultivated land occupies perhaps only 5 per cent of the whole country, about the same as pasture. But rich soil in the volcanic foothills can yield two crops of beans, corn, or sorghum in a year. The chief crops are sugar cane, corn, sorghum, cotton, coffee, rice, and beans. Other crops include bananas, cocoa, sesame, and tobacco.

An early 1980s estimate gave 2.3 million cattle and 500,000 pigs. Nicaragua ranks third for beef output in Central America, behind Guatemala and Costa Rica.

Fish provide most of the protein eaten on the Caribbean coast. The commercial fishery depends mainly on shrimps.

Mineral resources include gold, silver, copper, salt, tungsten, and natural gas off the Pacific coast. Lack of mined fossil fuel or hydroelectric plant contributes to low electricity output.

Manufacturing accounts for nearly one-third of gross domestic product according to one estimate (another gives less than one-fifth). Food processing is the chief sector, with factories refining sugar, processing meat, and producing drinks, dairy products, and instant coffee. Others make cement, cigarettes, leather goods, textiles, chemicals, and metal goods. There is an oil refinery.

Trade, tourism, and transportation account for nearly one-third of the gross domestic product. The main exports are cotton, coffee, meat, chemicals, and sugar. Major imports include machinery, transportation equipment, chemicals, oil, and food.

Nicaragua's chief trading partners have included the U.S., West Germany, Japan, Italy, Venezuela, Costa Rica, and Guatemala.

A cotton plant, one of Nicaragua's chief crops.

©DIAGRAM

Costa Rica

OFFICIAL NAME
República de Costa Rica

Above Flag of Costa Rica
State: Five horizontal bands of blue, white, red, white, blue. To the staff side of center the red band has a white disk with the coat of arms. Civil: As above but with no coat of arms.

Slightly larger than Vermont and New Hampshire together (A)

AREA	**19,650** square miles (50,900sq.km.)
POPULATION	**2,378,000** (1983 preliminary figure)
POPULATION DENSITY	**121.0** per square mile
CURRENCY	**Colón** (1 colón = 100 centimos)
PRINCIPAL RELIGION	**Roman Catholic**
OFFICIAL LANGUAGE	**Spanish**
CAPITAL	**San José**
ADMINISTRATIVE DIVISIONS	**7 provinces**

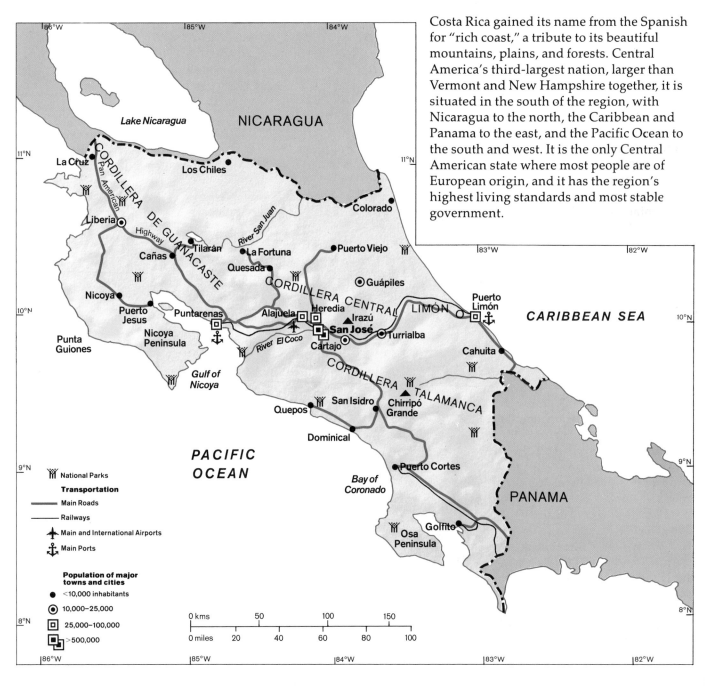

Costa Rica gained its name from the Spanish for "rich coast," a tribute to its beautiful mountains, plains, and forests. Central America's third-largest nation, larger than Vermont and New Hampshire together, it is situated in the south of the region, with Nicaragua to the north, the Caribbean and Panama to the east, and the Pacific Ocean to the south and west. It is the only Central American state where most people are of European origin, and it has the region's highest living standards and most stable government.

National Parks

Transportation
Main Roads
Railways
Main and International Airports
Main Ports

Population of major towns and cities
● <10,000 inhabitants
◉ 10,000–25,000
▣ 25,000–100,000
▣ >500,000

HISTORICAL REVIEW

1821	Costa Rica gains independence.
1824	Costa Rica joins Mexico in the Central American Federation.
1838	Costa Rica leaves the Federation.
1871	New constitution introduced.
1896	Treaty signed over disputed boundary with Nicaragua.
1913	Alfredo Gonzáles Flores becomes President.
1917	General Federico Tinoco Granados stages a successful revolution.
1919	Julio Acosta Garcia is elected President.
1941	Costa Rica declares war on Japan, Germany and Italy.
1948	Serious political crisis. José Figueres becomes chairman of the ruling junta.
1949	New constitution is adopted.
1950	Industrialization strategy begins.
1953	José Figueres, a socialist landowner, is legally elected President. Nationalization policies are introduced.
1955	Costa Rica, aided by the OAS, repel an invasion by exiles in Nicaragua.
1963	Mt. Irazú erupts.
1970	José Figueres is again elected President.
1985	U.S. advisers trained an anti-terrorist force.

History Indian farmers were living in the area when Christopher Columbus discovered it in 1502. Spanish colonists settled the central highlands and controlled the country by the 1570s. Many Indians were killed by warfare and imported diseases, depriving colonists of the cheap native labor exploited in Spain's other Central American colonies. As a result, unlike them, Costa Rica did not become a land run by a few, wealthy plantation owners; instead it gained many small, poor, Spanish peasant farmers.

Colonial Costa Rica came under Spain's Captaincy General of Guatemala. Like the rest of Central America, Costa Rica broke away from Spain in 1821. It joined Mexico briefly, and then was a member of the United Provinces of Central America from 1823 to 1838. Surviving dictators and civil wars (the last in 1948-49), Costa Rica emerged as Central America's most soundly-based democracy.

Prosperity dates from the 1840s, when coffee was first exported. Export earnings underpinned the development of transportation, education, and (after 1950) fast industrial and urban growth.

Land Costa Rica is relatively long and narrow, with low coasts and a mountain spine. Its irregular Pacific Coast measures 631 miles (1016km.), nearly five times longer than the 132 miles (212km.) of straighter Caribbean coast. From coast to coast is 74–175 miles (119–282km.).

Three-tenths of Costa Rica consists of the thinly peopled, swampy Caribbean coastal plain.

To its south three mountain ranges with large volcanoes cross the center of the country. From northwest to southeast these ranges are the Guanacaste, Central, and Talamanca. Chirripó Grande, in the Talamanca range, is the highest peak, at 12,529ft. (3819m.). In this area high mountains flank tablelands made fertile by volcanic ash. A devastating ashfall covered much of the thickly populated Meseta Central, the largest tableland, when Irazú erupted in 1963–64.

The hilly Nicoya and Osa peninsulas are features of the mostly low Pacific coast.

Costa Rica's largest river is the navigable San Juan, shared with Nicaragua.

Climate Like the rest of Central America, Costa Rica has hot, humid coasts and cooler uplands. Average temperatures range from more than 80°F (27°C) on the coasts, through 69°F (21°C) in the capital, San José, at 3800ft. (1158m.), to 59°F (15°C) at twice that altitude. The so-called "temperate" and "cold" zones start about 1000ft. (3048m.) lower on Pacific than on Caribbean slopes.

Parts of the southern Pacific and Caribbean coasts receive over 126 inches (3200mm.) of rain a year. On the Pacific coast the rainy season can last from April to December. On the Caribbean side, moist northeast winds can bring rain 300 days a year.

Vegetation and animals About half the land is forested. Tropical - broadleaf - forest covers moist, warm areas. Trees include mahogany and rosewood, and there are mountain stands of evergreen oaks. Palms and mangroves thrive on coasts, whereas deciduous forest or savanna covers dry Pacific slopes.

Costa Rica has a wealth of wildlife. South American mammals include anteaters, armadillos, monkeys, sloths, and tapirs. North American forms include coyotes, deer, foxes, otters, and wild cats. Nature reserves hold all these and many of Costa Rica's 900

Juan Rafael Mora, president following the power struggles between the landowning clans from 1842–1870.
(stamp issued 1907)

©DIAGRAM

57

Costa Rica

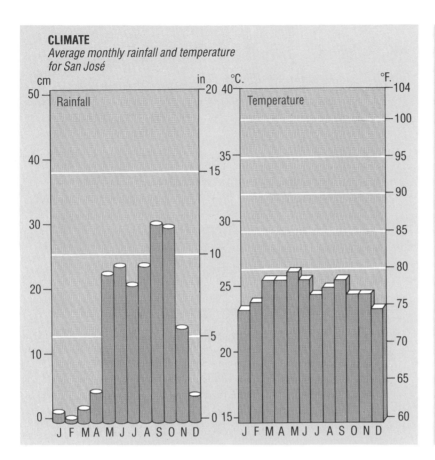

CLIMATE
*Average monthly rainfall and temperature
for San José*

Rainfall

Temperature

J F M A M J J A S O N D

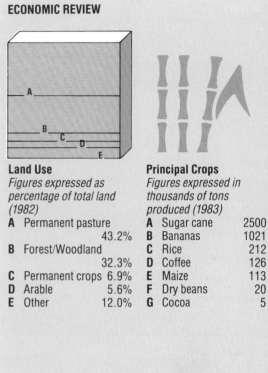

ECONOMIC REVIEW

Land Use
*Figures expressed as
percentage of total land
(1982)*

A	Permanent pasture	43.2%
B	Forest/Woodland	32.3%
C	Permanent crops	6.9%
D	Arable	5.6%
E	Other	12.0%

Principal Crops
*Figures expressed in
thousands of tons
produced (1983)*

A	Sugar cane	2500
B	Bananas	1021
C	Rice	212
D	Coffee	126
E	Maize	113
F	Dry beans	20
G	Cocoa	5

bird species – more than in the whole of the U.S. Tropical tree frogs, snakes, and turtles live in the hot forests, and the country teems with lovely butterflies.

People More than nine-tenths of the population is of Spanish or Mestizo (Spanish-Indian) origin, with tiny minorities of Negroes and Indians. But Negroes make up one-third of the inhabitants of the thinly populated Caribbean province of Limón. The population is more than 90 per cent Roman Catholic; there are some Protestants, and a few Jews. Spanish is the official language, although many of Limón's Negroes speak Jamaican English.

Costa Rica's population of less than three million is the third-smallest in Central America. Two-thirds of the people live in rural areas, and more than half the total population dwells in the fertile Meseta Central and nearby valleys.

Social conditions About one-third of the population works in agriculture, two-fifths in industry and commerce, and one-quarter in services and government. Average income is the highest in Central America, but is only one-quarter that in the U.S.

It has long been government policy to raise standards of education, housing, and health. The 90 per cent literacy rate is among the highest in Central America. There is six years' compulsory education, and over 20,000 people attend the University of Costa Rica.

Malnutrition, vitamin deficiences, and goiter remain problems. But Costa Rica has more doctors and hospital beds per 100,000 citizens than most Central American states, and the region's highest life expectancy.

The birth rate is still high, although low for Central America. Infant mortality has been reduced and population growth is rapid. In the mid 1980s, the annual population increase of 2.7 per cent was four times that of the U.S.

Government All citizens aged over 20 are eligible to vote every four years to choose a President and Legislative Assembly. The President is chosen by direct popular vote; the 57 deputies of the Assembly by proportional representation. The Assembly chooses magistrates of the Supreme Court for extendable eight-year terms. Governors appointed by the President run Costa Rica's

A banana plant, one of the chief Costa Rican exports.

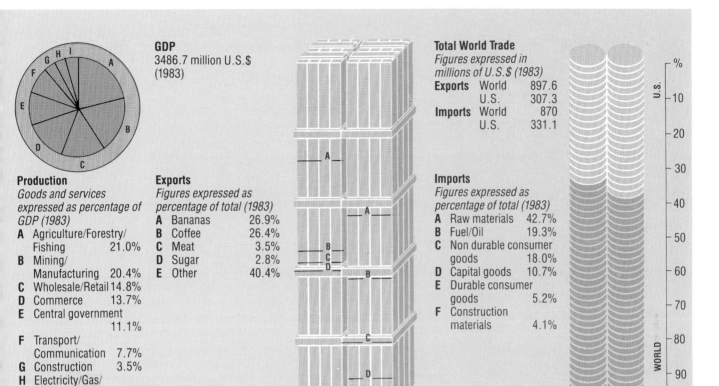

GDP
3486.7 million U.S.$
(1983)

Production
Goods and services
expressed as percentage of
GDP (1983)

A	Agriculture/Forestry/ Fishing	21.0%
B	Mining/ Manufacturing	20.4%
C	Wholesale/Retail	14.8%
D	Commerce	13.7%
E	Central government	11.1%
F	Transport/ Communication	7.7%
G	Construction	3.5%
H	Electricity/Gas/ Water	3.5%
I	Other	4.3%

Exports
Figures expressed as
percentage of total (1983)

A	Bananas	26.9%
B	Coffee	26.4%
C	Meat	3.5%
D	Sugar	2.8%
E	Other	40.4%

Total World Trade
Figures expressed in
millions of U.S.$ (1983)

Exports	World	897.6
	U.S.	307.3
Imports	World	870
	U.S.	331.1

Imports
Figures expressed as
percentage of total (1983)

A	Raw materials	42.7%
B	Fuel/Oil	19.3%
C	Non durable consumer goods	18.0%
D	Capital goods	10.7%
E	Durable consumer goods	5.2%
F	Construction materials	4.1%

EXPORTS IMPORTS

EXPORTS IMPORTS

seven provinces. There is a Civil Guard but no army.

Communications and transportation There are several television stations and a great many radio stations. Costa Rica has more telephones than any other Central American state and the region's largest readership of daily newspapers.

Nearly one-quarter of the 17,100 miles (27,500km.) of road is surfaced, and the Pan-American Highway links Costa Rica with Nicaragua and Panama. Railroads cross the country, linking San José with the Pacific port of Puntarenas (and soon with its replacement Caldera) and Puerto Limón on the Caribbean coast. Other railroads serve plantations. San José has an international airport.

Economy Costa Rica's gross domestic product ranked third in value in Central America in the early 1980s. It was also growing at the fastest rate. But there was a marked trade imbalance, and Costa Rica's inflation rate was by far the region's highest.

Nearly one-quarter of the gross domestic product comes from agriculture: arable farming takes up 10 per cent of the land and

pasture occupies 25 per cent, and has been much increased by forest clearance.

Fishing also contributes to the economy.

Mining takes place for gold, silver, sea salt, manganese, and mercury. There are deposits of iron ore, sulfur, and bauxite.

Costa Rica produces more energy than any other country in Central America: most comes from hydroelectricity. Much sugar cane is now grown for use as fuel.

One-fifth of the gross domestic product is accounted for by manufacturing. Products include sugar, coffee, beer, meat, clothing, wood, cement, and chemicals.

Coffee and bananas together usually account for more than half the value of all exports. Other exports include cattle, meat, cocoa, sugar, and fertilizers. Tropical scenery and political stability encourage tourism, another source of foreign earnings.

Machinery, transportation equipment, manufactured goods, chemicals, oil, and food account for most imports.

Up to one-third of Costa Rica's trade is with the U.S. West Germany, Japan, El Salvador, Guatemala, and the Netherlands are other leading trading partners.

A colon coin, named after the Spanish for Columbus.

©DIAGRAM

Panama

OFFICIAL NAME
República de Panamá

Above Flag of Panama
This has four quarters. Top, next staff: white with a blue star. Top, outer: red. Below, next staff: blue. Below, outer: white with a red star. Colors symbolize political groups; stars, qualities.

SIZE IN RELATION TO U.S. STATE

A

Slightly larger than Maine (A)

AREA	**33,569** square miles (87,176 sq.km.)
POPULATION	**1,964,000** (1983 preliminary figure)
POPULATION DENSITY	**58.5** per square mile
CURRENCY	**Balboa** (1 balboa = 10 centesimos)
PRINCIPAL RELIGION	**Roman Catholic**
OFFICIAL LANGUAGE	**Spanish**
CAPITAL	**Panama City**
ADMINISTRATIVE DIVISIONS	**9 provinces**

The republic of Panama is Central America's fourth-largest nation – a little larger than Maine – and the region's southernmost state. It lies east of Costa Rica, west of Colombia, south of the Caribbean Sea, and north of the Pacific Ocean. The Panama Canal cuts across its center. The country's position astride the canal and between North and South America have earned it the nickname "crossroads of the world." Its real name comes from an old Indian word meaning "fishermen."

Panama is Central America's narrowest country, and has the longest coastlines.

Inland are low mountains, dense tropical forests, and fertile plains and valleys.

History More than 60 Indian tribes inhabited the Isthmus of Panama in 1501, when the Spanish explorer Rodrigo de Bastidas discovered Panama's Caribbean coast. Spanish colonists arrived in 1509, and crushed the Indians. In 1513 Governor Vasco Núñez de Balboa discovered the Pacific coast; his successor founded Panama City in 1519.

Thereafter Panama became a springboard for Spanish colonists thrusting west through

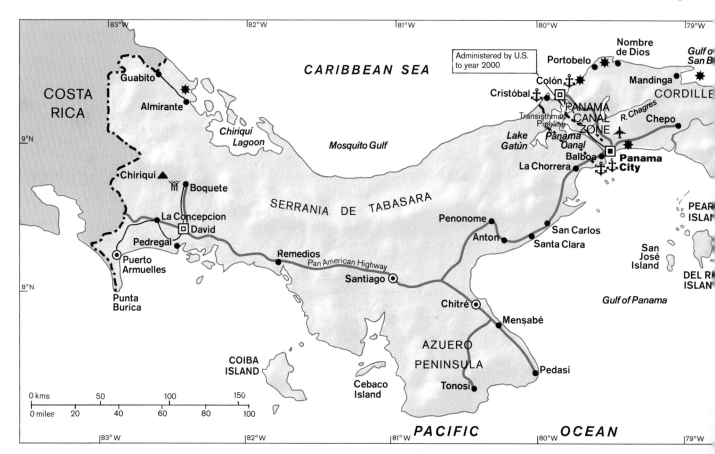

HISTORICAL REVIEW

1821	Panama proclaims its independence from Spain. Voluntarily joins the Colombian Union.
1855	Panama Railroad is completed.
1901	U.S. and Great Britain sign the Hay-Pauncefote Treaty, allowing the U.S. to build the Panama Canal.
1903	Panama proclaims its independence from Colombia.
1904	New constitution. Manuel Amador Guerrero becomes first President.
1914	Construction of the Canal is completed.
1940	Pro fascist Arnulfo Arias becomes President.
1941	War declared on Japan, Germany and Italy.

1951	Constitution is suspended.
1954	U.S.-Panama Treaty renegotiated.
1955	Ricardo Arias Espinosa becomes President. Work on the Inter-American Highway begins.
1960	Roberto Francisco Chiari is elected President.
1964	Marco A. Robles is elected President.
1968	Coup by the National Guard brings Col. José M. Pinilla to power as President.
1979	The U.S. formally handed Canal sovereignty to Panama.
1981	"Strong man" President Omar Torrijos killed in an air crash.

Central America and south to Peru. It was also a major transshipment route for gold and silver flowing back to Spain.

In 1717 Panama joined Colombia as part of Spain's Viceroyalty of New Granada, but in 1821 Panama broke with Spain and became a province of Colombia. After revolts, it gained independence in 1903, with U.S. support.

The U.S.-sponsored Panama Canal opened in 1914. This brought increased prosperity, but with it came discontent with U.S. control of the Canal Zone. In 1979 sovereignty of the zone reverted to Panama, but U.S. administration is to run until the year 2000.

Land Panama is a long, narrow isthmus shaped like a letter S on its side. At its narrowest, the country is only 31 miles (49km.) across. Yet its Pacific coastline extends for 760 miles (1223km.), and the Caribbean coast is 470 miles (756km.) long.

Three-fifths of Panama is mountainous: low ranges run the length of the land. The tallest summits are in the west, including the highest peak, the volcano Chiriquí at 11,411ft (3478m.). Between the parallel ranges lie fertile valleys and plains, and there is a low-lying, sometimes swampy, coastal strip. Chief rivers include the Chagres, Chepo, and Tuira. Man-made Gatún is the only big lake.

The southern (Pacific) coast is much indented. Here the chunky Azuero Peninsula forms the western side of the great Gulf of Panama. Coiba Island lies west of the peninsula, and the Gulf of Panama contains the Pearl Islands archipelago.

Climate This is largely tropical and rainy. Lowland temperatures average over 80°F (27°C), with a drop at night; uplands are cooler at 66°F (19°C) or less. Much of the Caribbean coast and high mountains has more than 120 inches (3048mm.) of rainfall a year – rain falls on most days and at any time of year. Parts of the Pacific coast around the Gulf of Panama have less than 60 inches (1524mm.) and have a dry season lasting from January to April.

Panama is outside the hurricane belt.

Vegetation and animals More than half of Panama is forest wilderness. Moist inland lowlands support tropical-broadleaf-forest trees such as mahogany, while deciduous-temperate-forest trees including oaks grow on the high western mountains. Savanna

Map

DE SAN BLAS

River Chepo

9°N

Pito

La Palma

San Miguel Gulf

River Tuira

8°N

COLOMBIA

Jaque

78°W · 77°W

Tourist Centres

National Parks

Transportation
— Main Roads
— Railways
✈ Main and International Airports
⚓ Main Ports

Population of major towns and cities
- ● <10,000 inhabitants
- ◉ 10,000–25,000
- ▣ 25,000–100,000
- ■ 100,000–500,000

Governor Vasco Núñez de Balboa, discoverer of the Pacific coast in 1513. *(stamp issued 1909–10)*

© DIAGRAM

61

Panama

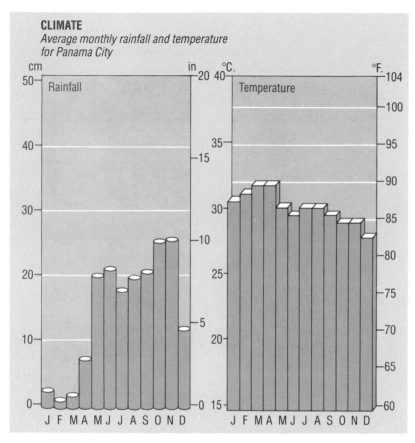

CLIMATE
Average monthly rainfall and temperature for Panama City

Rainfall

Temperature

J F M A M J J A S O N D

J F M A M J J A S O N D

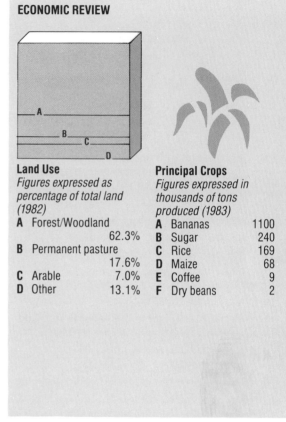

ECONOMIC REVIEW

Land Use
Figures expressed as percentage of total land (1982)

A Forest/Woodland
62.3%
B Permanent pasture
17.6%
C Arable   7.0%
D Other   13.1%

Principal Crops
Figures expressed in thousands of tons produced (1983)

A Bananas	1100
B Sugar	240
C Rice	169
D Maize	68
E Coffee	9
F Dry beans	2

grassland covers some of the drier Pacific areas.

Tropical forest animals include armadillos, deer, monkeys, jaguars, opossums, porcupines, raccoons, and tapirs. Panama has 850 species of birds, along with innumerable tropical insects from gaudy butterflies to ants that give a painful bite. Reptiles include crocodilians, lizards, snakes, and turtles; amphibians feature small, brilliantly colored frogs. The waters contain a wealth of fishes.

People Panamanians are mainly Mestizos (of mixed White and Indian stock) and Mulattoes (of mixed White-Negro stock). There are also Negroes, Chinese, Jews, Hindus, and three aboriginal Indian tribes: the Chocó, Cuna, and Guaymí. Many U.S. citizens live and work in the former Canal Zone.

More than 90 per cent of Panamanians are Roman Catholics; there is a small Protestant minority. Spanish is the official language, but English is also spoken by many.

Panama has the second-smallest population in Central America. Three-quarters of the land is uninhabited. Most people inhabit the Canal region and the southwest: almost two-fifths of the population live in or near the capital, Panama City (pop. 655,000), at the Pacific end of the Panama Canal, or in or near Colón (pop. 117,000) at the other end.

Social conditions Agriculture employs more than twice as many people as industry. Average income is a fraction that of the U.S., but higher than in most of Central America. There is a minimum wage law, and a state social security system provides hospitals and other benefits. Improved social conditions show in population statistics: by the mid 1980s Panama had the second-highest life expectancy in Central America, and the infant mortality rate was the region's second-lowest though more than twice as high as that of the U.S.

Nearly one-quarter of the national budget goes on education. Elementary education is compulsory and 85 per cent of the population can read and write. Higher education centers on two universities in Panama City.

Government Citizens aged over 18 are eligible to vote every five years to elect a President and ministers. Elections were

GDP
4391.8 million U.S.$ (1983)

Production
Goods and services expressed as percentage of GDP (1983)

A Transport/
Communication 15.9%
B Government 12.5%
C Commerce 12.1%
D Agriculture 10.0%
E Finance 9.9%
F Manufacturing/
Mining 9.3%
G Construction 5.9%
H Electricity/Gas/
Water 3.4%
I Other 21.0%

Exports
Figures expressed as percentage of total (1983)

A Bananas 23.4%
B Shrimps 16.0%
C Sugar 12.9%
D Petroleum 11.1%
E Other 36.6%

Total World Trade
Figures expressed in millions of U.S.$ (1983)

Exports World 479.6
U.S. 186.9
Imports World 2868.2
U.S. 572.8

Imports
Figures expressed as percentage of total (1983)

A Manufactures 29.8%
B Oil 24.6%
C Industrial machinery/
equipment 21.1%
D Chemicals 11.3%
E Food 8.4%
F Other 4.8%

EXPORTS IMPORTS

EXPORTS IMPORTS

resumed in 1984 after a break since 1968. A National Assembly of Boroughs is chosen by popular vote. There is also a National Legislative Commission. Panama has nine provinces with governors appointed by the President, and three Indian reservations. Judicial power rests with the Supreme Court and lesser tribunals.

Communications and transportation There are many commercial radio stations and several television channels. Panama has more business telephones than any other Central American state, and one of the highest newspaper readerships.

At least half of Panama's 5220 miles (8400km.) of road is surfaced. The Pan-American Highway links Panama City with Costa Rica. Another paved road crosses the isthmus from Panama City to Colón. Eastern Panama remains mostly trackless forest, but there are plans to continue the Pan-American Highway to Colombia. Railroads serve western farming areas, and the Panama–Colón line crosses the country. There are many domestic airports and an international airport near Panama City.

The U.S.-administered Panama Canal is one of the world's great engineering feats. Each year, up to 14,000 sea-going ships pass through its three sets of locks on the 51-mile (82km.) transit between the Atlantic and Pacific oceans. Cristóbal at the Atlantic (Caribbean) end and Balboa at the Pacific end are Panama's chief ports.

Economy Panama's gross domestic product ranked only fifth in value in Central America in the mid 1980s. But per head of population economic output was among the highest in the region. Unlike most neighbors, Panama showed real economic growth, and its inflation rate was very low. But one-fifth of the workforce was unemployed.

Farms occupy only 8–10 per cent of the land, while another 10–12 per cent is pasture. Panama is nonetheless a major banana producer; other leading crops are rice, corn, sugar cane, beans, tobacco, coffee, coconuts, and potatoes. There are about 1.5 million cattle and 200,000 pigs.

Panama has much the largest fish catch in Central America, made up predominantly of shrimps.

Minerals include one of the world's largest copper deposits with the potential for

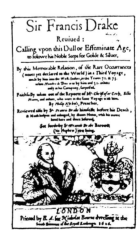

A review of the successful attack on Nombre de Dios, in 1572, during Drake's third voyage to the West Indies.

©DIAGRAM

63

Panama

The Panama Canal Zone
The Panama Canal Commission, a U.S. Government agency, presently operates the Canal Zone. The Commission replaced the former Panama Canal Company on October 1, 1979, when sovereignty of the Zone reverted to Panama. On December 31, 1999, the U.S. will transfer control of the Canal Zone to Panama.

development, as well as gold, coal, manganese, sand, and gravel. Hydroelectric power plants are making the country self-sufficient for electricity.

Factories produce mostly clothing, furniture, processed foods, and building materials.

The main exports are petroleum products, bananas, shrimps, fish meal, sugar, and coffee. Panama also receives revenue from canal tolls, oil passing through the Transisthmus Pipeline, and reexports handled by the Colón Free Zone, the largest

such center in the Western Hemisphere. Sizable invisible earnings come from hundreds of international banking and other financial institutions attracted by tax incentives and other advantages. Invisible earnings usually balance a visible trade deficit.

Panama's main imports are oil, machinery, transportation equipment, basic manufactured goods, chemicals, and food.

Major trading partners are the U.S. West Germany, Japan, and Latin American countries.

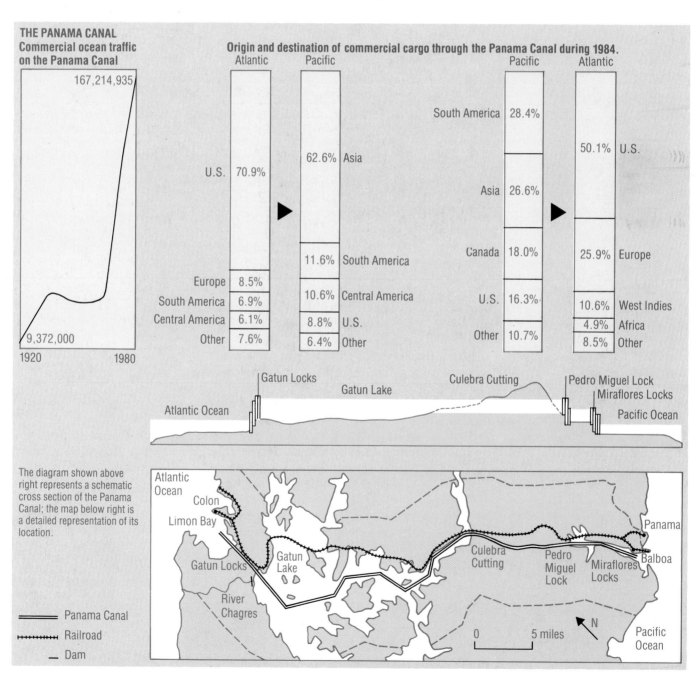

THE PANAMA CANAL
Commercial ocean traffic on the Panama Canal

167,214,935

9,372,000

1920 — 1980

Origin and destination of commercial cargo through the Panama Canal during 1984.

Atlantic:
- U.S. 70.9%
- Europe 8.5%
- South America 6.9%
- Central America 6.1%
- Other 7.6%

Pacific:
- Asia 62.6%
- South America 11.6%
- Central America 10.6%
- U.S. 8.8%
- Other 6.4%

Pacific:
- South America 28.4%
- Asia 26.6%
- Canada 18.0%
- U.S. 16.3%
- Other 10.7%

Atlantic:
- U.S. 50.1%
- Europe 25.9%
- West Indies 10.6%
- Africa 4.9%
- Other 8.5%

Gatun Locks — Gatun Lake — Culebra Cutting — Pedro Miguel Lock / Miraflores Locks

Atlantic Ocean — Pacific Ocean

The diagram shown above right represents a schematic cross section of the Panama Canal; the map below right is a detailed representation of its location.

Atlantic Ocean — Colon — Limon Bay — Gatun Locks — Gatun Lake — River Chagres — Culebra Cutting — Pedro Miguel Lock — Miraflores Locks — Panama — Balboa — Pacific Ocean

═══ Panama Canal
+++++ Railroad
— Dam

0 — 5 miles

N

PART THREE

THE CARIBBEAN REGION

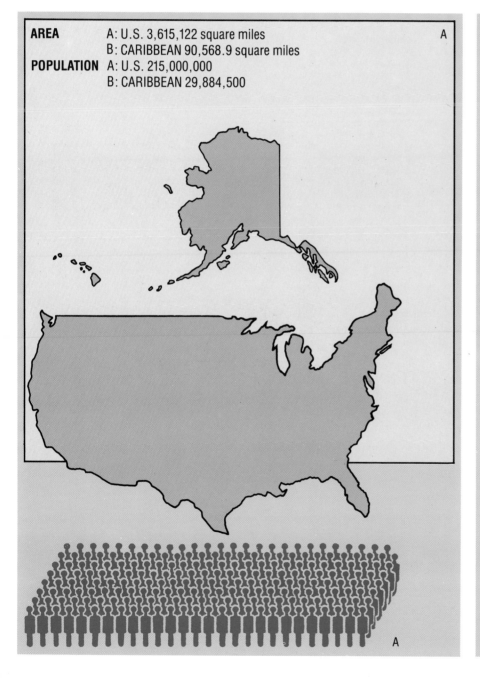

AREA	A: U.S. 3,615,122 square miles
	B: CARIBBEAN 90,568.9 square miles
POPULATION	A: U.S. 215,000,000
	B: CARIBBEAN 29,884,500

A

A

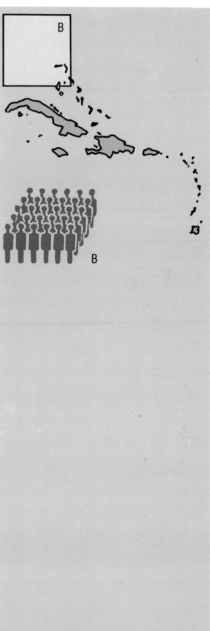

B

B

The People 1 (Lands and Peoples)

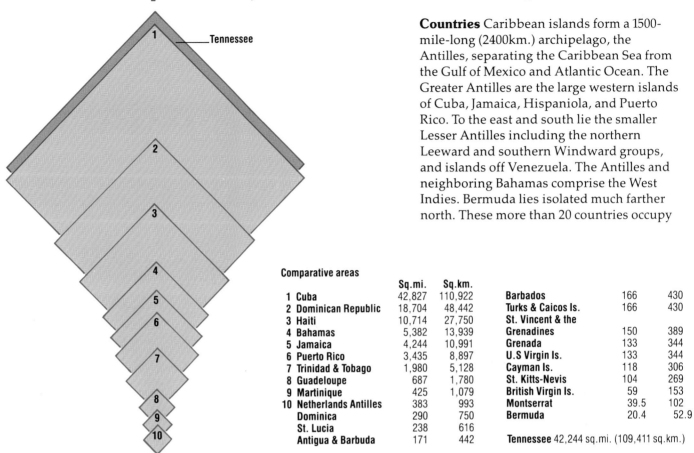

Tennessee

Countries Caribbean islands form a 1500-mile-long (2400km.) archipelago, the Antilles, separating the Caribbean Sea from the Gulf of Mexico and Atlantic Ocean. The Greater Antilles are the large western islands of Cuba, Jamaica, Hispaniola, and Puerto Rico. To the east and south lie the smaller Lesser Antilles including the northern Leeward and southern Windward groups, and islands off Venezuela. The Antilles and neighboring Bahamas comprise the West Indies. Bermuda lies isolated much farther north. These more than 20 countries occupy

Comparative areas

		Sq.mi.	Sq.km.
1	Cuba	42,827	110,922
2	Dominican Republic	18,704	48,442
3	Haiti	10,714	27,750
4	Bahamas	5,382	13,939
5	Jamaica	4,244	10,991
6	Puerto Rico	3,435	8,897
7	Trinidad & Tobago	1,980	5,128
8	Guadeloupe	687	1,780
9	Martinique	425	1,079
10	Netherlands Antilles	383	993
	Dominica	290	750
	St. Lucia	238	616
	Antigua & Barbuda	171	442

	Sq.mi.	Sq.km.
Barbados	166	430
Turks & Caicos Is.	166	430
St. Vincent & the Grenadines	150	389
Grenada	133	344
U.S Virgin Is.	133	344
Cayman Is.	118	306
St. Kitts-Nevis	104	269
British Virgin Is.	59	153
Montserrat	39.5	102
Bermuda	20.4	52.9

Tennessee 42,244 sq.mi. (109,411 sq.km.)

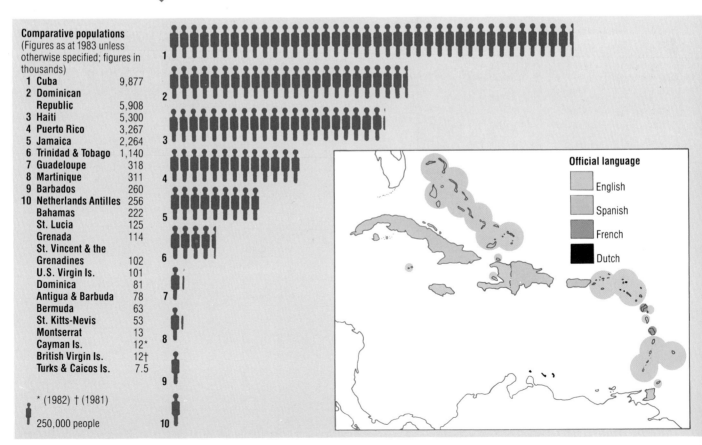

Comparative populations
(Figures as at 1983 unless otherwise specified; figures in thousands)

1	Cuba	9,877
2	Dominican Republic	5,908
3	Haiti	5,300
4	Puerto Rico	3,267
5	Jamaica	2,264
6	Trinidad & Tobago	1,140
7	Guadeloupe	318
8	Martinique	311
9	Barbados	260
10	Netherlands Antilles	256
	Bahamas	222
	St. Lucia	125
	Grenada	114
	St. Vincent & the Grenadines	102
	U.S. Virgin Is.	101
	Dominica	81
	Antigua & Barbuda	78
	Bermuda	63
	St. Kitts-Nevis	53
	Montserrat	13
	Cayman Is.	12*
	British Virgin Is.	12†
	Turks & Caicos Is.	7.5

* (1982) † (1981)

▮ 250,000 people

Official language

- English
- Spanish
- French
- Dutch

about 92,000 square miles (238,000 sq.km.): less land than Oregon and less than half the area of Central America.

Population In the mid 1980s the region's 30 million people outnumbered those of California or Central America. Ten million lived in Cuba – one of only six countries with more than a million inhabitants.

Population density and distribution There are heavy concentrations of people in Bermuda, northern Cuba, Haiti, Puerto Rico, and most of the larger Lesser Antilles. But concentration varies. Population density in Bermuda – one of the world's most thickly populated countries – is 60 times greater than in the sparsely peopled Turks and Caicos Islands.

By the mid 1980s population growth and the drift to towns produced million plus agglomerations centered on Havana, Santo Domingo, and San Juan, yet in most countries most people were classified as rural.

Ethnic groups Most West Indians are of Negro or mixed origin, descended at least partly from West African slaves. The rest are mainly Whites descended from Spanish, British, French, Dutch, or other European colonists. There are also Asians whose ancestors were shipped in to provide cheap labor for plantations after slavery had been abolished and the African slaves released.

Despite their diversity, Caribbean peoples share a common, so-called Creole, culture with lively dances and carnivals, and distinctive foods and drinks.

Languages Most Caribbean peoples speak Spanish (notably in Cuba, the Dominican Republic, and Puerto Rico); but Puerto Ricans also speak English, the official language in the U.S. Virgin Islands, and in Jamaica, Trinidad, Bermuda, and other past or present British colonies. French and Dutch are officially spoken respectively in the French and Dutch Antilles. There are also many local tongues, especially Afro-European forms collectively called Creole. Versions of French Creole are much used in Haiti and the French Antilles.

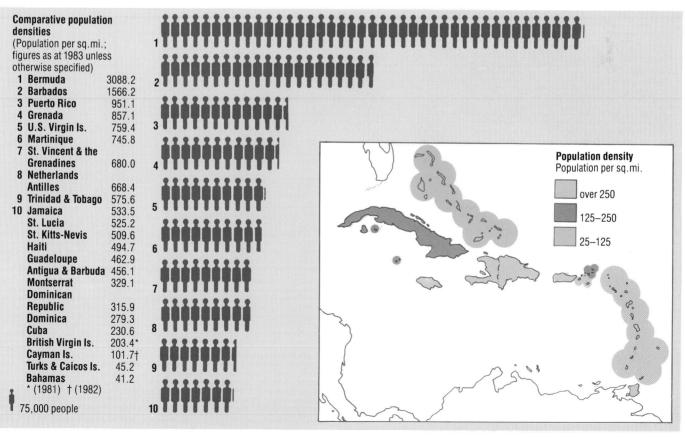

Comparative population densities
(Population per sq.mi.; figures as at 1983 unless otherwise specified)

1	Bermuda	3088.2
2	Barbados	1566.2
3	Puerto Rico	951.1
4	Grenada	857.1
5	U.S. Virgin Is.	759.4
6	Martinique	745.8
7	St. Vincent & the Grenadines	680.0
8	Netherlands Antilles	668.4
9	Trinidad & Tobago	575.6
10	Jamaica	533.5
	St. Lucia	525.2
	St. Kitts-Nevis	509.6
	Haiti	494.7
	Guadeloupe	462.9
	Antigua & Barbuda	456.1
	Montserrat	329.1
	Dominican Republic	315.9
	Dominica	279.3
	Cuba	230.6
	British Virgin Is.	203.4*
	Cayman Is.	101.7†
	Turks & Caicos Is.	45.2
	Bahamas	41.2

* (1981) † (1982)

75,000 people

Population density
Population per sq.mi.

over 250

125–250

25–125

The People 2 (Population Trends)

Like Central America, the Caribbean area has broad-based population pyramids typical of developing economies. But pyramids shown here differ more than those of Central America. For instance, birth control and welfare programs help to give Cuba relatively fewer children but more old people than impoverished Haiti. Similarly, Bermuda's top-heavy population pyramid owes something to Bermuda's status as a wealthy tourist and financial center.

Of the 17 Caribbean countries listed in one 1985 estimate, 12 showed a drop in death rate since the early 1970s, four revealed no change, and only one produced a slight increase. Some reductions were dramatic. The death rate was halved in Dominica and was nearly halved in the Dominican Republic. Haiti, with 13 deaths per 1000, retained the worst mortality rates – almost twice as high as most countries in the area. In fact 15 of the 17 had death rates of 8 or less – about or lower than the death rate in the U.S.

Countries with a large, young, healthy population can have low death rates even if few people reach old age. But by 1985 life expectancy was 70 years or more in over half the Caribbean lands.

Birth rates fell in 15 out of 17 countries between the early 1970s and mid 1980s. At the low end of the range, Cuba's rate of 17 births per 1000 population showed a one-third drop to the level of the U.S. At 36 per 1000, Haiti's birth rate stayed the highest.

In most Caribbean countries, declining death rates more than made up for a falling birth rate. The result was population growth. Indeed between the early 1970s and 1985 more than half the Caribbean countries showed an increase in the rate of growth. The rate ranged from 2.5 per cent in the Dominican Republic down to 1.0 per cent in Antigua and Barbuda, and the Bahamas. Even the highest rate was less than that in most Central American republics, though the lowest stood above that of the U.S. Projections made in 1985 forecast a doubling of population in all Caribbean lands by 2057 if current rates of growth continued. Haiti's population (put at 5.8 million in 1985) seemed set to soar to more than 14 million by A.D. 2020. But even the fastest estimated growth (the Dominican Republic's and St. Lucia's) lagged compared with most of Central America's.

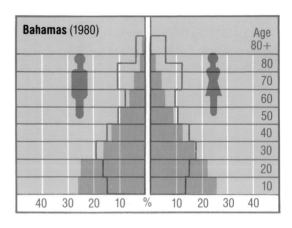

Bahamas (1980)

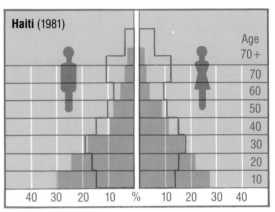

Haiti (1981)

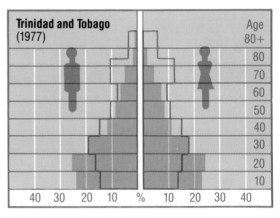

Trinidad and Tobago (1977)

Population pyramids
Pyramids show composition by age and sex of populations in eight Caribbean countries and Bermuda. Each stage represents a 10-year age group. The lowest stage is the youngest group. The wider a stage, the higher the percentage of the population in that age group. The left side of each pyramid consists of males; the right side, of females.
Broad-based pyramids show that young people form the vast majority in the Dominican Republic, Jamaica, and Haiti. (Under-10s reportedly account for nearly half the citizens of the Dominican Republic.) Barbados, Bermuda, Cuba, Puerto Rico, and Trinidad and Tobago are perched on relatively narrow bases. This feature usually indicates a recent drop in birth rate. The solid areas in the pyramids represent the population figures for the particular country; the outlined areas those for the U.S. by comparison.

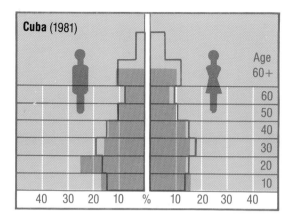

Cuba (1981)

Age 60+ 60 50 40 30 20 10

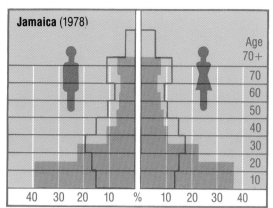

Jamaica (1978)

Age 70+ 70 60 50 40 30 20 10

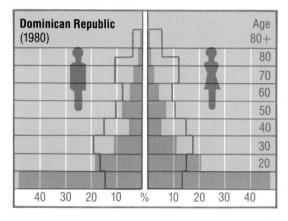

Dominican Republic (1980)

Age 80+ 80 70 60 50 40 30 20

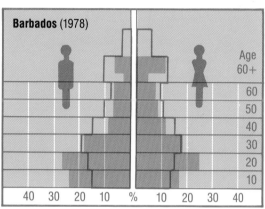

Barbados (1978)

Age 60+ 60 50 40 30 20 10

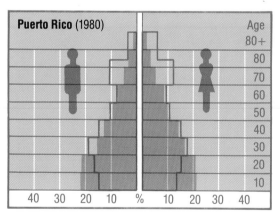

Puerto Rico (1980)

Age 80+ 80 70 60 50 40 30 20 10

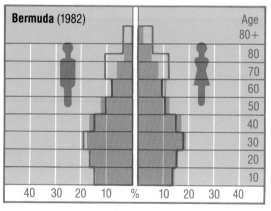

Bermuda (1982)

Age 80+ 80 70 60 50 40 30 20 10

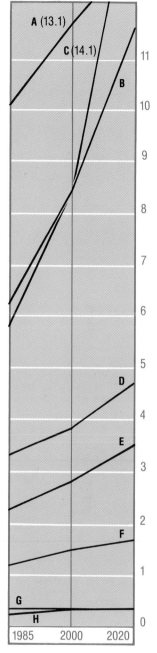

A (13.1)
C (14.1)
B
D
E
F
G
H

1985   2000   2020

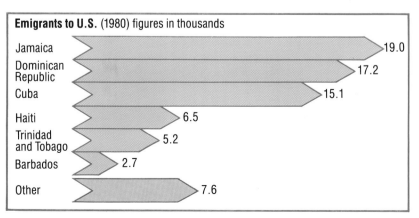

Emigrants to U.S. (1980) figures in thousands

Jamaica — 19.0
Dominican Republic — 17.2
Cuba — 15.1
Haiti — 6.5
Trinidad and Tobago — 5.2
Barbados — 2.7
Other — 7.6

Emigration to the U.S.
The table shown left gives estimates (in thousands) of numbers emigrating to the U.S. in 1980. Only the main sources of origin are listed individually. The table excludes emigration from Puerto Rico because this U.S. possession is omitted from the U.S. Immigration and Naturalization Service listings.

Growth to A.D. 2020
Lines on the diagram above show the projected growth in population of eight Caribbean countries between A.D. 1985 and A.D. 2020. Numbers represent millions of individuals.
A Cuba
B Dominican Republic
C Haiti
D Puerto Rico
E Jamaica
F Trinidad and Tobago
G Barbados
H Bahamas

©DIAGRAM

Land Use and Economy

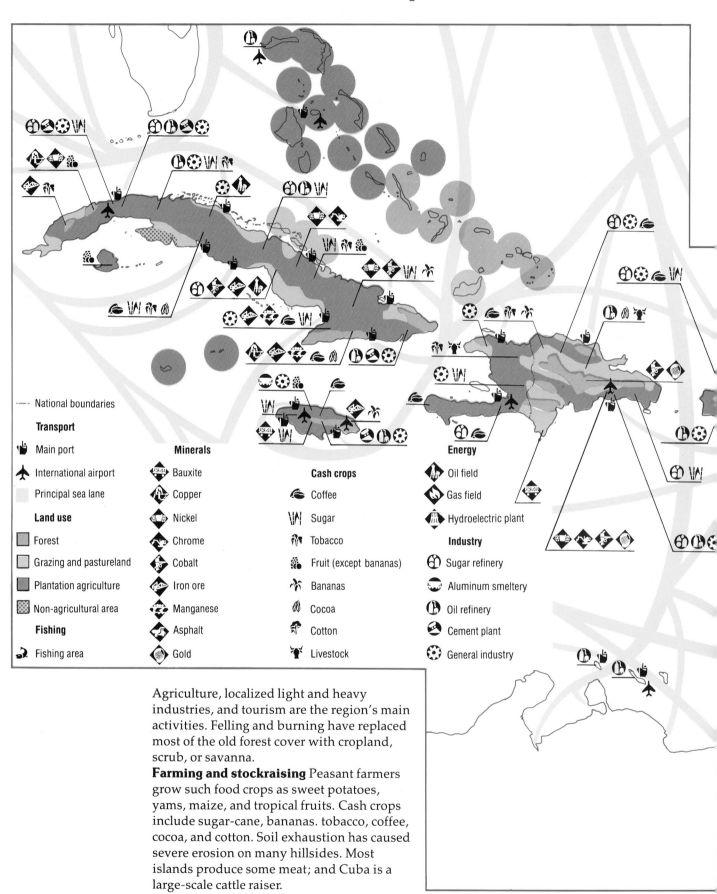

National boundaries

Transport
- Main port
- International airport
- Principal sea lane

Land use
- Forest
- Grazing and pastureland
- Plantation agriculture
- Non-agricultural area

Fishing
- Fishing area

Minerals
- Bauxite
- Copper
- Nickel
- Chrome
- Cobalt
- Iron ore
- Manganese
- Asphalt
- Gold

Cash crops
- Coffee
- Sugar
- Tobacco
- Fruit (except bananas)
- Bananas
- Cocoa
- Cotton
- Livestock

Energy
- Oil field
- Gas field
- Hydroelectric plant

Industry
- Sugar refinery
- Aluminum smeltery
- Oil refinery
- Cement plant
- General industry

Agriculture, localized light and heavy industries, and tourism are the region's main activities. Felling and burning have replaced most of the old forest cover with cropland, scrub, or savanna.

Farming and stockraising Peasant farmers grow such food crops as sweet potatoes, yams, maize, and tropical fruits. Cash crops include sugar-cane, bananas. tobacco, coffee, cocoa, and cotton. Soil exhaustion has caused severe erosion on many hillsides. Most islands produce some meat; and Cuba is a large-scale cattle raiser.

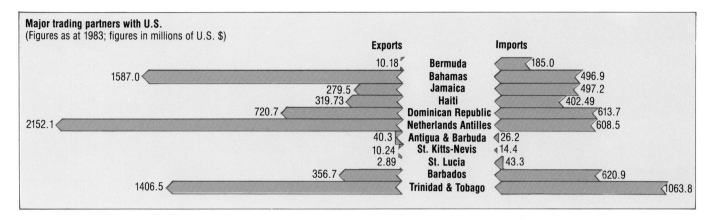

Major trading partners with U.S.
(Figures as at 1983; figures in millions of U.S. $)

	Exports		Imports
Bermuda	10.18		185.0
Bahamas	1587.0		496.9
Jamaica	279.5		497.2
Haiti	319.73		402.49
Dominican Republic	720.7		613.7
Netherlands Antilles	2152.1		608.5
Antigua & Barbuda	40.3		26.2
St. Kitts-Nevis	10.24		14.4
St. Lucia	2.89		43.3
Barbados	356.7		620.9
Trinidad & Tobago	1406.5		1063.8

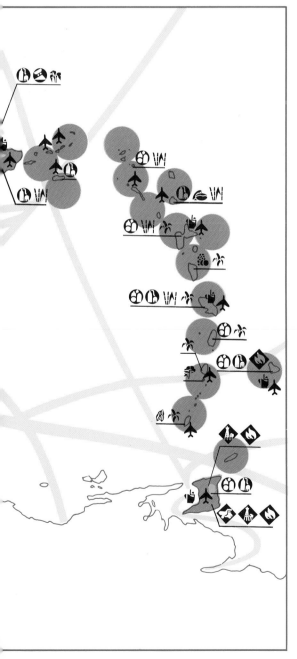

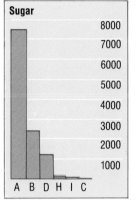

Sugar

8000
7000
6000
5000
4000
3000
2000
1000

A B D H I C

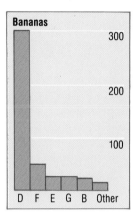

Bananas

300

200

100

D F E G B Other

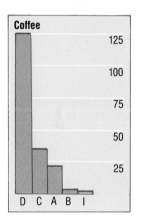

Coffee

125

100

75

50

25

D C A B I

Forestry and fisheries There is no large-scale forestry, but there are some cutting and planting programs. Excepting Cuba, fisheries are mostly small scale.

Minerals and energy The major mineral deposits are Trinidad's oil and gas, and Jamaica's bauxite. Apart from Trinidad the region lacks abundant energy supplies. Fuelwood burning has contributed to severe deforestation on Haiti.

Manufacturing Puerto Rico leads in light industrial development; and there are oil refineries in Puerto Rico, Jamaica, Grand Bahama, and elsewhere. But the small local market has hindered the development of heavy industry.

Trade and transportation Chief exports include cane sugar, bananas, tobacco, coffee, bauxite, oil, and assembled products. Substantial earnings come from tourism and, on some islands, from offshore financial services. The region imports food, fossil fuels, and a wide range of manufactured goods.

An extensive network of air and sea routes links the islands.

Crop production
The diagrams above compare the production by country of the three principal crops of the region. Figures are as at 1983 unless otherwise stated below, and are in thousands of tons produced.
A Cuba
B Jamaica
C Haiti (1982)
D Dominican Republic (1982)
E Dominica
F St. Lucia
G St. Vincent & The Grenadines
H Barbados
I Trinidad & Tobago

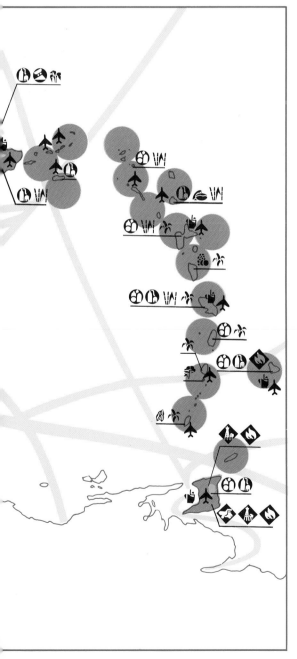

© DIAGRAM

Current Political Situation

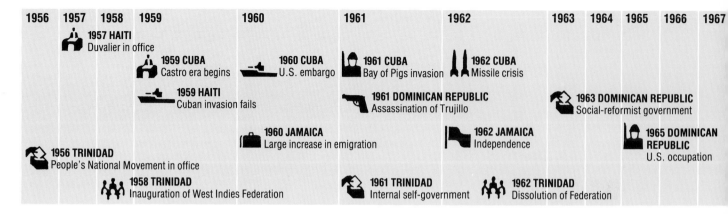

| 1956 | 1957 | 1958 | 1959 | 1960 | 1961 | 1962 | 1963 | 1964 | 1965 | 1966 | 1967 |

1957 HAITI Duvalier in office

1959 CUBA Castro era begins

1960 CUBA U.S. embargo

1961 CUBA Bay of Pigs invasion

1962 CUBA Missile crisis

1959 HAITI Cuban invasion fails

1961 DOMINICAN REPUBLIC Assassination of Trujillo

1963 DOMINICAN REPUBLIC Social-reformist government

1960 JAMAICA Large increase in emigration

1962 JAMAICA Independence

1965 DOMINICAN REPUBLIC U.S. occupation

1956 TRINIDAD People's National Movement in office

1958 TRINIDAD Inauguration of West Indies Federation

1961 TRINIDAD Internal self-government

1962 TRINIDAD Dissolution of Federation

By the middle 1980s the Caribbean region with the Bahamas and Bermuda comprised more than three times as many countries as Central America lying to its west, although its population was not much larger than that region's and its area was only half as great.

Most of the two dozen countries fell into three main political categories: (1) 11 colonies or other territories formally attached to larger outside powers; (2) 10 recently independent ex-colonies – most very small; (3) 3 long-established nations: Cuba, Haiti, and the Dominican Republic. These three groups feature countries where political concerns include, respectively, winning independence, keeping independence, and influencing lesser states. From outside the region, the U.S. stands ready to step into its Caribbean backyard to block destabilizing acts.

In the 1980s most of the colonies and other territories attached to outside powers appeared politically stable. Independence seemed unimportant to the majority of the six British holdings, some arguably too small or too economically weak to run themselves. Anguilla's elected government had a no-independence policy. In the British Virgin Islands people voted for political personalities rather than political parties. The Cayman Islands was determined to remain a British dependency. The Turks and Caicos Islands seemed too tiny to set out on its own. In 1982 a U.N. Decolonization Mission to Montserrat found independence generally unwanted there; and Bermudan independence talk died down with the election of a new progressive and multiracial government.

Similar conditions existed in the Commonwealth of Puerto Rico and the U.S.

Virgin Islands. In Puerto Rico the old idea of independence from the U.S. attracted less than 5 per cent support, while the U.S. Virgin Islands remained politically and economically tied to the U.S.

Independence aroused stronger feelings in the French and Netherlands Antilles. In the early 1980s small separatist groups launched bombing campaigns in the French Antilles, though there seemed little general support for nationhood.

Elsewhere, there have been some dramatic political and even military events among the region's 10 Commonwealth members which were granted independence by Britain after the early 1960s. Antigua and Barbuda; the Bahamas; Barbados; Dominica; Grenada; Jamaica; St. Kitts-Nevis; St. Lucia; St. Vincent and the Grenadines; and Trinidad and Tobago all inherited the British form of parliamentary democracy. In most countries this works effectively enough, but financial adventurers, "bought" politicians, mercenaries, and "legal" invasions have shown how easily outsiders can manipulate or even seize control of some small island states.

The worst experiences had been those of Dominica and Grenada. Dominica suffered three attempted coups in 18 months after Miss Eugenia Charles's Dominica Freedom Party had won power in a 1980 election. French, U.S., and British aid helped her government to survive. As forceful chairperson of the Organization of East Caribbean States, Miss Charles later called for U.S. military aid to topple Grenada's revolutionary leftist regime.

For a while, in 1983, Grenada's problems and U.S. intervention in them dominated world news. Grenada's difficulties sprang

1971 HAITI
Duvalier dies

1973 PUERTO RICO
Workers' strikes

1979 GRENADA
Revolution

1983 GRENADA
American invasion

1980 FRENCH ANTILLES
Nationalist bombing

1971 DOMINICAN REPUBLIC
Failed coup

1976 CUBA
Socialist constitution

1980 DOMINICA
Three attempted coups

1986 NETHERLANDS ANTILLES
Aruba secedes

1972 JAMAICA
People's National Party takes office

1980 JAMAICA
Jamaica Labor Party regains office

1973 THE BAHAMAS
Independence

1971 U.S. VIRGIN ISLANDS
First U.S. governor elected

1976 TRINIDAD
Republic

1980 TOBAGO
Self-government

1984 HAITI
Riots

from government mismanagement which had led to an almost bloodless revolution in 1979. This resulted in power being seized by the so-called New Jewel Movement, seeking egalitarianism, social and economic progress, and international non-alignment.

In 1983, though, Grenada obtained military help from several communist states – Cuba, the Soviet Union, and North Korea; and hundreds of Cuban technicians helped to build Grenada's big new airport. To the U.S. its size suspiciously suggested a military base for Cuban-Soviet subversion in Central America. At first Washington just watched uneasily. Then came an unexpected chance to claim legitimate involvement: a Grenadan power struggle culminating in an October military coup in which Prime Minister Maurice Bishop was first overthrown, then murdered, together with a number of supporters. Within days, more than 6000 U.S. troops invaded, with air support and armor, soon followed by a token force of troops and police drawn from member nations of the Caribbean Community (Caricom).

Grenada's Revolutionary Military Council was swiftly crushed, and Cuban workers were deported. By December 1983 most U.S. forces had withdrawn, and elections a year later gave power to Grenada's middle-of-the-road New National Party.

The repercussions that ensued threatened to break-up Caricom. On one hand there were Caribbean nations like Barbados, Dominica, and Jamaica that had backed the U.S. military action. In another camp stood the Bahamas and Trinidad and Tobago, which had both withheld support. For a while Jamaica's anticommunist Premier, Edward Seaga, argued for the creation of a new right-wing Caribbean grouping of Jamaica, Haiti, the Dominican Republic, Puerto Rico, and some of the small Commonwealth islands. If formed, this bloc would have brought about Caricom's demise. Instead, a Nassau Summit Meeting widened membership to take in Haiti, the Dominican Republic, and Surinam.

The Grenada affair marked a setback for communism in the Caribbean region. However, captured documents from Grenada showed that the Soviet Union had known that this must stay a U.S. sphere of influence. Also, while Cuba had helped Maurice Bishop, it did refuse military aid for the extremists who succeeded him. Cuba remains the Western Hemisphere's only major communist power (bolstered by the economic support of the Soviet Union and other East European powers). As such, Cuba traditionally offers technical and sometimes military aid to rebel groups or leftist regimes as far apart as Ethiopia and Nicaragua. Cubans know that their very role in helping leftist revolution incurs hostility from their powerful northern neighbor just across the Gulf of Mexico. The Grenada affair renewed old Cuban fears of U.S. invasion, and led Cuba to increase its territorial troop militia to 1,200,000 armed forces, and 190,000 reservists, so strengthening the Western Hemisphere's best equipped and largest military force outside the U.S.

East of Cuba internal problems dominate the politics of those other old-established Caribbean nations, the Dominican Republic and Haiti. In the mid 1980s both countries suffered riots: Haiti's against continued authoritarian rule; the Dominican Republic's against price rises imposed to prop up the recession-hit economy.

©DIAGRAM

Government Finances

In the 1980s most Caribbean countries at least partly shared the financial problems that racked most of Central America. For like that region much of the Caribbean has depended heavily on exported commodities – cash crops such as sugar cane, mineral oil, and bauxite. All suffered from a recession-triggered drop in demand, reflected in price slumps. To take the most extreme example: in 1975 a pound of sugar cost 75 cents on the open market; in 1985 it cost just 4.

Yet many countries in the region enjoyed three benefits not found in much of Central America. These three were a relatively large tourist income; high revenues from offshore financial services; and cash aid from the powers to which the islands do or did belong.

Even so, many islanders suffered a fall in living standards as their governments raised taxes, cut jobs, and devalued currencies. Only such strict financial management persuaded international creditors to make much-needed loans or to extend repayment times for loans or interest already overdue.

Most of the six British dependencies remained financially sound, thanks largely to tourism and/or offshore financial services. In the early 1980s, for example, company fees and customs duties helped give the Cayman Islands enough income to more than fill a yawning import-export gap. Bermuda, the British Virgin Islands, and Montserrat were also prosperous by Caribbean standards, and the Turks and Caicos Islands expected to be self-sufficient from 1985 onward. But Anguilla still depended on British and other outside aid to help finance capital spending.

Direct and indirect U.S. economic aid assisted Puerto Rico and the U.S. Virgin Islands. But while Treasury aid was helping to balance the Islands' budget, new import regulations threatened to cut Puerto Rico's income from exports to the U.S. mainland.

The French and Dutch territories faced difficulties, too. Shrinking incomes from oil refining and tourism hit the Netherlands Antilles; and only huge supplies of capital from mainland France kept Guadeloupe and Martinique financially afloat.

Cuba's economy, the region's largest, seemed likely to survive, for Cuba mainly traded with socialist member countries of the Council for Mutual Economic Assistance

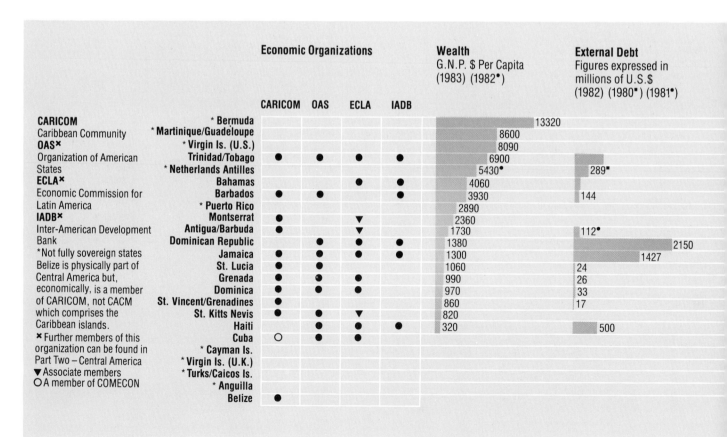

		Economic Organizations				Wealth G.N.P. $ Per Capita (1983) (1982•)	External Debt Figures expressed in millions of U.S.$ (1982) (1980■) (1981•)
		CARICOM	OAS	ECLA	IADB		
CARICOM Caribbean Community	* Bermuda					13320	
OAS✗	* Martinique/Guadeloupe					8600	
Organization of American States	* Virgin Is. (U.S.)					8090	
	Trinidad/Tobago	●	●	●	●	6900	
ECLA✗	* Netherlands Antilles					5430•	289■
Economic Commission for Latin America	Bahamas			●	●	4060	
	Barbados	●	●	●	●	3930	144
IADB✗	* Puerto Rico					2890	
Inter-American Development Bank	Montserrat	●		▼		2360	
	Antigua/Barbuda	●		▼		1730	112•
* Not fully sovereign states	Dominican Republic		●	●	●	1380	2150
Belize is physically part of Central America but,	Jamaica	●	●	●	●	1300	1427
economically, is a member	St. Lucia	●	●			1060	24
of CARICOM, not CACM	Grenada	●	●	●		990	26
which comprises the	Dominica	●	●	●		970	33
Caribbean islands.	St. Vincent/Grenadines	●				860	17
✗ Further members of this	St. Kitts Nevis	●	●	▼		820	
organization can be found in	Haiti		●	●	●	320	500
Part Two – Central America	Cuba	○	●	●			
▼ Associate members	* Cayman Is.						
○ A member of COMECON	* Virgin Is. (U.K.)						
	* Turks/Caicos Is.						
	* Anguilla						
	Belize	●					

(Comecon) and its credits helped Cuba to maintain its industrial development.

Elsewhere in the Caribbean, only the Bahamas, Trinidad and Tobago, and Grenada (before Maurice Bishop's overthrow in 1983) were returning budget surpluses. Of the larger islands, impoverished Haiti received huge sums in aid, and Jamaica and the Dominican Republic reluctantly imposed harsh austerity measures in return for IMF and other credits.

Debts also weighed down most small East Caribbean nations. Only British aid balanced the St. Kitts-Nevis budget. Dominica leaned financially on half a dozen outside sources. Two of these – Britain and the Caribbean Development Bank – also helped support St. Lucia. Meanwhile France and Taiwan enabled St. Vincent to pay for capital expenditure which otherwise it could not afford. And economically weak Barbados relied on IMF cash and a credit squeeze to turn a real trading deficit into apparent surplus.

In many of these countries improvement in government finances hinged on an increase in commodity prices, but that increase had not happened by the middle 1980s.

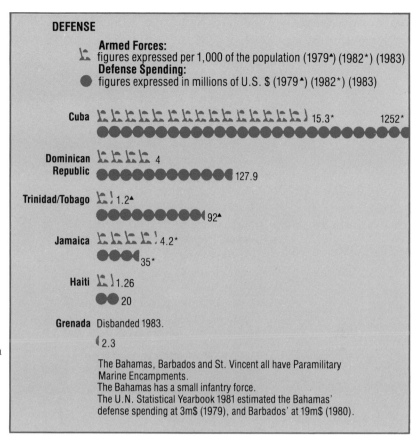

DEFENSE

Armed Forces: figures expressed per 1,000 of the population (1979▲) (1982*) (1983)
Defense Spending: figures expressed in millions of U.S. $ (1979▲) (1982*) (1983)

Cuba 15.3* 1252*

Dominican Republic 4 127.9

Trinidad/Tobago 1.2▲ 92▲

Jamaica 4.2* 35*

Haiti 1.26 20

Grenada Disbanded 1983. 2.3

The Bahamas, Barbados and St. Vincent all have Paramilitary Marine Encampments.
The Bahamas has a small infantry force.
The U.N. Statistical Yearbook 1981 estimated the Bahamas' defense spending at 3m$ (1979), and Barbados' at 19m$ (1980).

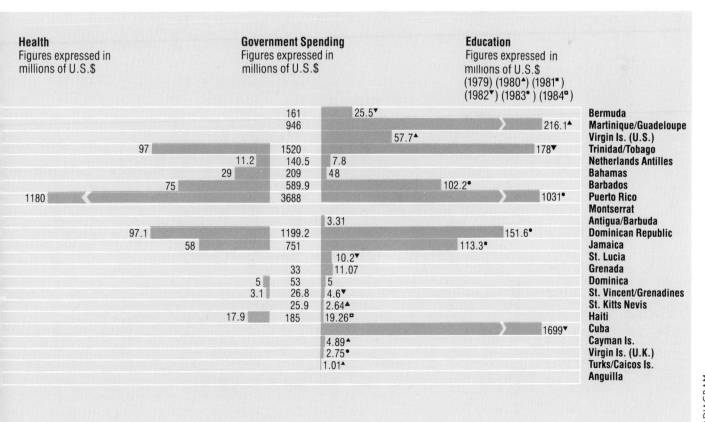

Health Figures expressed in millions of U.S.$	Government Spending Figures expressed in millions of U.S.$	Education Figures expressed in millions of U.S.$ (1979) (1980▲) (1981■) (1982▼) (1983●) (1984□)	
	161	25.5▼	Bermuda
	946	216.1▲	Martinique/Guadeloupe
		57.7▲	Virgin Is. (U.S.)
97	1520	178▼	Trinidad/Tobago
11.2	140.5	7.8	Netherlands Antilles
29	209	48	Bahamas
75	589.9	102.2●	Barbados
1180	3688	1031●	Puerto Rico
			Montserrat
		3.31	Antigua/Barbuda
97.1	1199.2	151.6●	Dominican Republic
58	751	113.3■	Jamaica
		10.2▼	St. Lucia
	33	11.07	Grenada
5	53	5	Dominica
3.1	26.8	4.6▼	St. Vincent/Grenadines
	25.9	2.64▲	St. Kitts Nevis
17.9	185	19.26□	Haiti
		1699▼	Cuba
		4.89▲	Cayman Is.
		2.75●	Virgin Is. (U.K.)
		1.01▲	Turks/Caicos Is.
			Anguilla

Bermuda

OFFICIAL NAME
Bermuda

Above: **Flag of Bermuda**
Red with the Union Flag in the
top staff corner, and
Bermuda's badge toward the
outer edge. Shown left is the
Bermudan coat of arms.

SIZE IN RELATION TO U.S. CITY

Slightly smaller than the Borough of Manhattan, New York City (A)

AREA	**20.4** square miles (52.9sq.km.)
POPULATION	**63,000** (1983 preliminary figure)
POPULATION DENSITY	**3088.2** per square mile (1983)
CURRENCY	**Bermuda dollar** (Ber.$ 1 = 100 cents)
PRINCIPAL RELIGION	**Anglican**
OFFICIAL LANGUAGE	**English**
CAPITAL	**Hamilton**
ADMINISTRATIVE DIVISIONS	**9 parishes and 2 municipalities**

Bermuda is the oldest self-governing British colony. It lies in the Atlantic, 800 miles (1290km.) southeast of New York and 750 miles (1210km.) northeast of the Bahamas. Its 145 islands and rocks roughly equal the size of Manhattan. Its subtropical climate and idyllic beaches attract many tourists.

History Juan de Bermúdez, a Spanish sea captain, reputedly sighted Bermuda soon after A.D. 1500. Settlement began in 1609 with the shipwreck off St. George's Island of Admiral Sir George Somers's ship *Sea Venture*, taking English colonists to Virginia.

Two stayed. Many more came with the forming of the Somers Islands Company in 1612. They imported African slaves to work tobacco plantations. In 1684 Bermuda came under joint Crown and Company rule. In 1815 Hamilton on Bermuda Island replaced St. George on St. George's Island as capital. Full internal self government came in 1968.

Land Bermuda is the world's northernmost group of coral islands. The 145 islands and rocks form a fishhook-shaped chain 23 miles (37km.) long and half a mile (0.8km.) wide. Bermuda Island (also called Main Island) makes up most of the hook and its shank. To its northeast, St. George's and St. David's islands form the head of the shank. In the southwest, Somerset and Ireland islands form the tip of the hook, pointing northeast. The hook and its two "barbs" (peninsulas) enclose Great and Little Sound.

Climate This is humid and subtropical. Temperatures average 70°F. (21°C.), with an August high of 90°F. (32°C.) and a February low of about 47°F. (8°C.). The annual rainfall of about 57 inches (1448mm.) is spread throughout the year: more than 140 days usually have at least some rain. Hurricanes can strike in summer or fall.

Vegetation and animals There are said to be more than 900 kinds of shrubs, trees, and other plants. Flowering species such as bougainvillea and hibiscus have been introduced. But disease has killed many of the Bermuda cedars, a species of juniper, that once covered most of the islands.

The few native animals include a lizard, a few land birds, and a scarce seabird, the cahow or Bermuda petrel. There are also rats, mice and frogs. Bermuda has no poisonous reptiles or insects. Marlin,

Map

64°50 W — 64°40 W

★ Tourist Centres

Transportation

— Main Roads

✈ Main and International Airports

⚓ Main Ports

Population of major towns and cities

● <10,000 inhabitants

ATLANTIC OCEAN

32°20 N

ST.GEORGE'S ISLAND — ★● St. George

ST. DAVID'S ISLAND

Castle Harbour — NONSUCH ISLAND — **Castle Point**

32°20 N

Harrington Sound

Shelly Bay — Flatts — ●Tucker's Town

IRELAND ISLAND ●Freeport

Spanish Point

●Somerset Village — ▲Town Hill — **BERMUDA**

SOMERSET ISLAND — ★⚓Hamilton

Great Sound

Little Sound — Warwick Long Bay

High Point

0 kms		5		10
0 miles	20	40		60

64°50'W — 64°40'W

HISTORICAL REVIEW

1503	Discovered by Juan de Bermúdez.	**1963**	Formation of Progressive Labor Party.
1511	Italian map showed position of islands.	**1964**	Formation of United Bermuda Party.
1609	Sir George Somers landed on previously uninhabited islands.	**1973**	Governor, Sir Richard Sharples, shot.
1612	James I granted charter to Virginia Company.	**1978**	Royal Commission recommended independence.
1616	Slaves introduced.	**1980**	Elections. PLP won led by Mrs Browne Evans.
1620	Legislative assembly set up.	**1982**	John Swan made premier.
1834	Abolition of slavery.	**1983**	General election. UBP re-elected for sixth time running.
1941	Air and naval bases leased to U.S. for 99 years.	**1984**	Resignation of Finance Minister, David Gibbons. General election won by UBP with an increased majority.
1957	British garrison withdrawn.		

barracuda, and lobsters abound in the sea.

People Sixty per cent of the population are black descendants of African slaves. The rest are of British or Portuguese origin. Half belong to the Church of England. There are also Roman Catholics, Methodists, and others. English is the chief language, but some Bermudans speak Portuguese.

Social conditions High average incomes from tourism and foreign investment have produced high living standards. The birth rate is accordingly lower and life expectancy higher than in most of the Caribbean countries, to the south.

More than one-third of the labor force works in hotels, restaurants, or stores. More than one-seventh works in finance, insurance, real estate, or business services. Less than 3 per cent works in manufacturing. Unemployment is low.

Education is free and compulsory between ages 5 and 16 and illiteracy is negligible. But students wanting further education must go abroad for it.

Babies and children are entitled to free medical aid. There is one general hospital.

Government Bermuda is a British colony with internal self government. The Head of State is the British monarch, represented by a Governor appointed by the Crown. Internal government is by an elected 40-member House of Assembly and an appointed 11-member Senate. The Premier can choose ministers from both houses. A Court of Appeal, Supreme Court, and Magistracy comprise the judiciary.

Communications and transportation Bermuda has two television stations, five radio stations, a daily newspaper, and international telephone links.

There are about 130 miles (209km.) of public roads. Bridges and causeways link the 10 largest islands, and there are ferries. Hamilton is the main port. Bermuda has U.S. naval and air stations. The air station serves as Bermuda's international airport.

Economy Bermuda has enjoyed steady economic growth, a dwindling national debt, and a balance of payments surplus.

Bermuda's wealth comes mainly from commerce, trade, and tourism.

Bermuda's chief trading partner is the U.S.

A silver crown which commemorates the 350th anniversary of the founding of Bermuda.

ECONOMIC REVIEW

Land Use	Principal Crops	Production	Exports	Imports	Total World Trade
Figures expressed as percentage of total land (1982)	*Figures expressed in thousands of tons produced (1984) (Total arable area only 674 acres)*	*Goods and services expressed as percentage of GDP (1983)*	*Figures expressed as percentage of total (1983)*	*Figures expressed as percentage of total (1982)*	*Figures expressed in millions of U.S.$ (1983)*
20% Forest/ Woodland		32.4% Tourism International	90% Oil	20.5% Machinery/Transport Equipment	**Exports** World 53.4
80% Other	1 Potatoes	24.9% finance	10% Other	20.3% Food/Beverages	U.S. 10.18
	4 Mixed vegetables	42.7% Other		14.1% Petroleum	**Imports** World 439.2
	1 Bananas			13.6% Manufactures	U.S. 185.0
	1 Citrus fruits			31.5% Other	**GDP** 674.2 million US$

©DIAGRAM

The Bahamas

SIZE IN RELATION TO U.S. STATE

A

Slightly larger than Connecticut (A)

Above: **Flag of the Bahamas**
Equal horizontal bands of
aquamarine, gold, and
aquamarine, with a black
triangle against the staff side.

OFFICIAL NAME
Commonwealth of the Bahamas

AREA	**5382** square miles (13,939sq.km.)
POPULATION	**222,000** (1983 preliminary figure)
POPULATION DENSITY	**41.2** per square mile (1983)
CURRENCY	**Bahamian dollar** (Bah.$ 1 = 100 cents)
PRINCIPAL RELIGIONS	**Baptist, Anglican, Roman Catholic**
OFFICIAL LANGUAGE	**English**
CAPITAL	**Nassau**
ADMINISTRATIVE DIVISIONS	**18 districts**

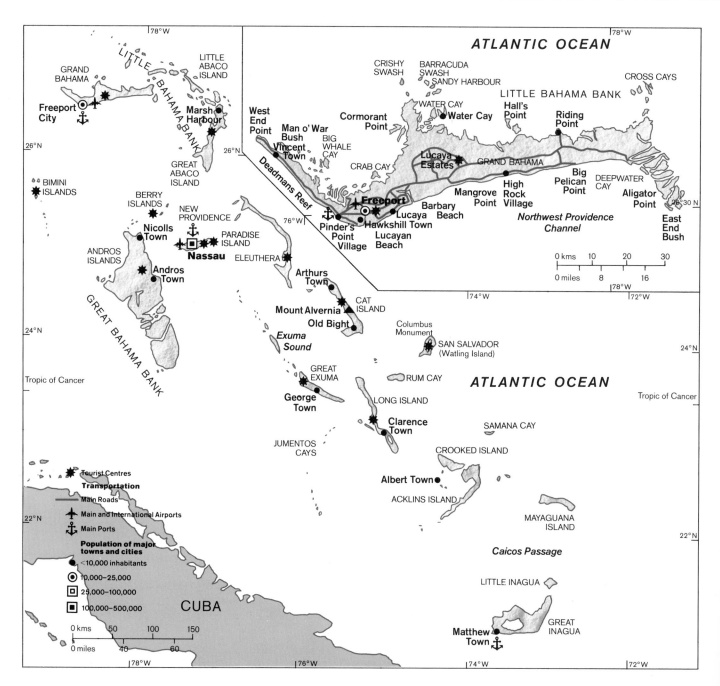

The Commonwealth of the Bahamas is a young island nation in the Atlantic Ocean off southeast Florida and northern Cuba. Its hundreds of low coral islands and thousands of islets match California for length yet add up to the size of Connecticut. The islands rise from submarine shelves, hence their name from the Spanish *bajamar*: "shallow water." They are now best known for their tourist attractions of sunshine, magnificent beaches, and transparent sea.

History Peaceful Arawak Indians peopled the Bahamas in Pre-Columbian times. In 1492 Christopher Columbus probably made his first New World landfall on San Salvador (Watling Island). The Spanish claimed but did not colonize the Bahamas; in fact they depopulated the islands by deporting Indians to work elsewhere.

English settlers arrived from Bermuda in 1648. The Bahamas became a haunt for pirates. Captain Woodes Rogers suppressed these on becoming first Royal Governor in 1718. In 1776 the U.S. Navy briefly held Nassau, and Spain seized the islands in 1782, but lost control to Britain next year. Loyalists and their black slaves enlarged the islands' population after the American Revolution. Tourism transformed the economy after World War II. Internal self government came in 1964, full independence in 1973.

Land There are about 700 islands and 2000 tiny cays. They are spread over an area of ocean nearly 17 times their own size – and larger than all of New England. From Grand Bahama, 60 miles (80km.) east of Florida, the archipelago extends southeast for about 760 miles (1223km.) to Great Inagua, 50 miles (80km.) northeast of eastern Cuba. It stands on two shallow submarine banks, part of North America's continental shelf. Coral reefs fringe the coasts, and deepwater channels divide island groups.

The Bahamas comprise geologically young coral and other limestone. Coral sand from the dazzling beaches blows inland to form dunes and lines of low hills. Mt. Alvernia on Cat Island is the highest point: only 206 feet (63m.) above sea level. Soil is mostly thin, but fertile in places. There are no freshwater rivers and Great Inagua has the only large lake, but brackish swamps occupy many limestone depressions.

Climate Lying in a subtropical high-pressure belt, and washed by the Gulf Stream, the Bahamas enjoy a warm, sunny climate. Temperatures seldom exceed 90°F. (32°C.) or fall below 60°F. (16°C.). They average about 80°F. (27°C.) in summer, and 70°F. (21°C.) in winter. Annual rainfall averages 46 inches (1168mm.), but Great Inagua and some other islands get only half that much. Most rain falls as heavy showers from May through October.

In summer, trade winds blow from the southeast; in winter, from the northeast. Hurricanes sometimes occur in the early fall.

Vegetation and animals Low scrub covers much of the land, but there are large tracts of Caribbean pine on four northern islands: Grand Bahama, Great Abaco, New Providence, and Andros. Low-growing tropical hardwood forest flourishes on Mayaguana and some other southern islands. Mangrove swamp fringes calm shores.

Human activity has much affected animal life, too. Wild horses and other farm creatures run wild on some islands. There are raccoons, agoutis (large rodents) and bats, but no large native land mammals. Flamingos – the national bird – and parrots

Queen Elizabeth II, ruler of the Bahamas until full independence was granted in 1973.
(stamp issued 1959)

©DIAGRAM

The Bahamas

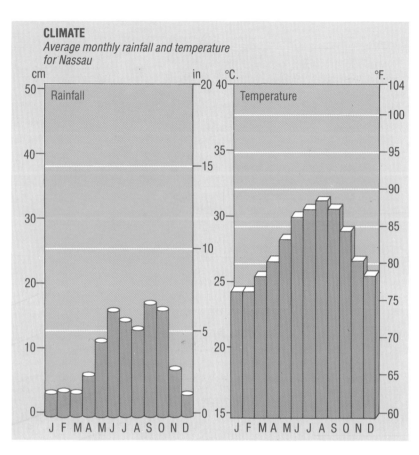

CLIMATE
Average monthly rainfall and temperature for Nassau

Rainfall

Temperature

J F M A M J J A S O N D

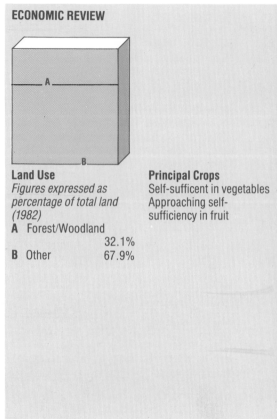

ECONOMIC REVIEW

Land Use
Figures expressed as percentage of total land (1982)
A Forest/Woodland
32.1%
B Other
67.9%

Principal Crops
Self-sufficent in vegetables
Approaching self-sufficiency in fruit

occur on some islands. The Bahamas have frogs, iguanid lizards and boid snakes, and sea turtles nest on some beaches. Colorful reef fishes, big-game fishes, crayfish and sponges live in the warm, limpid sea.

People Eighty-five per cent of Bahamians are black descendants of African slaves. The rest are Caucasians of British, Canadian, and U.S. origin. Most people are Baptist or Anglican Protestants, but more than one-fifth of the population is Roman Catholic. English is the official language, but imported Haitian laborers speak a dialect of French.

Almost all the quarter of a million Bahamians are concentrated on about two dozen islands. In fact more than half the entire population lives in the capital, Nassau (pop. 140,000 in 1982), on New Providence Island. The other main center is the resort, port, and industrial complex of Freeport City (pop. 16,000) on Grand Bahama.

Social conditions Two-thirds of the employed workforce is involved in tourism, one-fifth in industry, and 5 per cent in agriculture. But in the early 1980s unemployment had grown sharply.

At more than one-third the U.S. figure, the national average income is high for the region.

Education is compulsory from 5 to 14 and by the early 1980s the literacy rate reached 89 per cent. There are no universities.

In the mid 1980s a high birth rate and low death rate was increasing population by 1.9 per cent a year. Half that increase came from Haitian immigrants who made up only 15 per cent of the population.

Government This is a parliamentary democracy based on the British system. The Head of State is the British monarch (as head of the Commonwealth) represented by a Governor General. Executive power rests with the Prime Minister and ministers. The Prime Minister belongs to the 43-member House of Assembly, elected by popular vote at least every five years. A Senate with limited powers serves a similar term. Most of its 16 members are appointed by the Governor General, on the Prime Minister's advice. Bahamian law is based on the English legal system. For local government, the Bahamas are divided into 18 districts.

Communications and transportation There

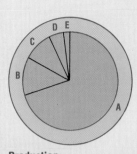

GDP
1449 million U.S.$
(1982)

Total World Trade
Figures expressed in millions of U.S.$ (1983)

Exports	World	1961.9
	U.S.	1587.0
Imports	World	3061.8
	U.S.	496.9

Production
Goods and services expressed as percentage of GDP (1983)

A	Tourism	70.0%
B	Banking and finance	13.0%
C	Manufacturing	10.0%
D	Agriculture	5.0%
E	Other	2.0%

Exports
Figures expressed as percentage of total (1983)

A	Oil	81.7%
B	Other	18.3%

Imports
Figures expressed as percentage of total (1983)

A	Oil	90.5%
B	Other	9.5%

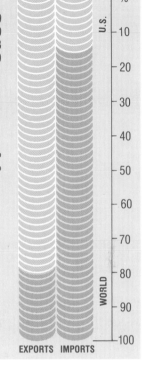

EXPORTS   IMPORTS

EXPORTS   IMPORTS

are three radio channels, one television channel, three daily newspapers, and an automatic telephone system, with inter-island radio-telephone links. Surfaced roads serve the main centers but there are no railroads. Nassau and Freeport have international airports, and dozens of airports and landing strips make even small obscure islands easy to reach. Nassau, Freeport, and Matthew Town on Great Inagua are the chief ports.

Economy For value of economic output the Bahamas rank seventh among West Indian nations. Tourism, banking, and oil refining underpin the economy.

Agriculture makes the Bahamas self-sufficient for eggs, poultry, meat and most vegetables, and nearly self-sufficient for fruit, pork, and sheep meat. Crops include cucumbers, grapefruit, guavas, mangoes, pineapples, and tomatoes.

The shallow Great Bahama Bank to the west and Little Bahama Bank to the north are rich fishing grounds; the catch includes crab, crayfish, grouper, and red snapper.

Minerals include salt and aragonite. Salt pans annually produce 1.6 million tons (1.5 million metric tons) of sea salt by evaporation. Dredging at Ocean Cay produces aragonite, used in making glass and cement. There is oil prospecting.

Manufacturers are mostly concentrated in the Freeport area where industries will operate tax free until A.D. 2054. Products include cement, steel piping, pharmaceuticals, processed foods, rum, furniture, and handicrafts. Freeport's oil refinery is one of the world's largest.

The Bahamas reexport oil and oil products and export pharmaceuticals, rum, aragonite, salt, steel piping, and cement. Oil refining contributes 12–15 per cent of the gross domestic product, but the main source of revenue is tourism followed by banking and other financial services.

The main imports include oil, food, machinery and transportation equipment, manufactured goods, and chemicals.

The chief suppliers of imports are oil-producing Arab and African nations and the U.S. The main export markets are the U.S. mainland, Puerto Rico, and the United Kingdom.

The flamingo, the national bird of the Bahamas.

Turks and Caicos Islands; Cayman Islands

OFFICIAL NAME
Turks and Caicos Islands

Above: **Flag of the Turks and Caicos Islands**
Blue with the Union Flag in the top staff-side corner and a yellow shield toward the outer edge.

SIZE IN RELATION TO U.S. CITY

Slightly larger than San Jose, California

AREA	**166** square miles (430sq. km.)
POPULATION	**7,500** (1983 estimate)
POPULATION DENSITY	**45.2** per square mile (1983)
PRINCIPAL RELIGIONS	**Roman Catholic, Protestant**
OFFICIAL LANGUAGE	**English**
CAPITAL	**Grand Turk**
CURRENCY	**U.S. dollar** (U.S.$1 = 100 cents)

The Turks and Caicos Islands, southeast of the Bahamas, and the Cayman Islands, northwest of Jamaica, are two British crown colonies. In both island groups combined, fewer than 30,000 people inhabit a total area about that of New York City.

History Arguably sighted by Christopher Columbus in 1492, the Turks and Caicos were settled from Bermuda in 1678; invaded by the French and Spanish in the 1700s; then part of the Bahamas (1799–1848); then separate (1848–74); next a Jamaican dependency (1874–1962). They have been a separate British colony since 1962, with ministerial government from 1976.

The Caymans were seen by Columbus in 1503; ceded (with Jamaica) by Spain to England in 1670; pirate-haunted; then seriously settled about 1734. Severing their Jamaican links in 1959 they stayed British after Jamaican independence (1962).

Land Both colonies feature groups of small, low limestone islands fringed by coral reefs. Most of the 30 or so Turks and Caicos Islands lie in the Caicos group, separated from the Turks Islands to the east by a broad, deep channel. A wide gap also separates Grand Cayman from Cayman Brac and Little Cayman to its northeast.

Climate Both colonies have a tropical climate tempered by Northeast Trade Winds.

Vegetation and animals Scrub, pines or mangroves cover large areas.

People On the Turks and Caicos most people are Negroes; the Caymans have a more mixed population. Both islands have Roman Catholics and Protestants and their official language is English. Only eight of the Turks and Caicos Islands are inhabited and half of the roughly 8500 islanders live on

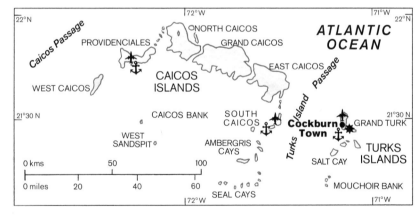

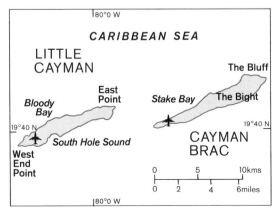

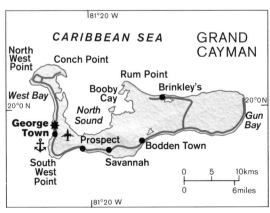

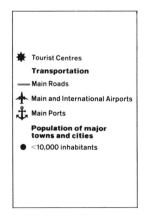

Tourist Centres
Transportation
— Main Roads
✈ Main and International Airports
⚓ Main Ports
Population of major towns and cities
● <10,000 inhabitants

OFFICIAL NAME
Cayman Islands

Above: **Flag of the Cayman Islands**
Blue with the Union Flag in the top staff-side corner, and a disk containing the coat of arms toward the outer edge.

SIZE IN RELATION TO U.S. CITY

Same as Austin, Texas (A)

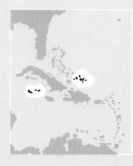

AREA	**118** square miles (306sq.km.)
POPULATION	**12,000** (1982 estimate)
POPULATION DENSITY	**101.7** per square mile (1982)
PRINCIPAL RELIGIONS	**Anglican, Roman Catholic**
OFFICIAL LANGUAGE	**English**
CAPITAL	**George Town**
CURRENCY	**Cayman Islands dollar** (C.I.$1 = 100 cents)

Grand Turk and Salt Bay. Cockburn Town (1980 pop. 3146) on Grand Turk is the capital. More than four-fifths of the roughly 19,000 Cayman islanders live on Grand Cayman, site of the Caymans' capital George Town (1981 pop. 8200).

Social conditions The Caymans' high living standards could soon be matched on the Turks and Caicos where poor job prospects formerly led to much emigration. Both colonies have free education, but only the Caymans offer higher education; they also have more advanced health care.

Government In each colony the head of state is the British monarch represented by a Governor.

Communications and transportation The Turks and Caicos have one radio station, no television stations, a weekly newspaper, and fewer than 1000 telephones. There are 75 miles (121km.) of roads; three main airports; and ports on Grand Turk, South Caicos, and Providenciales islands. The Cayman Islands have two radio stations; an incipient television station; several newspapers; and over 6000 telephone subscribers. There are more than 108 miles (175km.) of roads; two international airports; and one port: George Town.

Economy In the mid 1980s, the Turks and Caicos Islands – least developed of the British West Indies – seemed set to follow the example of the Cayman Islands, where tourism and financial services have built a booming economy. More than 300,000 tourists a year have visited the Cayman Islands; and these hold more than 450 banks, attracted to a tax-free country with strict laws of confidentiality. Other economic sectors are much less developed. The Turks and Caicos have some subsistence farming, hampered

by a lack of rain; but the Caymans produce fruit, vegetables, and livestock commercially. Conch and crawfish are important to the Turks and Caicos, and sportfishing is a feature of the Caymans. The Turks and Caicos once produced sea salt and have started mining seabed aragonite. Both colonies have little manufacturing, and import almost everything they use. The Turks and Caicos export conch and crawfish. The vast bulk of the Caymans' foreign earnings come from invisible exports such as financial services and tourism.

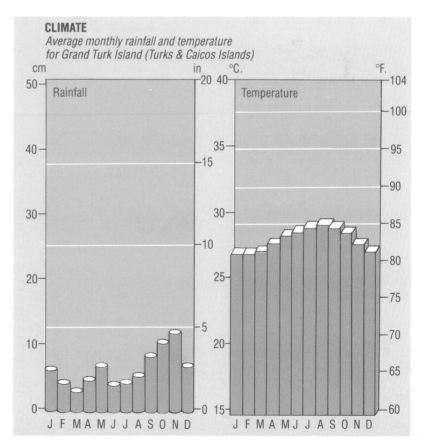

CLIMATE
Average monthly rainfall and temperature for Grand Turk Island (Turks & Caicos Islands)

Cuba

OFFICIAL NAME
República de Cuba

Above: **Flag of Cuba**
Equal horizontal bands of
blue, white, blue, white, blue;
with a staff-side red triangle
containing a white star. Shown
left is the Cuban coat of arms.

SIZE IN RELATION TO U.S. STATE

A

Slightly larger than Tennessee (A)

AREA	**42,827** square miles (110,922 sq.km.)
POPULATION	**9,877,000** (1983 preliminary figure)
POPULATION DENSITY	**230.6** per square mile (1983)
CURRENCY	**Peso** (1 peso = 100 centavos)
PRINCIPAL RELIGION	**Roman Catholic**
OFFICIAL LANGUAGE	**Spanish**
CAPITAL	**Havana**
ADMINISTRATIVE DIVISIONS	**14 provinces**

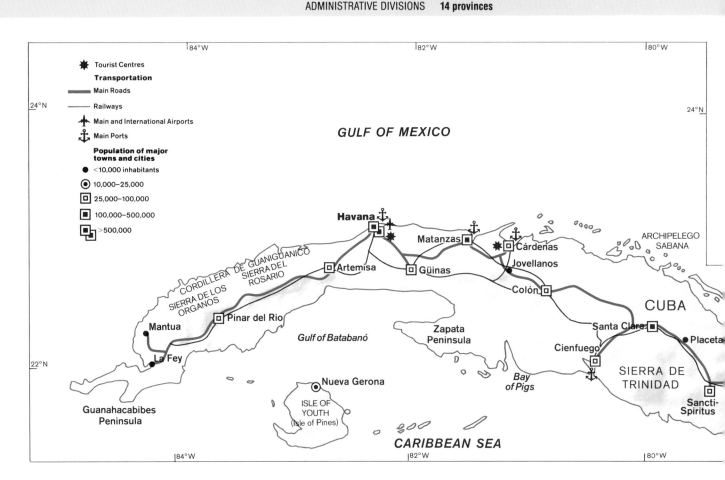

Cuba is best known as the only powerful American nation where communism shapes the people's way of life – with implications far beyond the Caribbean region.

In size this Caribbean island almost equals all the rest, and occupies an area a little larger than Tennessee. Cuba resembles an alligator located just inside the tropics, dominating sea lanes linking the Atlantic, Caribbean, and Gulf of Mexico. It lies east of Mexico, south of Florida and the Bahamas, west of Haiti, and north of Jamaica – an appropriately central place for a land whose name comes from the Indian *cubanacan*: "center place".

Long, narrow Cuba is mostly rolling lowland, with some narrow mountain ranges. Fertile soil, warm climate, and adequate rain help to make this one of the world's top producers of cane sugar.

With about one-third of the West Indies' entire population, Cuba has far more people than any other Caribbean country – almost as many as Florida. Its authoritarian regime has reduced personal freedom but raised living standards.

HISTORICAL REVIEW

1510	Diego Velázquez commissioned to conquer and settle Cuba.		"26th of July Movement".
1868	Beginning of the Ten Years War.	**1956**	Castro leads an unsuccessful expedition back to Cuba aboard the Yacht Granma.
1879–80	"La Guerra Chiquita": The Little War.	**1959**	Batista falls; Castro era begins.
1895	The War of Independence begins.	**1960**	U.S. embargo on Cuba.
1898	U.S. intervention; the war ends and military occupation begins.	**1961**	C.I.A. backed unsuccessful invasion of the Bay of Pigs.
1901	Cuba's first constitution.	**1962**	Cuban missile crisis.
1906–09	Second U.S. intervention.	**1973**	Cuba and U.S. reached an extradition agreement on hijackers.
1940	New constitution introduced.	**1976**	Cuba's new Socialist Constitution in force.
1953	Fidel Castro organizes unsuccessful attack on the Moncada Barracks in Santiago.	**1983**	Twenty four Cubans killed in the U.S. invasion of Grenada.
1955	Castro, exiled in Mexico, establishes the		

History Several groups of Indians inhabited Cuba when Christopher Columbus discovered it in 1492: the Ciboney and Guanahatabey (in the west) were outnumbered by the Arawakan Taino Indians who had a more complex culture based on farming and fishing.

Spanish colonization began in 1511 with a colony founded in the northeast by Diego Velázquez. In 1519 he also established Havana as the capital on its present site.

In the 1500s Cuba became a major staging post for Spanish expeditions to Mexico, Florida, and the southern Mississippi, and Havana emerged as a key transshipment center between Spain's American colonies and Spain.

Early economic growth was slowed by hurricanes, pirate attacks, and diseases that decimated the Indian labor force. By 1850, though, imported African slaves cultivating canefields were helping to make Cuba a world leader in sugar production, forging an economy linked to the U.S.

Increased Spanish taxation and Spain's refusal to concede self-government provoked

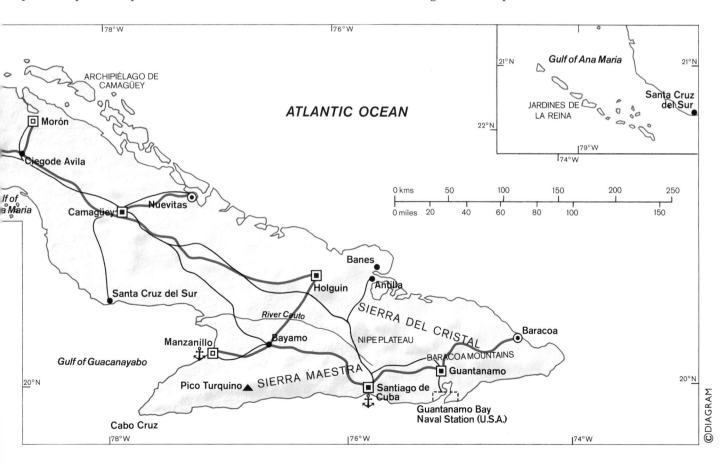

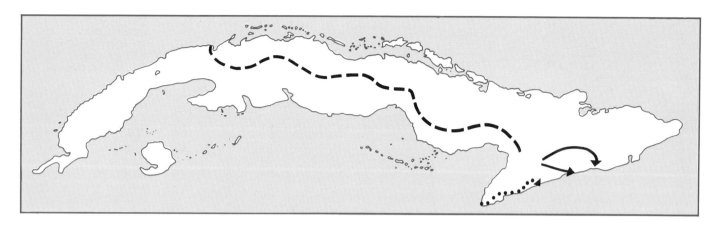

Cuban revolution

••••• Castro's route from coast to Sierra Maestra

━━━ Route of Castro's successful attack on Santiago de Cuba

━ ━ ━ Route of Castro's advance on Havana

July 26, 1953
Castro leads unsuccessful attack on Moncada barracks at Santiago de Cuba. Castro captured, imprisoned, later released in general amnesty. (Later, successful revolution is named "26th July Movement" after this attack.)

1955
Castro in Mexico planning new attempt to overthrow Batista regime.

December 2, 1956
Castro lands in Oriente province with small force including Che Guevara. Most of force killed by Cuban army, survivors escape into Sierra Maestra. Set up headquarters of guerilla force launching attacks on chosen targets.

August 1958
Castro begins final drive against Batista regime.

January 1, 1959
Castro takes Santiago de Cuba. Batista flees abroad.

January 8, 1959
Castro enters Havana.

two independence wars (1868–78 and 1895–98) culminating in 1898 in U.S. military intervention and Cuban independence. A "protective" U.S. military force occupied Cuba until 1901, establishing the Guantanamo Bay naval station (still held by the U.S.), and Americans invested heavily in Cuba. There followed a second occupation (1906–09), but Cuba stayed independent.

Between 1909 and 1959 the republic endured rule by corrupt politicians largely serving U.S. and other foreign interests. Most Cubans suffered poverty, and Afro-Cubans faced severe racial persecutions.

In 1959, after two years' grueling guerrilla warfare, rebel leader Fidel Castro toppled Cuba's then dictator, Fulgencio Batista. Becoming Premier, Castro established a communist regime that launched sweeping socio-political reforms to benefit the poor and end foreign ownership of Cuban assets. The Government seized farms, banks, and industries, mostly without compensation payments; and dealt harshly with the disaffected of whom 700,000 eventually emigrated, mainly to the U.S.

Cuba's leftist aims and growing ties with the Soviet Bloc aroused U.S. opposition. In the early 1960s came U.S. trade embargoes that damaged the economy. In 1961, CIA-trained Cubans unsuccessfully invaded Cuba from Guatemala. Next year, the U.S. forced Russia to withdraw nuclear missiles newly based on Cuban soil. Despite some limited agreements between the U.S. and Cuba, Fidel Castro continued giving military aid to leftist rebels and regimes worldwide. Cuba's military strength and internationalism explain why the U.S. sees this small southern neighbor as the main threat to Western Hemisphere security.

Under communism, Cubans have suffered shortages and lost liberties, but seen improvements in education, health, and housing. In those terms Cuba is among the most successful nations of the Caribbean.

Land Cuba consists of more than 3700 islands and islets. By far the biggest is the island of Cuba, the largest and most westerly of all the Great Antilles: 780 miles (1255km.) from northwest to southeast, and from 20 to 120 miles (32–193km.) across. The country's second largest island is the Isle of Youth (once called the Isle of Pines), off southwest Cuba. Many tiny islands form several offshore archipelagoes, notably the northern Archipiélago de Camaguey.

Much of Cuba is a mass of folded rocks upraised above the sea some 20 million years ago, and since subjected to erosion.

Three-quarters of the land is rolling plains or coastal swamps. Large tracts of lowland soil are deep, fertile, well-drained reddish clay overlying limestone.

There are several mountain ranges. The two highest rim most of the southeast coast. Here, Cuba's most rugged range, the Sierra Maestra, rises to 6476 feet (1974m.) at Pico Turquino, Cuba's highest point. East of the Sierra Maestra, beyond the Nipe plateau, lie the Baracoa mountains. Lesser mountains rise much farther west. The Sierra de Trinidad stands in southern-central Cuba, while the far west has the isolated limestone summits of the Sierra de los Organos and the ridged Rosario mountains – collectively called the Cordillera de Guaniguanico.

Most Cuban rivers flow briefly north or south across the island. The longest river is the 230-mile (370-km.) Cauto, which drains the Sierra Maestra's northern slopes.

A varied coastline of more than 3550 miles

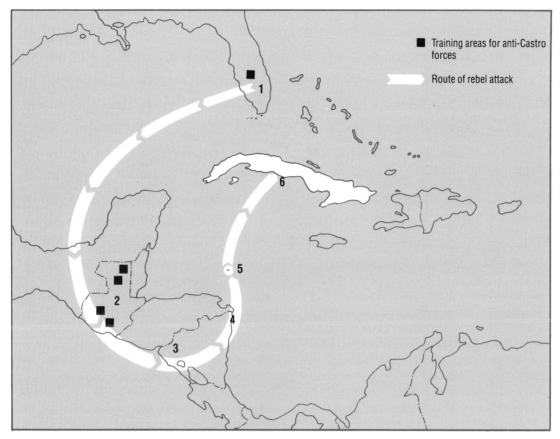

Bay of Pigs invasion
January 3, 1961
U.S. government severs all diplomatic relations with Cuba, later sanctions CIA planned invasion of Cuba by anti-Castro exiles.
January–April 1961
Anti-Castro forces train in Florida (**1**), Guatemala (**2**), and Nicaragua (**3**), assemble at Puerto Cabezas (**4**), and transfer to Swan Island. (**5**).
April 17, 1961
Invasion force lands at Bahia de los Cochinos (the Bay of Pigs) (**6**).
April 17–19, 1961
Invasion force holds beachhead. Invasion fails – most of the force is captured and imprisoned.
December 1962–July 1965
U.S. ransoms survivors.

■ Training areas for anti-Castro forces

➤ Route of rebel attack

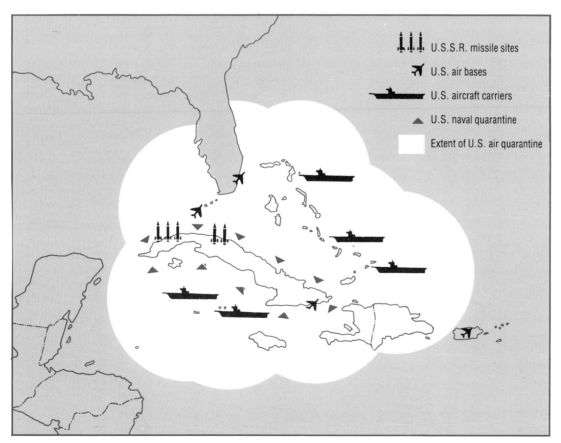

Cuban missile crisis
July 1962
U.S. government learns of U.S.S.R. shipments of ballistic nuclear missiles to Cuba.
August 29, 1962
U2 spy planes spot weapons site construction
October 14, 1962
U2 planes spot missiles on launch pads.
October 22, 1962
President Kennedy announces naval and air quarantine of Cuba, demands that missiles are withdrawn.
October 28, 1962
Soviet Premier Khrushchev announces that construction work has ceased and missiles will be withdrawn. In return U.S. promises not to invade Cuba.
November 20, 1962
U.S. lifts quarantine.

U.S.S.R. missile sites

✈ U.S. air bases

U.S. aircraft carriers

▲ U.S. naval quarantine

Extent of U.S. air quarantine

Cuba

(5713km.) has bays, beaches, cliffs, coral reefs, lagoons, and mangrove swamps.

Climate Cuba has a warm, humid, subtropical climate. The mean annual temperature is about 78°F. (26°C.). August, the hottest month, averages 82°F. (28°C.) and January, the coolest, 72.5°F. (22.5°C.). Temperatures seldom exceed 95°F. (35°C.) or drop below 66°F. (19°C.), but temperature varies more between day and night than on the smaller Caribbean islands. Also, winter winds from the U.S. can send lowland temperatures down to 39°F. (4°C.), causing mountain frosts. Rainfall averages 54 inches (1380mm.) a year. Some southeastern coastal areas get less, while high mountains in the southeast receive more than 98 inches (2500mm.). May through October is the rainy season, when Cuba can expect three-quarters of its annual rainfall. Severe hurricanes can strike between June and October.

Vegetation and animals The country's natural plant cover (much of it replaced by crops and pastures) ranges from forests to savanna, scrub, and swamp.

Forests once sprawled over more than half the land, but those on fertile plains were cleared for farming. The surviving 10–15 per cent of forest cover should reach 20 per cent under Government reforestation schemes. Most forest is concentrated on the mountains. There is a small patch of evergreen tropical rain forest in the southeast; otherwise most trees are semi-deciduous, although pine forests flourish in the west and southeast and on the Isle of Youth. Tree species include the kapok and that stately national tree the royal palm – both left standing on the cultivated plains; also such valuable timber trees as ebony and mahogany.

Savanna grasses cover some lowland tracts. There is a coastal strip of thorn scrub in the southeast, mixed scrub and forest on many offshore islands, and a great deal of mangrove swamp along low-lying coasts.

Like other West Indian islands, Cuba lacks large native mammals. But there are 30 kinds of bats; 6 rodent species; the Cuban solenodon (a rare, ratlike insectivore); and the manatee, or sea cow.

Cuba's birds include flamingos, the royal thrush, and hummingbirds. Many birds are North American migrants.

Among the reptiles and amphibians are

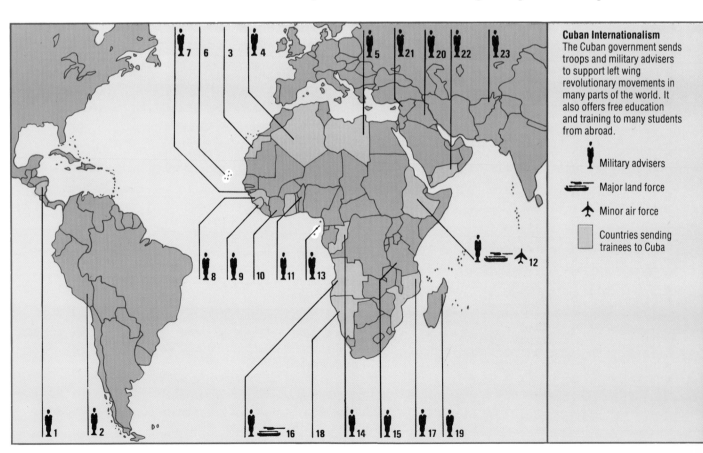

Cuban Internationalism
The Cuban government sends troops and military advisers to support left wing revolutionary movements in many parts of the world. It also offers free education and training to many students from abroad.

Military advisers

Major land force

Minor air force

Countries sending trainees to Cuba

two crocodilians, turtles, iguanid lizards, the Cuban boa – Cuba's largest snake – and five dozen kinds of frogs and toads.

Shallow offshore waters teem with many hundred kinds of fishes.

People More than 70 per cent of Cubans declare themselves as Whites, descended mainly from Spanish colonists and other immigrants. Self-declared Blacks descended from African slaves make up about one-quarter of the population, and there is a tiny Chinese minority. In fact, many Cubans are the product of mixed marriages. But disease and ill-treatment wiped out the native Indians long ago.

Roughly half of all Cubans claim no religious belief, a reflection of the Government's communist philosophy. About 40 per cent are Roman Catholics, and there are Protestants and others.

Spanish is the official language, but spoken with a local accent.

With more than 10 million people by the middle 1980s, Cuba had the largest population anywhere inside the Caribbean region or Central America. But population density is low compared to that in other of the larger Caribbean states, and because the area of cultivable land is relatively large, Cuba does not suffer the overpopulation pressures of such nations as Haiti.

One mid '80s estimate suggested that 70 per cent of Cubans lived in towns and cities. In fact the capital Havana and its suburbs held an estimated two million – nearly one-fifth of the whole population, and more people than any other city in the Caribbean region or Central America. Of the more than a dozen cities with populations of 100,000 or more, the two largest were Santiago de Cuba (1961 pop. 345,000) and Camaguey (pop. also 345,000).

Social conditions About half the labor force works in agriculture or industry – rather more on farms than in factories. All large farms are state controlled, and small farms sell produce to the state.

Average annual earnings remain a fraction of those in the U.S.; yet despite consumer goods shortages, general living standards have improved greatly since the 1950s. Rents are low, transportation is cheap, and most Cubans have access to a television and refrigerator.

Government schemes have hugely improved standards of education, housing, and health.

Cuba spends more on education than any other state in Latin America, and has that region's best teacher-pupil ratio and highest literacy rate (about 96 per cent). Education is compulsory between ages 6 and 14 and free at every level. Besides schools there are many day care centers, several universities, and agricultural and school projects. About 50,000 teenagers (14,000 from abroad) study agriculture on the Isle of Youth.

Cuba has built more than 2.4 million housing units since 1959, four-fifths with electricity. Havana has a housing shortage but lacks the shantytowns that disfigure most other big Latin American cities.

Medical care is free and extensive. Cuba has a better ratio of doctors and hospital beds per 100,000 population than most other Caribbean countries and claims to have wiped out the chief epidemic diseases. Infant mortality is higher than in the U.S., but low for the region, and no Caribbean nation has a higher life expectancy. At the same time birth control keeps the rate of population increase the lowest anywhere in Latin America.

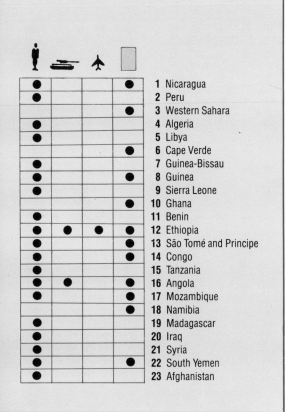

👤	🚂	✈	▯	
●			●	1 Nicaragua
●			●	2 Peru
			●	3 Western Sahara
●				4 Algeria
●				5 Libya
			●	6 Cape Verde
●				7 Guinea-Bissau
●			●	8 Guinea
●				9 Sierra Leone
			●	10 Ghana
●				11 Benin
●	●	●	●	12 Ethiopia
●			●	13 São Tomé and Principe
●			●	14 Congo
●				15 Tanzania
●	●		●	16 Angola
●			●	17 Mozambique
			●	18 Namibia
●				19 Madagascar
●				20 Iraq
●				21 Syria
●			●	22 South Yemen
●				23 Afghanistan

A tobacco plant, one of Cuba's principal cash crops.

Cuba

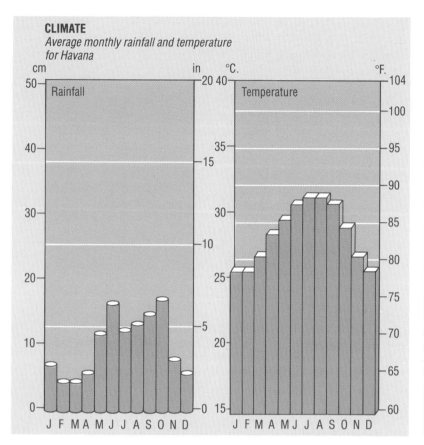

CLIMATE
Average monthly rainfall and temperature for Havana

Rainfall

Temperature

J F M A M J J A S O N D

J F M A M J J A S O N D

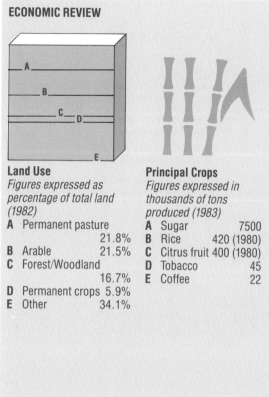

ECONOMIC REVIEW

Land Use
Figures expressed as percentage of total land (1982)

A	Permanent pasture	21.8%
B	Arable	21.5%
C	Forest/Woodland	16.7%
D	Permanent crops	5.9%
E	Other	34.1%

Principal Crops
Figures expressed in thousands of tons produced (1983)

A	Sugar	7500
B	Rice	420 (1980)
C	Citrus fruit	400 (1980)
D	Tobacco	45
E	Coffee	22

Government The 1976 constitution instituted a system of government involving national, provincial, and municipal assemblies. Voters (aged 16 and over) elect delegates to 169 municipal assemblies, choosing candidates only from the Communist Party and government-approved mass organizations representing workers and Cuban women. Municipal assemblies in turn elect the 481-member National Assembly which meets twice a year and appoints a Council of State and a Council of Ministers to conduct daily administration. As President of the former and Chairman of the latter, Premier Fidel Castro became Head of State and Head of Government.

Local government comes under the 169 municipal assemblies and they choose the delegates for the 14 provincial assemblies.

A four-chamber Tribunal Supremo Popular is the chief judicial body, but provincial tribunals handle relatively minor cases.

Communications and transportation In the early 1980s there were several radio stations and two television channels; about one radio for every five people, and one television set for every 10. Most of the 400,000 telephones were in Havana.

According to one estimate there were some 18,640 miles (30,000km.) of roads. Most were unsurfaced but engineers were building an island-long eight-lane highway. Public track accounted for about 3100 miles (5000km.) of the 11,200 miles (18,000km.) of railroads.

Havana's international airport serves scheduled flights to the Americas and Europe, and there are also local airports.

Havana is the major port. Other leading ports include Matanzas and Cárdenas in the north, and Cienfuegos, Manzanillo, and Santiago de Cuba in the south.

Economy Cuba's economy is centralized and state controlled on Marxist-Leninist lines, apart from the 12 per cent of arable land that belongs to small farmers. Cuba depends on sugar cane and – especially when sugar prices are low – on subsidized exports to its main trading partners, other socialist members of Comecon (the Council for Mutual Economic Assistance). Since 1970 Cuba has tried to reduce its dependence on sugar by growing "new" crops, and

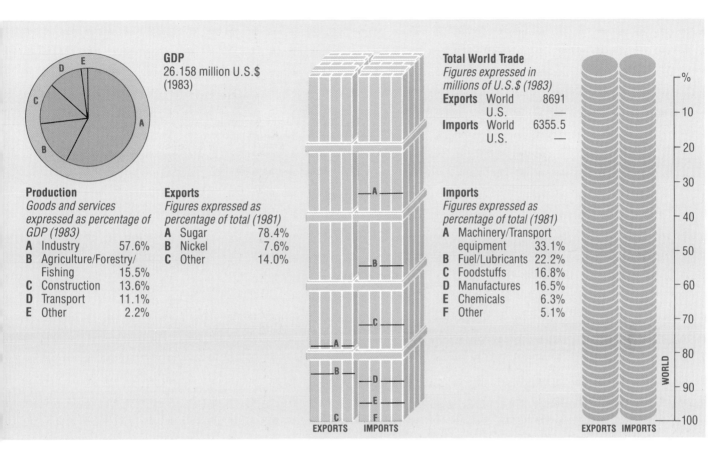

GDP
26.158 million U.S.$
(1983)

Production
Goods and services expressed as percentage of GDP (1983)

A	Industry	57.6%
B	Agriculture/Forestry/ Fishing	15.5%
C	Construction	13.6%
D	Transport	11.1%
E	Other	2.2%

Exports
Figures expressed as percentage of total (1981)

A	Sugar	78.4%
B	Nickel	7.6%
C	Other	14.0%

Total World Trade
Figures expressed in millions of U.S.$ (1983)

Exports	World	8691
	U.S.	—
Imports	World	6355.5
	U.S.	—

Imports
Figures expressed as percentage of total (1981)

A	Machinery/Transport equipment	33.1%
B	Fuel/Lubricants	22.2%
C	Foodstuffs	16.8%
D	Manufactures	16.5%
E	Chemicals	6.3%
F	Other	5.1%

EXPORTS   IMPORTS

EXPORTS   IMPORTS

expanding manufacturing, fishing, and tourism. But in the mid 1980s at least 75 per cent of national earnings came from sugar.

Increasingly helped by machinery, Cubans cultivate more than one-third of their country. In the early 1980s Cuba ranked as the world's third-largest cane sugar producer with 8 per cent of world output – mostly for export. The other main cash crops are tobacco and (increasingly) citrus fruits. Farms also yield tropical fruits, cassava, cotton, tomatoes, vegetables, and coffee grows on eastern mountain plantations. The six million cattle grazing on eastern and central savannas make meat the second most valuable farm product.

An expanding deep-sea fishing fleet has greatly increased Cuba's fish catch and fish exports since the mid 1970s.

Forestry features a wide range of native timber trees such as cedar, pine, and mahogany; but replanting programs include eucalyptus and other species.

Cuba's mines have made this one of the world's major nickel producers, with the world's fourth-largest nickel reserves. Other, but largely unexploited, minerals include copper, iron, gold, lead, manganese, and zinc. Cuba produces some offshore oil but imports most of the oil it consumes.

Manufactured goods range from processed foods, shoes, cotton textiles, and shoes to cement, steel, farm machinery, and fishing boats.

Cuba's chief exports are sugar, nickel, tobacco, and fish. The country imports mainly machinery, basic manufactured goods, food, fuel, and chemicals.

Cuba's chief trading partner is the Soviet Union followed by other East European states, Japan, Spain, and Canada.

Diego de Velásquez and a view of the coast of Cuba, which he conquered in 1511.

©DIAGRAM

Jamaica

OFFICIAL NAME
Jamaica

Above: **Flag of Jamaica**
A gold diagonal cross
(sunlight), green triangles
above and below (hope), and
black triangles at the sides
(hardship). Shown left is the
coat of arms.

SIZE IN RELATION TO U.S. STATE

Smaller than Connecticut (A)

AREA	**4,244** square miles (10,991sq.km.)
POPULATION	**2,264,000** (1983 preliminary figure)
POPULATION DENSITY	**533.5** per square mile (1983)
CURRENCY	**Jamaica dollar** (Jam.$1 = 100 cents)
PRINCIPAL RELIGIONS	**Anglican, Baptist**
OFFICIAL LANGUAGE	**English**
CAPITAL	**Kingston**
ASMINISTRATIVE DIVISIONS	**12 parishes and Kingston & St. Andrew corporate area**

Jamaica is a parliamentary state within the Commonwealth. One of the Greater Antilles, this is the third largest island of the West Indies, only a little smaller than Connecticut. It lies entirely in the Caribbean Sea, 90 miles (145km.) south of Cuba and 100 miles (161km.) west of Haiti.

Once notorious as the haunt of hard-drinking pirates, Jamaica is now noted for its farms, mines, and rapidly expanding tourist industry. The multiracial inhabitants depend on these as a source of income, and now form one of the region's fastest growing populations, larger than those of all other Caribbean members of the Commonwealth combined.

This is one of the loveliest of the West Indies, with mountains, lush valleys, broad plains, and soft, white, sandy beaches. All bask beneath a tropical sun. Indeed Jamaica's name comes from the old Indian word *Xaymaca*: "land of wood and water." Dazzling blooms and hummingbirds enliven the tropical greenery, and the air throbs with the sounds of birds, frogs, and the reggae and calypso beat.

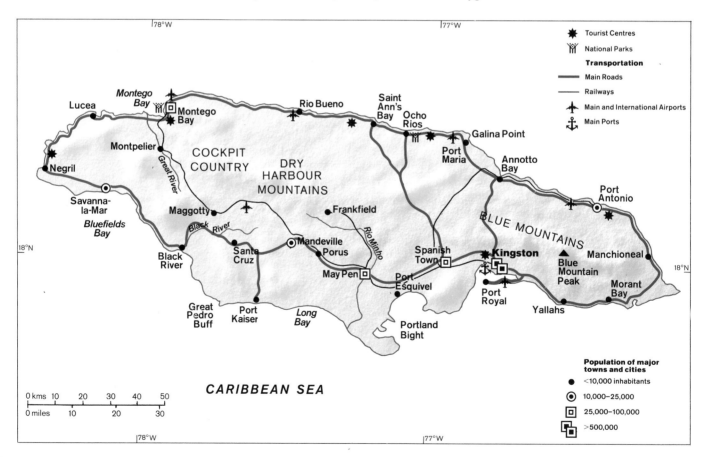

HISTORICAL REVIEW

1494 Christopher Columbus discovers the island and calls it Santiago.

1509 Spanish colonization of the island begins.

1655 A formal British expedition invades the island.

1838 Abolition of slavery leads to the collapse of the plantation system.

1865 The Morant Bay Rebellion occurs.

1866 Jamaica becomes a crown colony.

1938 Disaffection with the crown colony system and worldwide economic recession leads to serious, widespread rioting and the growing demand for self-determination.

1944 New constitution, universal adult suffrage, and a two party house of representatives are introduced.

1958 Jamaica becomes a founding member of the Federation of the West Indies.

1960 Period of high emigration to Great Britain, the U.S., and Canada begins.

1962 Independence is granted. The Jamaica Labor Party wins the elections.

1972 Michael Manley's People's National Party takes office.

1980 Edward Seaga's Jamaica Labor Party regains office.

History Peaceful Arawak Indians colonized Jamaica by A.D. 1000. Christopher Columbus discovered the island in 1494 and in 1509 Juan de Esquivel started Spanish occupation. The Arawaks soon died out, and the Spanish imported black slave labor from Africa. Then an English expeditionary force landed in 1655, and by 1660 had driven out the Spanish. However, many of their slaves escaped into the mountains and, as so-called Maroons, waged war against the English for the next 140 years or so.

Under English occupation, Jamaica became a base for merchants and planters, doubling as buccaneers or pirates until these were suppressed in 1670. In 1692 an earthquake shattered Port Royal, but nearby Kingston later developed into a major Caribbean port (although itself badly damaged by another earthquake, which struck in 1907). By the early 1800s plantations of sugar cane and coffee and the African slave trade had made Jamaica Britain's richest colony.

Prosperity collapsed with the end of slavery in 1838. Many freed slaves left the plantations and occupied idle land in the hills. Planters imported Asian Indians to fill the labor gap, but maladministration and poverty culminated in an 1865 uprising that led indirectly to government reform. Jamaica lost its self-governing House of Assembly, becoming a Crown Colony run by a Governor appointed by Britain.

In 1938 Jamaicans rioted against colonial status and low earnings. Political rivals Norman Manley and Alexander Bustamante led a freedom movement that by 1962 helped make Jamaica an independent member of the Commonwealth. Since then, mines, hotels, and factories have supplemented farming.

Land Jamaica has been described as looking like a lozenge, or more fancifully, a turtle swimming west. The island is about 146 miles (235km.) long and 51 miles (82km.) across at its broadest.

Most of Jamaica is basically a vast hogback of limestone overlying older rocks; seamed by faults, and deeply bitten into by erosion, The island's three main regions are the eastern mountains, central hills and plateaus, and the coastal plains.

The eastern mountains are the highest area. In the Blue Mountains four peaks exceed 6000 feet (1829m.) and Blue Mountain Peak is Jamaica's highest point at 7402 feet (2256m.). From the Blue Mountains, rugged spurs and gullies jut north and south.

Two-thirds of the island is a rugged platform of limestone. Limestone plateaus and hills cover most of inland central and western Jamaica. They include the strange, trackless Cockpit Country, covering almost one-eighth of the entire island. Here, the rainwater has gnawed into the limestone surface, producing thousands of "cockpits" or hollows, some 500 feet (152m.) deep, and many flanked by wooded cliffs.

Broad alluvial plains cover much of the southern part if the island, and a narrow strip of lowland rims the north coast. This gently curving shore has most of the island's best sandy beaches, The southern coast is deeply notched by coves and bays.

More than 100 streams and rivers flow swiftly from the highlands to the sea. Some plunge down limestone caverns and travel miles underground before they reappear. Jamaica's fast-flowing rivers are mostly unsuitable for navigation, but tourists find the island's springs and waterfalls among its main attractions.

Port Royal in 1853, once notorious as a pirate's haunt. *(stamp issued 1921–23)*

©DIAGRAM

Jamaica

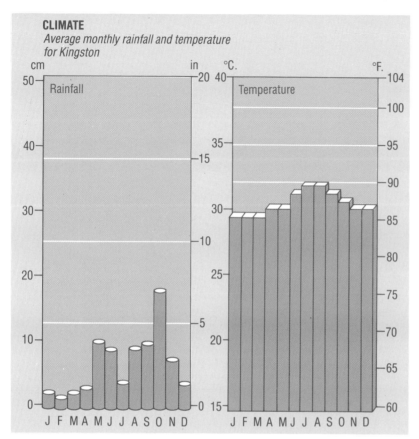

CLIMATE
Average monthly rainfall and temperature for Kingston

Rainfall

Temperature

J F M A M J J A S O N D

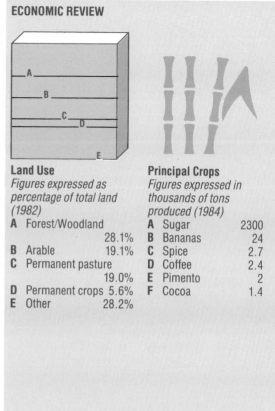

ECONOMIC REVIEW

Land Use
Figures expressed as percentage of total land (1982)

A	Forest/Woodland	
		28.1%
B	Arable	19.1%
C	Permanent pasture	
		19.0%
D	Permanent crops	5.6%
E	Other	28.2%

Principal Crops
Figures expressed in thousands of tons produced (1984)

A	Sugar	2300
B	Bananas	24
C	Spice	2.7
D	Coffee	2.4
E	Pimento	2
F	Cocoa	1.4

Climate The heat is tropical but moderated by sea breezes and, on mountains, by the altitude. Temperatures do not vary greatly with the seasons. At sea level Kingston's daily "high" averages 88°F. (31°C.) and its daily low, 71°F. (22°C.), but high mountains have a cooler, more refreshing climate than the hot, humid coasts.

Annual rainfall averages 77 inches (1956mm.) but mountainous parts of the northeast receive over 200 inches (5080mm.) – ten times more than the dry plains of the south and west. Rainfall peaks in May and October, and thunderstorms bring heavy showers in intervening summer months.

Besides the year-round Northeast Trade Winds, coasts receive fresh onshore breezes by day, and cooling offshore breezes by night. Rarely are there summer hurricanes and cool winter winds called Northers.

Vegetation and animals In 1500 forest covered almost all Jamaica. Now, only one-fifth of the land is forested – mostly the high mountain slopes, and parts of the hummocky Cockpit Country. Many of Jamaica's present trees were introduced by man. There are huge silk-cotton trees, lignum vitae, native palms, West Indian ebony, Caribbean pine, breadfruit, banyan, and many other species.

Drought-resistant cacti and other plants grow on dry uncultivated lowlands in the south, and low, sheltered coasts support big groves of mangrove trees.

Many roadsides are made picturesque by bamboo, hibiscus, poinsettia, the yellow-flowering *poui* and other shrubs or trees.

Jamaica does not have many native mammals. But there are 20 species of bats, a rare rodent called the hutia, and the manatee. The island echoes to the cries of some 200 kinds of birds including parrots, tanagers, and hummingbirds. Jamaica has eight species of snakes, all nonpoisonous: and there are many kinds of frogs. Fireflies and huge butterflies flutter through woodland glades, while offshore coral reefs are rich in brilliantly colored fishes. There are big-game fishes too: particularly bonito, kingfish, marlin, wahoo, and yellowtail.

People Jamaica is an ethnic melting pot with the apt motto "out of many, one people." Africa, Britain, India, China, Syria, Germany, and Portugal all contributed elements of the population which ranges

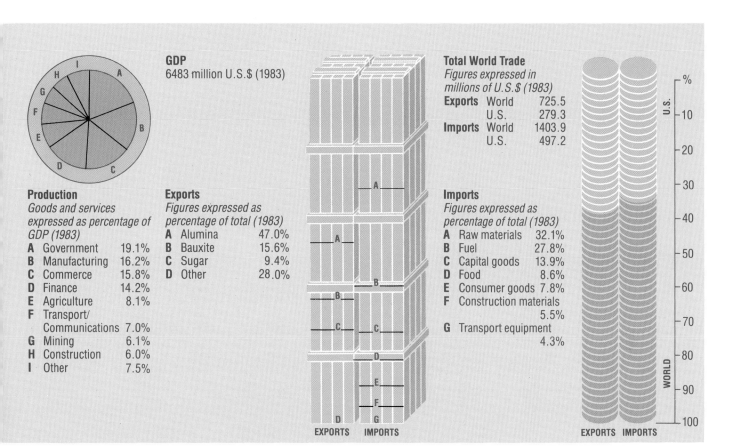

GDP
6483 million U.S.$ (1983)

Production
Goods and services expressed as percentage of GDP (1983)

A	Government	19.1%
B	Manufacturing	16.2%
C	Commerce	15.8%
D	Finance	14.2%
E	Agriculture	8.1%
F	Transport/Communications	7.0%
G	Mining	6.1%
H	Construction	6.0%
I	Other	7.5%

Exports
Figures expressed as percentage of total (1983)

A	Alumina	47.0%
B	Bauxite	15.6%
C	Sugar	9.4%
D	Other	28.0%

Total World Trade
Figures expressed in millions of U.S.$ (1983)

Exports	World	725.5
	U.S.	279.3
Imports	World	1403.9
	U.S.	497.2

Imports
Figures expressed as percentage of total (1983)

A	Raw materials	32.1%
B	Fuel	27.8%
C	Capital goods	13.9%
D	Food	8.6%
E	Consumer goods	7.8%
F	Construction materials	5.5%
G	Transport equipment	4.3%

EXPORTS   IMPORTS

EXPORTS   IMPORTS

from black to white and coffee colored. More than 90 per cent of Jamaicans are of African or Afro-European origin. One mid-1980s breakdown gave 76 per cent of African origin, and 15 per cent mixed.

British influence has largely shaped the island's faith and languages. Anglican Protestants predominate; but there are also Roman Catholics, Jews, Hindus, Moslems, Bahais, and Rastafarians. Although English is the official tongue, many people use "Jamaica Talk," an English-based Creole dialect with Ashanti, French and Spanish borrowings.

With more than two million people, Jamaica has the fifth largest population in the West Indies, but ranks only seventh for population density. The most thickly peopled parts are coastal lowlands, and some inland farming regions. By 1985 more than half the people were urbanized; almost one-third of all Jamaicans living on the south coast at the capital Kingston and its suburbs (pop. 800,000). Other important, but much smaller, towns include the north coast centers Montego Bay, Ocho Rios, and Port Antonio.
Social conditions Normally over one-third

of the labor force works in agriculture, nearly one-third in services, and about 15 per cent in industry and commerce. Earnings are low. In the mid 1980s a leading international aid organization, Oxfam, estimated that one-third of the labor force averaged less than U.S. $7 a week – a quarter of the cost of adequate food for an average family. In fact in the early 1980s more than a quarter of the labor force was out of work. There were as many as 50,000 malnourished young children and poverty, deepened by mid 1980s inflation, contributed to a high rate of crime. Even before the 1980s recession, thousands of Jamaicans had emigrated in search of better conditions abroad – to the U.S., Britain, Canada, and elsewhere.

Despite their social problems, Jamaicans have benefited from relatively advanced government programs of education, housing, pensions and health.

Education is free and compulsory between ages 5 and 16, and university and technical education is free. But a claimed literacy rate of over 80 per cent may be optimistic.

Housing development schemes have helped low-income groups, although all

Jamaica

homes still do not have their own water or electricity.

National insurance payments contribute to old age pensions, but there is no national scheme for unemployment pay.

A successful public health program has attacked malaria and major epidemic diseases. Thanks largely to improved medical aid, between 1960 and 1985 the death rate fell by more than one-third to 6 per 1000, and infant mortality dropped from 42.4 to 28 per thousand (though this was well over twice the U.S. figure). A nationwide family-planning scheme cut the birthrate by one-third. But Jamaica's 28 births per 1000 compared with only 11 in the U.S. The continuing high birth rate and reduced death rate kept population growing at a high annual rate of 2.2 per cent.

Government Jamaica is a parliamentary democracy in the Commonwealth. Its head of state is the British monarch represented by a Crown-appointed Governor General. The head of government is a Prime Minister chosen by the Parliamentary members of the leading political party. The legislature has

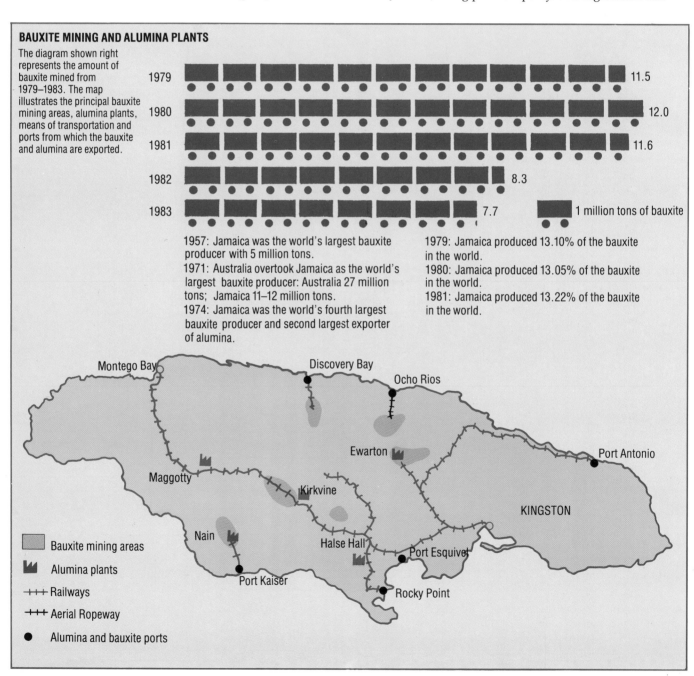

BAUXITE MINING AND ALUMINA PLANTS

The diagram shown right represents the amount of bauxite mined from 1979–1983. The map illustrates the principal bauxite mining areas, alumina plants, means of transportation and ports from which the bauxite and alumina are exported.

1979   11.5
1980   12.0
1981   11.6
1982   8.3
1983   7.7   ▬ 1 million tons of bauxite

1957: Jamaica was the world's largest bauxite producer with 5 million tons.
1971: Australia overtook Jamaica as the world's largest bauxite producer: Australia 27 million tons; Jamaica 11–12 million tons.
1974: Jamaica was the world's fourth largest bauxite producer and second largest exporter of alumina.

1979: Jamaica produced 13.10% of the bauxite in the world.
1980: Jamaica produced 13.05% of the bauxite in the world.
1981: Jamaica produced 13.22% of the bauxite in the world.

Montego Bay • Discovery Bay • Ocho Rios • Port Antonio
Ewarton
Maggotty • Kirkvine • KINGSTON
Nain • Halse Hall • Port Esquivel
Port Kaiser • Rocky Point

▬ Bauxite mining areas
🏭 Alumina plants
+++ Railways
+++ Aerial Ropeway
● Alumina and bauxite ports

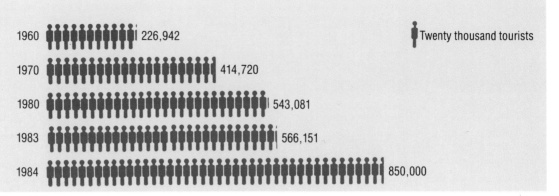

TOURISM
The figures shown on the right represent the number of tourists visiting Jamaica from 1960–1984.

1960 — 226,942
1970 — 414,720
1980 — 543,081
1983 — 566,151
1984 — 850,000

Twenty thousand tourists

two houses: a House of Representatives with 60 members elected every five years by universal adult suffrage (voters must be over 21), and a Senate of 21 appointed members. For local government, Jamaica is divided into parishes run by parish councils and the Kingston and St. Andrew Corporation.

Judicial power rests with a Supreme Court and lesser courts, and the legal system rests on English common law.

Communications and transportation
Jamaica has two government-supported radio services, some commercial services, and a single television station. In 1979 there were 750,000 radios but only 115,000 television sets. By 1982 there were 124,000 telephones, 75 per cent of them in Kingston. Daily newspaper circulation then averaged 137 per 100,000.

More than one-third of the country's 7500 miles (12,000km.) of roads have a hard surface, and the 186 miles (300km.) of railroad link Kingston, Montego Bay and Port Antonio – the chief three of Jamaica's 16 seaports. Kingston has an international airport and there are internal flights.

Economy This once-prosperous island was hard hit by recession in the mid 1970s and again in the early 1980s. Although becoming chief beneficiary of President Ronald Reagan's Caribbean Basin Initiative, Jamaica saw no economic growth in 1983 and in the mid 1980s the economy labored under production cutbacks, inflation, and a mountain of international debt.

Agriculture contributes less than 10 per cent of the gross domestic product, but generates much of the island's employment. Arable land covers 30 per cent of Jamaica (notably in alluvial basins) and about one-fifth of the island is in pasture. Most agricultural earnings come from crops grown by small and large farmers for home consumption. These crops include beans, yams, rice, potatoes, sweet potatoes, mangoes, avocados, cassava, breadfruit, and maize.

Sugar cane is the chief of those cash crops grown largely for export. It covers roughly one-fifth of all arable land. Others include bananas, cocoa, coffee, citrus fruits, pimento, ginger, and tobacco.

Livestock includes some 290,000 cattle, 375,000 goats, and 250,000 pigs.

Although one-fifth of Jamaica is wooded, and there are replanting schemes, it must import nine-tenths of the timber it uses.

Similarly, fishing and fish farming supply only about half the island's requirements.

Bauxite mining provides the island's chief source of export earnings. In the 1980s Jamaica was the world's third largest producer of this aluminum ore. Immense deposits in weathered limestone of the west central area cover more than one-fifth of Jamaica. Giant mechanical shovels stripmine the ore. Jamaica has at least five other ores and sand, gypsum, marble, and peat; but most deposits are unworked. There are small hydroelectric power plants, but energy comes largely from imported oil.

Factories (mostly in Kingston) produce processed foods, clothing, building materials, and industrial products, and major refineries extract alumina from bauxite.

Bauxite and alumina provide nearly two-thirds of foreign earnings, followed by tourism. Crude oil, basic manufactured goods, and food are the chief imports.

More than one-third of Jamaica's trade is with the U.S. Other trading partners include Britain, Venezuela, and Canada.

©DIAGRAM

Haiti

Above: Flag of Haiti
Two vertical bands of black (staff-side) and red. The state flag has a central white panel with the coat of arms (also shown left).

OFFICIAL NAME
République d'Haiti

SIZE IN RELATION TO U.S. STATE

Slightly larger than Maryland (A)

AREA	**10,714** square miles (27,750sq.km.)
POPULATION	**5,300,000** (1983 preliminary figure)
POPULATION DENSITY	**494.7** per square mile (1983)
CURRENCY	**Gourde** (1 gourde = 100 centimes)
PRINCIPAL RELIGION	**Roman Catholic**
OFFICIAL LANGUAGE	**French**
CAPITAL	**Port-au-Prince**
ADMINISTRATIVE DIVISIONS	**9 departments**, subdivided into communes

Haiti is the world's oldest Negro republic and the West Indies' third largest nation, the size of Maryland. Mist-shrouded ridges and plunging valleys make Haiti the region's most mountainous country, named from an Indian word for "high land." It lies in the north-central Caribbean, forming the west of Hispaniola island. The Dominican Republic lies to its east, the Caribbean Sea to its south and west, the Atlantic Ocean to its north.

Overcrowded Haiti is one of the poorest nations in the entire Western Hemisphere.
History Arawak Indians inhabited Haiti when Christopher Columbus discovered it in 1492. He named the whole island Española (anglicized as Hispaniola). Under Spanish colonial rule, disease and overwork soon killed off the Indians and Spain as good as abandoned Haiti. French buccaneers moved in, and the Treaty of Ryswick (1697) handed Haiti to France.

The French Revolution weakened France's hold on Haiti and a slave revolt broke out in 1791. Black leaders – including Toussaint L'Ouverture and Jean Jacques Dessalines – won independence by 1804. But war had

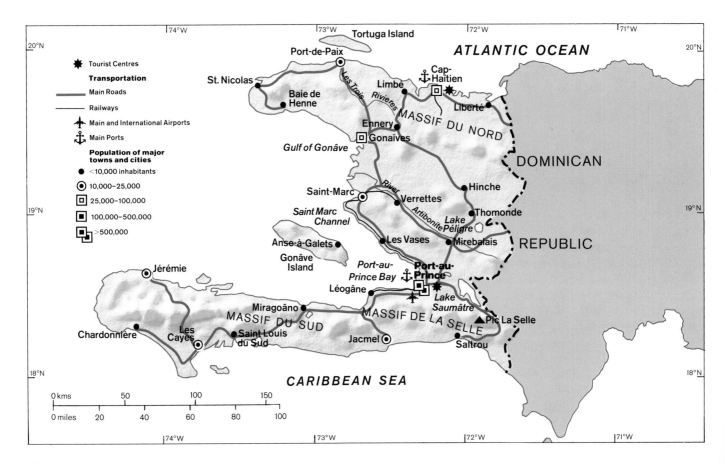

HISTORICAL REVIEW

1492	Columbus lands at Môle St. Nicolas.
1697	Treaty of Ryswick. Spain recognises France's claim to Western St. Domingue.
1797	Sonthonax appoints Toussaint L'Ouverture Commander in Chief of French Forces.
1801	Toussaint invades Santo Domingo and declares slavery abolished. New constitution.
1804	Dessalines declares Haitian independence, and is crowned Emperor Jacques I of Haiti.
1805	Dessalines launches unsuccessful invasion of Santo Domingo.
1806	Death of Dessalines. Haiti is declared a Republic.

1825	France grants independence to Haiti.
1888	Outbreak of civil war.
1915	U.S. Marines arrive to maintain law and order.
1929	Martial law is declared.
1934	End of U.S. occupation.
1941	Haiti declares war on Japan, Germany, Italy and all Axis powers.
1946	General strike. The army assumes power.
1957	Duvalier inaugurated as President.
1959	Attempted Castroite invasion in south fails.
1971	Death of Duvalier.
1984	Elections and riots.

savaged the economy and Negro-Mulatto civil strife followed.

U.S. Marines occupied Haiti from 1915 to 1934 to bring security and safeguard U.S. investments. President François Duvalier ("Papa Doc") ran a dictatorial police state from 1957 to 1971. Authoritarianism and poverty continued under his son, would-be reformer Jean-Claude ("Baby Doc").

Land Haiti forms the western third of Hispaniola island. It is up to 400 miles (644km.) long and 150 miles (241km.) wide. Four-fifths of the land is mountainous.

Haiti resembles the head of a long-jawed open-mouthed fish. The jaws make up most of the land. They are two long, westward-jutting peninsulas flanking a great bay, the Gulf of Gonave. East of the gulf, parallel ridges, plateaus, and valleys trend from northwest to southeast.

Haiti has three main mountain ranges. The Massif du Nord forms the spine of the northern peninsula. The Massif du Sud (also called the Massif de la Hotte) runs the length of the southern peninsula. To its east the Massif de la Selle rises to 8793 feet (2680m.) at the Pic la Selle, one of the highest points in Haiti.

Haiti's largest river, the Artibonite, crosses the country from east to west. There are two large lakes called the Saumâtre and Péligre. The coast has rocky cliffs and many small coastal plains. The largest offshore islands are the Île de Gonâves (Island of Gonave) in the Gulf of Gonave, and the Île de la Tortue (Tortuga Island) off the north coast.

Climate Haiti has a tropical climate but sea and mountains produce local differences. The humid sea-level capital, Port-au-Prince, has one of the Caribbean's highest average temperatures, reaching 98°F. (37°C.) in July.

But frost can occur on high mountains.

Mountains intercepting moist winds locally affect annual rainfall. This is more than 80 inches (2032mm.) in parts of the Artibonite Valley and Massif du Sud, but 20 inches (508mm.) in the far northwest. The north gets more rain in summer than winter; the south, more in winter than summer.

Winds are east and southeast in summer, northeast in winter. Severe hurricanes can strike from summer through fall.

Vegetation and animals Forests once covered Haiti. Deforestation has mostly destroyed them. Relics of lush tropical forest linger in some warm, moist lowlands. Drier areas have some thorn forest and savanna. A belt of cactus and thorn bushes covers much of dry northwest Haiti. There are some coastal mangrove swamps. A few pine forests survive on mountains, with alpine vegetation in cool, damp air higher up.

Little grows where severe erosion has ripped topsoil from steep slopes. Haiti lacks large native mammals, but has many rodents and the Indian mongoose. There are iguanid lizards, boas, crocodiles, over 200 bird species including flamingos, and even more kinds of sea fish including barracuda and tarpon.

People More than 90 per cent of Haitians are descended from African slaves imported by French colonists. Most of the rest are Mulattoes. Whites account for less than one per cent.

Four-fifths of the people are Roman Catholics, and Protestants make up one-tenth of the population. Voodoo is widespread.

French is the official language, but most Haitians speak Creole, with African ingredients.

Louis Borno, president during part of the U.S. occupation from 1915–1934.
(stamp issued 1924)

Haiti

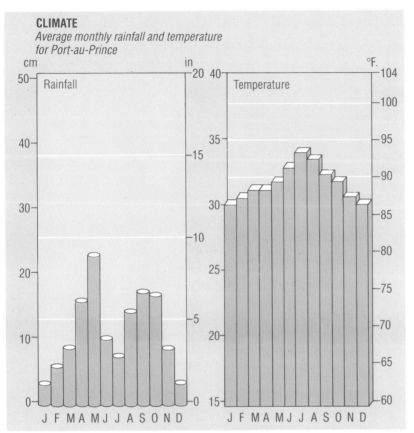

CLIMATE
Average monthly rainfall and temperature for Port-au-Prince

Rainfall

Temperature

J F M A M J J A S O N D

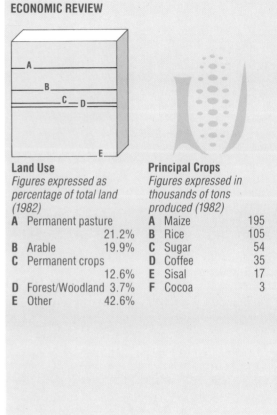

ECONOMIC REVIEW

Land Use
Figures expressed as percentage of total land (1982)

A Permanent pasture 21.2%
B Arable 19.9%
C Permanent crops 12.6%
D Forest/Woodland 3.7%
E Other 42.6%

Principal Crops
Figures expressed in thousands of tons produced (1982)

A Maize 195
B Rice 105
C Sugar 54
D Coffee 35
E Sisal 17
F Cocoa 3

Haiti has the third largest population in the Caribbean area. Population density is high almost everywhere, very high in parts of the north and south. Fewer than 30 per cent (one of the region's lowest urban percentages) live in towns, most of which stand on the coast. They include the capital and largest city Port-au-Prince (pop. 888,000 in 1982), Gonaïves, and Cap Haïtien.

Social conditions At least 70 per cent of people work on the land, the rest mostly in service industries and manufacturing. In the mid 1980s average income was little more than U.S. $300 a year. Overpopulation, lack of cheap power and raw materials, difficult terrain, and poor roads help to explain the deep poverty trap that engulfs the vast majority.

Health, housing, and education lack adequate funds. In the late 1970s there were 7 doctors per 100,000 people against 176 per 100,000 in the U.S. Towns suffer from poor, overcrowded housing conditions. About three quarters of the people are illiterate despite free, and in theory compulsory, elementary education. There is a university at Port-au-Prince.

Grim social conditions contribute to Haiti's depressing vital statistics. In the mid 1980s Haiti's annual death rate of 13 per 1000 was the second worst in the Western Hemisphere. Its birth rate of 36 per 1000 was the highest in the Caribbean.

Government The republic's executive power rests with a President-for-Life, who appoints cabinet ministers. The legislature is a 58-member National Assembly elected for six-year terms by all Haitians aged over 18. Thirty presidential supporters lost seats in the 1984 election despite government harassment of opposition leaders in a backlash following riots. Judicial power rests with a Supreme Court, courts of appeal, and local courts. The Head of State appoints judges. For local government Haiti is divided into nine departments subdivided into communes.

Communications and transportation There are many radio stations but the television service is limited, and in the mid 1980s fewer than 2 in 100 people had a telephone. There are several daily newspapers, with a very small circulation. By the early 1980s there were only about 2500 miles (4000km.) of roads,

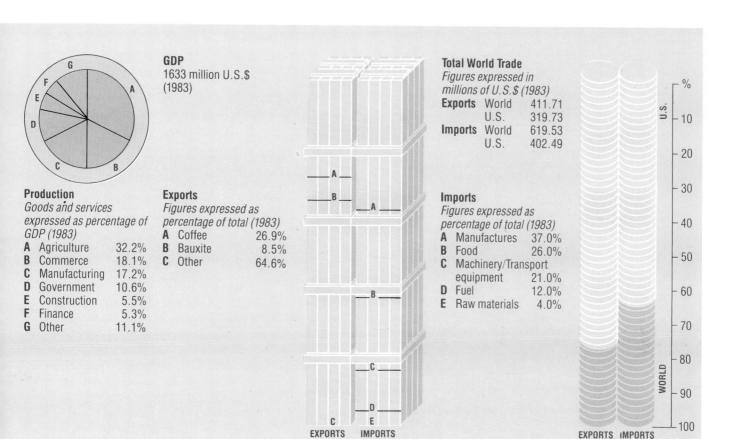

GDP
1633 million U.S.$
(1983)

Production
Goods and services expressed as percentage of GDP (1983)

A	Agriculture	32.2%
B	Commerce	18.1%
C	Manufacturing	17.2%
D	Government	10.6%
E	Construction	5.5%
F	Finance	5.3%
G	Other	11.1%

Exports
Figures expressed as percentage of total (1983)

A	Coffee	26.9%
B	Bauxite	8.5%
C	Other	64.6%

Total World Trade
Figures expressed in millions of U.S.$ (1983)

Exports	World	411.71
	U.S.	319.73
Imports	World	619.53
	U.S.	402.49

Imports
Figures expressed as percentage of total (1983)

A	Manufactures	37.0%
B	Food	26.0%
C	Machinery/Transport equipment	21.0%
D	Fuel	12.0%
E	Raw materials	4.0%

EXPORTS IMPORTS

EXPORTS IMPORTS

some of them impassable after rain. Three short railroads carry farm produce to Port-au-Prince. An international airport stands near that city and there are internal air services. Haiti's main ports are Port-au-Prince on the Gulf of Gonâve, and Cap Haïtien on the northern, Atlantic, coast.

Economy Output fell in value in the early 1980s for reasons including worldwide recession and hurricane damage to crops. In value, per capita output is the Western Hemisphere's lowest. But Haiti gets U.S. and other economic aid; and its low labor costs and lack of legal curbs encouraged foreign investment even before President Reagan's Caribbean Basin Initiative (CBI) offered exports duty-free entry to the U.S.

Agriculture underpins the economy, accounting for about 30 per cent of the gross domestic product. From 25 to 50 per cent of Haiti is arable land (estimates vary) and one-fifth is pasture. Most peasants work their own smallholdings, growing corn, millet, cassava, peas, sweet potatoes and other food crops. Cash crops include coffee, sugar cane, and rice. Haiti has about one million cattle, almost that many goats, and nearly two million pigs.

Forests now cover less than 10 per cent of Haiti. Fuelwood provides its main source of energy, but overfelling and soil erosion have removed most timber trees such as oak and mahogany.

Sea fishing supplies local demand.

Mining and manufacturing contribute about one-fifth of the gross domestic product. Haiti has some bauxite and copper, but useful bauxite reserves are used up. Manufacturing is mostly assembly work. Haiti makes textiles, sports goods, toys, electrical goods, and also other products from shoes to steel rods and sugar.

Most export earnings usually come from coffee and manufactured goods, but tourist income is growing. (Tourist attractions include voodoo ceremonies, and the Citadel, a spectacular old mountain fortress near Cap Haïtien.)

Imports include machinery and transportation equipment, basic manufactured goods, food, drinks, and oil.

Haiti's chief trading partners are the U.S., France, Italy, Belgium, the Netherlands, the Netherlands Antilles, and Canada.

President Geffrard, ruler of Haiti from 1859–67, as shown on a 10 centimes coin.

© DIAGRAM

101

Dominican Republic

OFFICIAL NAME
República Dominicana

Above: **Flag of the Dominican Republic**
State: Diagonal blue and red rectangles (blue, top staff-side), and a white cross bearing a coat of arms.
Civil: No coat of arms.

SIZE IN RELATION TO U.S. STATE

Slightly smaller than Vermont and New Hampshire together (A)

AREA	**18,704** square miles (48,442sq.km.)
POPULATION	**5,908,000** (1983 preliminary figure)
POPULATION DENSITY	**315.9** per square mile (1983)
CURRENCY	**Peso** (1 peso = 100 centavos)
PRINCIPAL RELIGION	**Roman Catholic**
OFFICIAL LANGUAGE	**Spanish**
CAPITAL	**Santo Domingo**
ADMINISTRATIVE DIVISIONS	**26 provinces and Santo Domingo**

This is the second-largest Caribbean country in size and population – a tropical land of forested mountains and lowland plantations edged by superb coves and beaches. It forms the eastern two-thirds of the central West Indian island of Hispaniola; bounded west by Haiti, north by the Atlantic, east by the Mona Passage with Puerto Rico beyond, and south by the Caribbean. Here are the oldest New World cities founded by Europeans; the West Indies' highest peak, and, less attractively, some of the region's worst social conditions.

History Carib and Taino Indians inhabited Hispaniola when Christopher Columbus discovered the island in 1492. By 1496 Spanish gold seekers were crushing the Indians and founding Santo Domingo. But by 1550 many had pulled out. Hispaniola became a Spanish colonial backwater raided by Dutch, English, and French pirates. Spain handed France western Hispaniola (Haiti) in 1697, and the rest in 1795.

In the early 1800s the country came under Haiti (1801–09), then Spain (1809–21), then, after the Dominican Republic declared

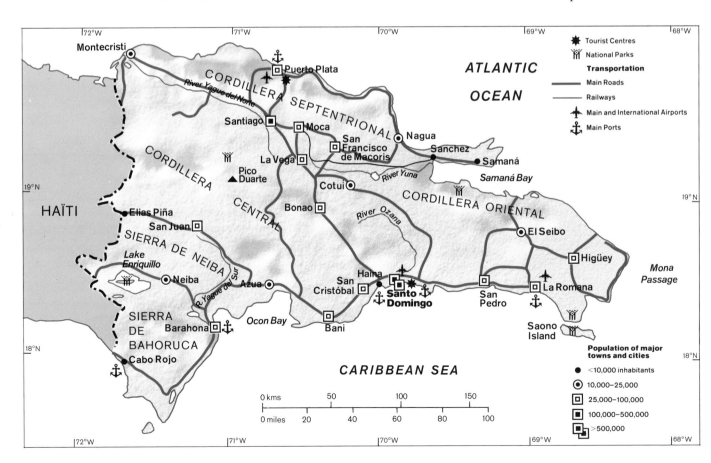

HISTORICAL REVIEW

1492	Christopher Columbus lands on Hispaniola.
1795	Spain cedes eastern two-thirds of Hispaniola to France.
1809	Colony reunited with Spain.
1821	Dominican Republic declares its independence from Spain.
1822	Haitian columns occupy the island.
1844	The Dominicans declare their independence from Haiti.
1861	Re-establishment of Spanish colonial rule.
1865	Withdrawal of Spanish forces.
1882	Ulises Heureaux gains control.
1916–24	U.S. occupation of the Dominican Republic.

1930	Rafael Leónidas Trujillo Molina elected President of the republic.
1961	Assassination of Trujillo.
1963	Juan Bosch becomes President.
1965	U.S. occupation.
1966	Joaquin Balaguer elected President. U.S. withdraw troops.
1970	Balaguer elected for a second term.
1971	Attempted right-wing coup is crushed.
1982	Partido Revolucionario Dominicano won election.

independence in 1821, under Haiti again (1822–44). For the rest of the century dictatorial presidents ruled, although fear of Haitian invasion led to a brief return of protective Spanish control (1861–65).

Civil disorders and mounting national debt led to U.S. occupation (1916–24) in a bid to restore order. Military leader Rafael Trujillo seized power in 1930, and ruled repressively until killed in 1961. There was more unrest and a fresh U.S. intervention (1965–66) but Trujillo's supporters held almost unbroken power until the Dominican Revolutionary Party won control in free elections in 1978

Land The republic is about 240 miles (386k.) from east to west and 170 miles (274km.) from north to south at its broadest. Five parallel mountain ranges run roughly from northwest to southeast. The Cordillera Central forms the country's (west-central) backbone, with Pico Duarte at 10,417 feet (3175m.) the highest West Indian summit. Lower ranges – the cordilleras Septentrional and Oriental respectively – parallel the northwest and northeast coast. Two more ranges – the sierras de Neiba and de Baharuco – dominate the southwest. Between ranges lie river valleys, and lowland takes up the southeast. The rivers Yaque del Norte and Yaque del Sur between them drain north and south slopes of the Cordillera Central; while the Yuna, Ozana, and others drain the east. The sub-sea-level Enriquillo salt lake is a large southwestern feature. Coasts include cliffs, coves, swamps, and beaches of pure white sand.

Climate This is basically humid and hot, for the republic lies inside the tropics. But mountains and the Northeast Trade Winds exert cooling influences. The temperature averages 77°F. (25°C.) and seldom exceeds 90°F. (32°C.) in summer, or falls below 60°F. (16°C.) in the cooler months, December through March.

Annual rainfall ranges from 100 inches (2540mm.) in the ocean-facing northeast to just over 30 inches (762mm.) in the far west. May through June, and September through November are the wettest months.

Tropical storms including hurricanes can strike between August and October.

Vegetation and animals Estimates suggest that forests still cover 25–40 per cent of the land, especially high mountain slopes. In the northeast, dense rainforest grows on slopes facing rainbearing winds. The chief trees are pines and tropical hardwoods such as mahogany, lignum vitae, and logwood. There are also scattered royal palms, and mangroves line tidal mudflats; but farm crops have replaced much forest on fertile plains and valleys. Dry land supports scrub and semiarid savanna.

There are no large native mammals, but the republic has a rare ratlike insectivore (the Haitian solenodon) and a rabbit-sized rodent (the Dominican hutia) – both at risk to the Indian mongoose. There are nonpoisonous snakes, and alligators inhabit some rivers. Birds, marine fishes, and mollusks abound in variety.

People About 70 per cent are Mulattoes (of mixed White-Negro origin); 16 per cent are Whites; and 11 per cent, Negroes. More than 90 per cent of the people are Roman Catholics, and there are tiny Jewish and Protestant minorities. Spanish is the official language, but some speak other tongues including a Creole patois.

With more than six million people by the mid 1980s, the republic has the West Indies' second largest population. Just over half lives

A coin commemorating the 25th year of the Trujillo Regime.

©DIAGRAM

Dominican Republic

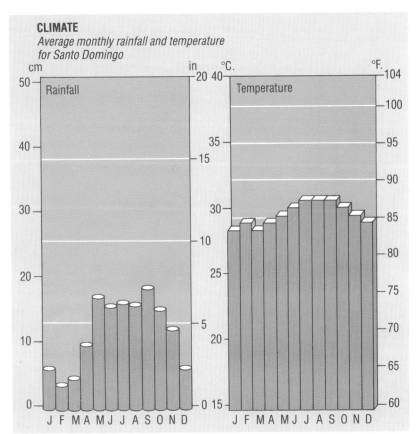

CLIMATE
Average monthly rainfall and temperature for Santo Domingo

Rainfall

Temperature

J F M A M J J A S O N D

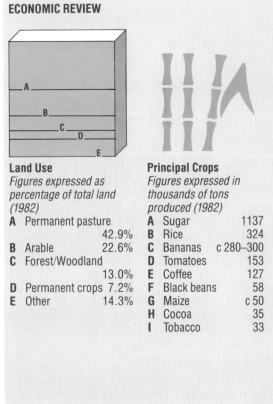

ECONOMIC REVIEW

Land Use
Figures expressed as percentage of total land (1982)

A	Permanent pasture	42.9%
B	Arable	22.6%
C	Forest/Woodland	13.0%
D	Permanent crops	7.2%
E	Other	14.3%

Principal Crops
Figures expressed in thousands of tons produced (1982)

A	Sugar	1137
B	Rice	324
C	Bananas	c 280–300
D	Tomatoes	153
E	Coffee	127
F	Black beans	58
G	Maize	c 50
H	Cocoa	35
I	Tobacco	33

in cities or towns, and there is a big concentration in the fertile northern area called the Cibao. Massive urban migration occurred in the 1970s. In 1981 the capital district of Santo Domingo held 1,551,000 people. Other major cities included Santiago (550,000), San Cristobal (446,000), La Vega (385,000), and San Francisco de Macoris (236,000).

Social conditions Agriculture usually employs up to half the productive labor force, and one-fifth works in industry; but by the mid 1980s, 25 per cent were officially jobless and the recession seemed likely to make matters worse. In the early 1980s average income was maybe one-eighth of the U.S. figure, even before the peso's buying power fell by one-third.

Education is theoretically compulsory and free from ages 7 through 14, but only 60 per cent attend school – about the same as the literacy rate. Of the three universities, the Universidad Autónoma de Santo Domingo, founded in 1538, is the New World's oldest university.

The poor – the majority – suffer nuritional deficiencies, bad housing, and inadequate

health care, so that infectious diseases are rife and infant deaths are appallingly high. In 1985 they were about 64 per 1000, the second worst in the Caribbean, as was the life expectancy: 63 years. But with 33 births per 1000 the population rose by an annual 2.5 per cent – the fastest rate in the region.

Government Under the 1966 Constitution executive power rests with a President elected for four years by popular vote (voters are those aged over 18, or younger if married). The legislature is a Congress elected for four years and comprising a Senate of 27 members, one from each province and one from Santo Domingo; and a Chamber of Deputies with 120 members, one per 50,000 inhabitants of each province.

Local government units are a National District and 26 provinces under governors appointed by the President, but split into municipalities with elected councils.

There is a Supreme Court of Justice and a series of regular courts; law is based on the Code Napoléon.

Communications and transportation There are more than 100 commercial radio stations, as well as 6 television channels and 10 daily

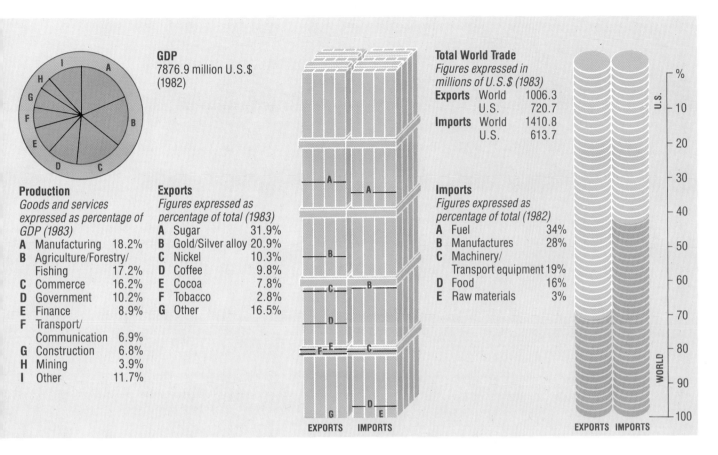

GDP
7876.9 million U.S.$
(1982)

Production
Goods and services
expressed as percentage of
GDP (1983)
A Manufacturing 18.2%
B Agriculture/Forestry/
 Fishing 17.2%
C Commerce 16.2%
D Government 10.2%
E Finance 8.9%
F Transport/
 Communication 6.9%
G Construction 6.8%
H Mining 3.9%
I Other 11.7%

Exports
Figures expressed as
percentage of total (1983)
A Sugar 31.9%
B Gold/Silver alloy 20.9%
C Nickel 10.3%
D Coffee 9.8%
E Cocoa 7.8%
F Tobacco 2.8%
G Other 16.5%

Total World Trade
Figures expressed in
millions of U.S.$ (1983)
Exports World 1006.3
 U.S. 720.7
Imports World 1410.8
 U.S. 613.7

Imports
Figures expressed as
percentage of total (1982)
A Fuel 34%
B Manufactures 28%
C Machinery/
 Transport equipment 19%
D Food 16%
E Raw materials 3%

EXPORTS IMPORTS

EXPORTS IMPORTS

newspapers, and the country had 175,000 telephones in 1982.

About half of the Dominican Republic's 7,500 miles (12,000km.) of roads are surfaced and highways link Santo Domingo with other centers. But the 365 miles (588km.) of railroad is used chiefly for farm produce. There are international airports for Santo Domingo, Puerta Plata, and La Romana. The chiefs ports are Santo Domingo, La Romana, San Pedro de Macoris, Puerto Plata, Barahona, Haina, and Las Calderas.

Economy Three categories – farming; mining and manufacturing; and trade, tourism, and transportation – normally each contribute about one-fifth of the gross domestic product. But the commodity-dependent economy has been hit by reduced world demand and prices, and the resulting withdrawal of some major U.S. investors in plantations and mines.

Agriculture usually contributes heavily to national wealth. Some 18–25 per cent of the country is arable land; much is fertile and well watered, and half is devoted to export crops. Chief of these is sugar cane, from the southeast. Others include coffee from low

mountain slopes, and cocoa and tobacco from the Cibao. Rice is the top cereal. Other crops include maize, beans, cassava, tomatoes, melons, and tropical fruits.

Mountain forests satisfy the home demand for timber, and there is an annual fish catch of around nine million tons.

There are substantial deposits of ferro-nickel and bauxite, but production had slumped by the mid 1980s. Copper, gold, and rock salt are less important and there are silver, platinum, and amber. Hydroelectric power plants supply some electricity.

Light-industry assembly plants have been opened in efforts to diversify the economy. Factories process foods, and make textiles, paper, bottles, cement, chemicals, and fertilizers.

The chief exports are sugar, coffee, and minerals. But in the mid 1980s, for the first time, tourism was the top earner of foreign exchange. Imports include oil, machinery, food, steel, and chemicals.

About half the country's trade is with the U.S. Among other trading partners are Venezuela, the Netherlands, Puerto Rico, Japan, and Spain.

Puerto Rico

OFFICIAL NAME
**Estado Libre Asociado
de Puerto Rico**

Above: Flag of Puerto Rico
Horizontal bands of red,
white, red, white, red, with a
staff-side blue triangle
containing a white star. Shown
left is the coat of arms.

SIZE IN RELATION TO U.S. STATE

Slightly more than two-thirds the size of Connecticut (A)

AREA	**3,435** square miles (8,897sq.km.)
POPULATION	**3,267,000** (1983 official estimate)
POPULATION DENSITY	**951.1** per square mile (1983)
CURRENCY	**U.S. dollar** (U.S. $1 = 100 cents)
PRINCIPAL RELIGION	**Roman Catholic**
OFFICIAL LANGUAGES	**Spanish, English**
CAPITAL	**San Juan**
ADMINISTRATIVE DIVISIONS	**76 municipalities**

Puerto Rico is the Caribbean region's fourth largest island – a warm, mostly well-watered land of green farms, steep mountain slopes, and rainforest remnants, all fringed by fine palm-lined beaches. It stands in the north central Caribbean, about 1000 miles (1600km.) southeast of Florida. The Dominican Republic lies to its west, the Virgin Islands to its east, the Caribbean Sea to its south, and the Atlantic Ocean to its north.

The Commonwealth of Puerto Rico is a self governing part of the U.S. Puerto Rico is Spanish for "rich coast" – the original name of its capital, San Juan. The island's old Spanish culture persists; this is the only part of the U.S. where the first language is Spanish. Once "the Poorhouse of the Caribbean," densely peopled Puerto Rico has the second highest per capita income in Latin America.

History Island-hopping Arawak Indians peopled Puerto Rico more than a thousand years ago. Christopher Columbus discovered the island in 1493 and claimed it for Spain; colonial settlement began 15 years later. In

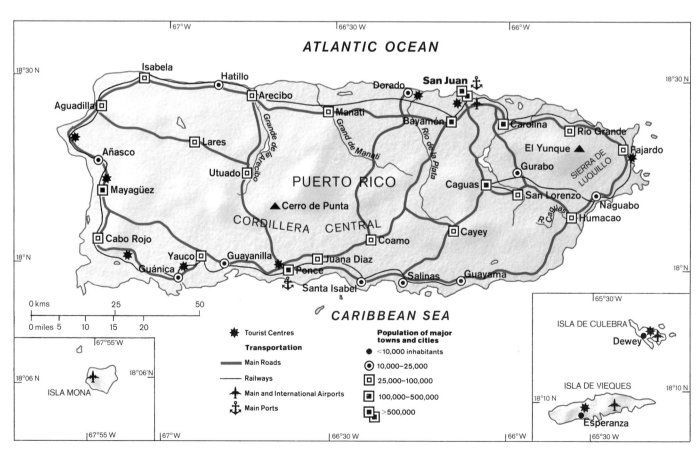

HISTORICAL REVIEW

1493	Columbus sights Puerto Rico.
1508	Juan Ponce De Leon begins Spanish occupation of Puerto Rico.
1812	New constitution introduced.
1814	Constitution abolished.
1820	Constitution reinstated.
1897	Puerto Rico is granted an autonomous charter by Spain.
1898	U.S. Spanish War. Puerto Rico is ceded to the U.S.
1900	The Foraker Act sets up civil government.
1917	Jones Act imposes U.S. citizenship on Puerto Ricans.
1941	Rexford Tugwell is named the last North American Governor of Puerto Rico.
1947	Operation Bootstrap begins: industrialization by invitation strategy.
1948	Luis Muñoz Marín becomes the first elected Governor in the history of Puerto Rico.
1952	The constitution of the commonwealth of Puerto Rico is approved.
1975	Puerto Rico's economy reels under the impact of U.S. recession.
1984	Carlos Romero Barcello as Governor. Elections pending.

1511 the Spanish crushed an Arawak uprising and by 1550 war and disease had almost wiped out the island's Indians. The Spanish shipped in others, and Africans, as slave labor for gold mines and farms.

Puerto Rico suffered centuries of plagues, hurricanes, and raids by Dutch, English, and French pirates; some even penetrated San Juan, fortified as an outpost of the Spanish empire.

By the early 1800s farming, commerce, and settlement were expanding. Spanish colonial rule proved less repressive here than elsewhere and Puerto Rico stayed loyal to Spain while other colonies broke away. In 1897 Spain gave it a form of self government.

Next year, though, the Spanish-American War ended Spain's rule. U.S. forces landed, and Puerto Rico became a U.S. colony. In 1900 came token self government, with the first U.S. appointed civil Governor. Puerto Ricans became U.S. citizens in 1917, and elected their own Governor from 1947. Rejecting independence or U.S. statehood, the islanders approved a constitution making Puerto Rico a self-governing commonwealth linked to the U.S. in 1952.

In the 1940s governors Luis Muñoz Marín and Rexford Tugwell had helped launch "Operation Bootstrap" to change Puerto Rico from a poor rural backwater to an industrialized state. But in the 1950s many thousands migrated to the U.S. mainland seeking work. Land, labor, tax, and other reforms encouraged U.S. investment and gave Puerto Ricans a larger share of the wealth they helped to create. Health, housing, education, and incomes sharply improved, although average pay remains well below that on the U.S. mainland.

Land Puerto Rico is the smallest and easternmost of the Greater Antilles, the large west Caribbean islands. It roughly resembles a rectangle aligned from west to east. The island measures about 110 miles (177km.) long and 40 miles (64km.) wide.

Half of the island is mountainous. The main mountain region, the Cordillera Central, forms a central chain of peaks crossing the south-central part of the island. Cerro de Punta at 4389 feet (1338m.) is the highest point in the country. The Caguas river valley separates these mountains from the Sierra de Luquillo in the northeast.

Foothills lie north and south of the mountains. The northwestern foothills have thousands of overgrown gullies and humps, known as haystacks. This is karst country – a limestone surface with pockets deeply eaten away by natural acid in water.

Lowlands rim the northern and southern coasts. The northern plain is the broader, more fertile of the two, up to 12 miles (19km.) across. In the east and west, river valleys have notched the mountains where these approach the sea.

Many small inlets and bays pierce the coast, producing a tidal shore 700 miles (1126km.) long. There are rock pools, and fine sandy beaches fringed by palm trees and mangroves.

Rivers mainly run north and south from the mountain spine. The longest streams, such as the Arecibo, are those that flow north. But none can carry large boats.

Besides the main island there are many smaller ones. The three largest are Mona to the west, and Culebra and Vieques to the east. Vieques (or Crab Island), is the biggest of the three. It measures 21 miles (34km.) long by 6 miles (10km.) wide.

King Alfonso XIII, ruler during the Spanish-American War in 1898.
(stamp issued 1898)

© DIAGRAM

107

Puerto Rico

Climate Puerto Rico's warm, equable climate owes much to its position just inside the tropics, where trade winds and sea buffer the country against seasonal temperature extremes. At sea level, temperature averages 76°F. (24°C.) and there are about 360 days' sunshine a year.

Seasonal sea-level temperatures range from 73°F. (23°C.) in January to 80°F. (27°C.) in July. Intense heat and frost are almost unknown – even high on the mountains inland. Annual rainfall averages about 74 inches (1880mm.), with a low of 30 inches (762mm.) in the southwest, and a high in some years of more than 200 inches (5080mm.) on El Yunque, a northeastern mountain. Much of the country receives rain almost daily, usually in short, heavy showers. But the main rainfall comes from May to November.

Trade winds blow over Puerto Rico from east or southeast during summer, from northeast in winter. Hurricanes are a threat from June to November, but severe winds occur only about once in 10 years.

Vegetation and animals Farming and soil erosion have removed most of Puerto Rico's native plant cover, but remnants of this great sea of trees survive in the Maricao, Río Abajo, and other national forests. The largest of all these is the El Yunque Rain Forest (or Caribbean National Forest), clothing peaks of the northeast's warm, rainy, Sierra de Luquillo. An average five showers a day soak the 240 species of tree that thrive here. Boxwood, calabash, cedar, ebony, lancewood, logwood, and palms crowd one another, as they thrust up into the light. Liana vines festoon the forest, while orchids and other flowers sprout from soaked mossy branches high above the ground. Ferns and shrubs smother the forest floor.

Elsewhere, dense greenery covers much of the northwest's hillocky karst land, and mangroves and coconut palms rim the coasts.

Puerto Rico has few native backboned land animals. One account sums them up as bats, birds, frogs, a nonpoisonous snake, and various lizards. The 200 or so kinds of bird include the rare Puerto Rico parrot and other species known nowhere else. Among creatures are rats, the Indian mongoose brought in to kill them, and South America's huge marine toad, which helps keep down insect pests.

The rare Puerto Rico parrot, one of the 200 or so species of birds to be found on the island.

Water life ranges in size from microorganisms that makes ships' wakes glow at night to offshore big-game fishes – kingfish, marlin, tuna, wahoo, and others. Black bass inhabit freshwater lakes.

People Puerto Ricans are an ethnic mixture derived mainly from Spanish colonists and African slaves, also from aboriginal Indians, European settlers, and white immigrants from North America. Accordingly, skin color ranges from pale white to jet black. Despite varying backgrounds, though, Puerto Ricans form a coherent people, and the islanders recognize no racial, or other minority groups.

Puerto Rican religion and language reflect Spanish colonial influence. Most people are Roman Catholics, but there are Lutherans, Episcopalians, Baptists and practicing Jews. The official language is Spanish, but many people speak English or "Spanglish" – a legacy of mass migration to and from the U.S. mainland.

Puerto Rico has the Caribbean's fourth largest population, crowded into its sixth largest country. The result is one of the region's highest population densities. But population is unevenly spread. The northern coast plain is most heavily peopled, while few live on the high mountain ranges. In fact only one-third of Puerto Ricans live rurally – mostly as farmers; two-thirds inhabit the cities and towns. Three of the largest lie in the northeast. In 1980 the capital San Juan held 435,000 people, but roughly one million including its urban agglomeration, Bayamón held 196,000 and Carolina 166,000.

Social conditions In 1983 nearly one-quarter of the employed labor force worked in public administration. Almost one-fifth worked in each of three other sectors: manufacturing; wholesaling and retailing; and service industries. Next came transportation and public utilities (6 per cent); agriculture (5 per cent); construction (4 per cent); and finance, insurance, and real estate (3 per cent).

The Government sets minimum wage levels covering mostly industrial and agricultural firms. Per capita income averaged about U.S. $3900 in 1983 – higher than in most Caribbean lands, but one-third the U.S. national average. More than 23 per cent of the labor force was unemployed, one reason for a high crime rate and emigration to the U.S. mainland by Puerto Ricans seeking work. About 1,500,000 now live on the mainland.

The Government has done much to develop public education, which receives up to one-third of the national budget. Between 1940 and the early 1970s illiteracy fell from 30 per cent to about 10 per cent. In the early 1980s public and private school enrollment stood at about one million, and more than 130,000 attended the state university and two private universities.

About one-fifth of the budget goes on health and welfare services. Between them these handle pure water supplies, sewage removal, and mosquito control, and provide clinics, health centers, and welfare payments to the needy.

Puerto Rico has one of the Caribbean's highest life expectancies (73 in the mid 1980s) and lowest death rates (6 per 1000). Infant mortality is roughly half as high again as on the continental U.S., but the rather high birth rate helps to cancel this out, so that population is rising at almost twice the rate on the mainland.

Government Under the constitution that came into force in 1952, the Commonwealth of Puerto Rico is a self-governing part of the U.S., with control over internal affairs similar to that of a U.S. state.

Executive power rests with a Governor elected for a four-year term by citizens aged over 18. A council of Secretaries comprising heads of departments forms the Governor's Advisory Council. There is a Legislative Assembly elected every four years and comprising two houses: a 27-member Senate of 11 senators at large and two from each of the eight senatorial districts; and a 51-member House of Representatives of 11 members at large and one from each of the 40 representative districts. The two main political parties are the New Democratic Party, which favors making Puerto Rico the fifty-first U.S. state, and the Popular Democratic Party which wants to keep commonwealth status. There is little support for pro-independence groups. Puerto Ricans may not vote in U.S. elections, and pay no federal taxes while on the island, but men may be drafted into the armed forces.

A Resident Commissioner represents Puerto Rico in Congress. The Commissioner has a seat in the House of Representatives,

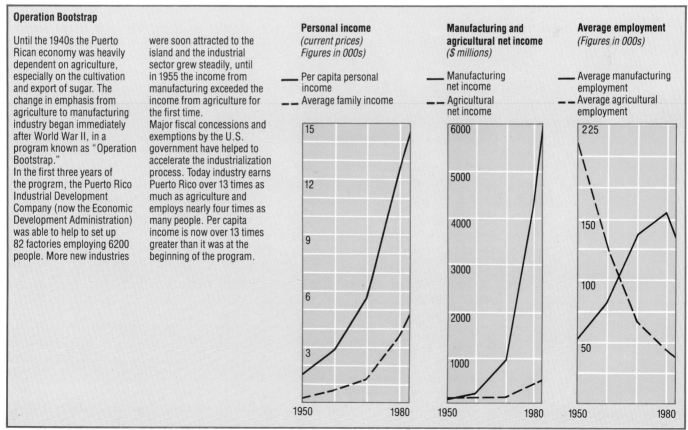

Operation Bootstrap

Until the 1940s the Puerto Rican economy was heavily dependent on agriculture, especially on the cultivation and export of sugar. The change in emphasis from agriculture to manufacturing industry began immediately after World War II, in a program known as "Operation Bootstrap."
In the first three years of the program, the Puerto Rico Industrial Development Company (now the Economic Development Administration) was able to help to set up 82 factories employing 6200 people. More new industries were soon attracted to the island and the industrial sector grew steadily, until in 1955 the income from manufacturing exceeded the income from agriculture for the first time.
Major fiscal concessions and exemptions by the U.S. government have helped to accelerate the industrialization process. Today industry earns Puerto Rico over 13 times as much as agriculture and employs nearly four times as many people. Per capita income is now over 13 times greater than it was at the beginning of the program.

Personal income
(current prices)
Figures in 000s

— Per capita personal income
-- Average family income

Manufacturing and agricultural net income
($ millions)

— Manufacturing net income
-- Agricultural net income

Average employment
(Figures in 000s)

— Average manufacturing employment
-- Average agricultural employment

© DIAGRAM

109

Puerto Rico

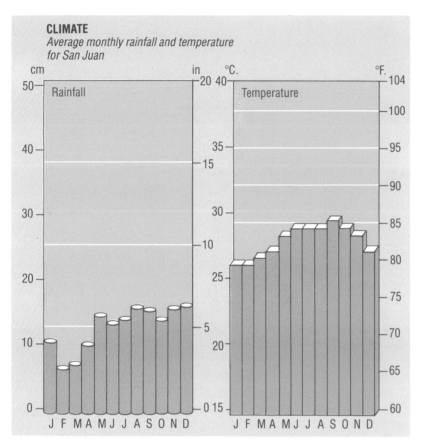

CLIMATE
Average monthly rainfall and temperature for San Juan

Rainfall

Temperature

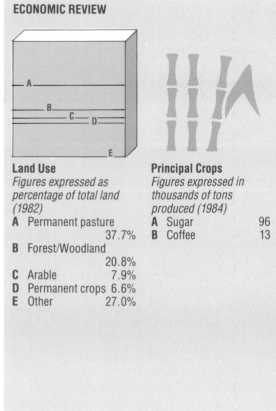

ECONOMIC REVIEW

Land Use
Figures expressed as percentage of total land (1982)
A Permanent pasture
    37.7%
B Forest/Woodland
    20.8%
C Arable   7.9%
D Permanent crops 6.6%
E Other   27.0%

Principal Crops
Figures expressed in thousands of tons produced (1984)
A Sugar   96
B Coffee   13

but may vote only in committees.

Heading the judiciary is a seven-member Supreme Court of judges appointed by the Governor. There are also superior and district courts.

San Juan is under city management. Other cities each have a popularly elected mayor and council.

Communications and transportation
Puerto Rico has one of the most intensive communication systems in the Caribbean. There are scores of radio stations, five regular television channels, and three major daily newspapers (two in Spanish). By the early 1980s, for every 10 Puerto Ricans there were roughly six radios, three television sets, and two telephones.

The island has an extensive network of all-weather roads, totalling over 7000 miles (11,263km.). Superhighways link major cities, but the large number of cars and trucks causes severe traffic jams, the worst of which are in San Juan. Puerto Rico has more than 1,200,000 registered motor vehicles.

There are no public railroads, but sugar corporations built local railroads to carry cane to sugar mills.

Puerto Rico has the Caribbean's most extensive air service, with direct flights to some 20 U.S. cities. San Juan is the region's busiest airport, handling millions of passengers a year. There are a number of smaller airports, mostly near coastal cities, and on Culebra and Vieques islands.

San Juan ranks first among the five modern sea ports, and is one of the world's 10 busiest container ports, handling incoming industrial raw materials and components, and shipping out manufactured goods. The second port is Ponce on the south coast; an exporter of sugar and rum, with an oil refinery.

Economy Puerto Rico has profited hugely from its place in the U.S. Free Trade area: its gross domestic product ranks easily first in the Caribbean. But in the mid 1980s the recession-hit economy showed few signs of returning to the fast rate of growth seen in the late 1970s.

In the early 1980s, agriculture provided only 3 per cent of the gross domestic product, although 15 per cent of Puerto Rico is cultivated. Sugar cane grows on the coastal plains, coffee, tobacco, and food crops

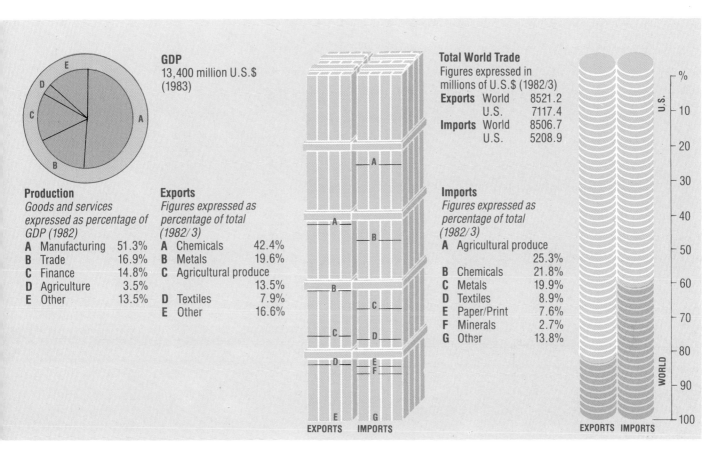

GDP
13,400 million U.S.$
(1983)

Production
Goods and services expressed as percentage of GDP (1982)

A Manufacturing	51.3%
B Trade	16.9%
C Finance	14.8%
D Agriculture	3.5%
E Other	13.5%

Exports
Figures expressed as percentage of total (1982/3)

A Chemicals	42.4%
B Metals	19.6%
C Agricultural produce	13.5%
D Textiles	7.9%
E Other	16.6%

Total World Trade
Figures expressed in millions of U.S.$ (1982/3)

Exports	World	8521.2
	U.S.	7117.4
Imports	World	8506.7
	U.S.	5208.9

Imports
Figures expressed as percentage of total (1982/3)

A Agricultural produce	25.3%
B Chemicals	21.8%
C Metals	19.9%
D Textiles	8.9%
E Paper/Print	7.6%
F Minerals	2.7%
G Other	13.8%

EXPORTS   IMPORTS

EXPORTS   IMPORTS

largely on hills and mountains inland. Diversification has increased pastureland for dairying at the expense of sugar cane. Cash crops include sugar cane, coffee, bananas, pineapples, oranges, tobacco, and coconuts; farms also grow such food crops as maize, sweet potatoes, yams, beans, and peppers. In the early 1980s Puerto Rico had about 530,000 cattle, 200,000 pigs and 7,500,000 poultry.

Population pressure on a limited land area has meant cultivating steep slopes subject to soil erosion. This affects more than half of the island, and is one reason why Puerto Rico must import much of its food.

Forestry plays no significant role, but commercial fisheries earned $9,000,000 in 1983.

Mineral resources include copper, iron, nickel, and stone building materials, but Puerto Rico is rich in few ores.

Electricity comes from hydroelectric, nuclear, and oil-fired power installations. Capacity has been sharply increased, and the Puerto Rico Electric Power Authority is the second largest state-owned utility in the U.S.

Manufacturing makes by far the largest single contribution to the island's economy. By 1982–83 it produced just over half the total gross product. U.S. and Puerto Rican tax concessions and low labor costs have spurred manufacturers to set up thousands of factories, many of them subsidiaries of U.S. mainland corporations. Firms make metal sheets, tubes, and castings; mold plastics; produce paper, pharmaceuticals, clothing, and rum; and assemble light machinery. Tax incentives introduced in 1978 saw the electronic/electrical sector grow by more than 40 per cent in five years.

Tourism is another significant source of income. Puerto Rico received 2,000,000 visitors in 1983, four-fifths of them from the U.S. mainland.

Puerto Rico's main exports include chemicals, petroleum products, clothing, and machinery. The country imports much crude oil, food, machinery, transportation equipment, and textiles.

About three-quarters of all trade is with the U.S. mainland. Other main trading partners are the U.S. Virgin Islands, Dominican Republic, Venezuela, the Netherlands Antilles, and France.

The Virgin Islands

SIZE IN RELATION TO U.S. CITY

Same as Detroit (A)

OFFICIAL NAME
Virgin Islands of the United States

Above: **Flag of the U.S. Virgin Islands**
White with the American Eagle flanked by the letters VI. Shown left is the U.S. Virgin Islands coat of arms.

AREA	**133** square miles (344sq.km.)
POPULATION	**101,000** (1983 preliminary figure)
POPULATION DENSITY	**759.4** per square mile (1983)
PRINCIPAL RELIGIONS	**Roman Catholic, Protestant, Jewish**
OFFICIAL LANGUAGE	**English**
CAPITAL	**Charlotte Amalie**
CURRENCY	**U.S. dollar** (U.S. $1 = 100 cents)

The Virgin Islands are scores of mostly uninhabited small, green, hilly islands set in a turquoise tropical sea. Although they are exposed tips of submerged mountains extending east from Puerto Rico in the Greater Antilles, they are sometimes grouped with the Lesser Antilles to their southeast. To the north is the Atlantic Ocean; to the south, the Caribbean Sea.

The whole group takes up less land than New Orleans, yet is politically divided into the (southwestern) U.S. Virgin Islands and (northeastern) British Virgin Islands.

History Arawak and Carib Indians lived here before Christopher Columbus arrived in 1493, naming the many islands in honor of St. Ursula's 11,000 martyred maidens. European settlement began in 1625 when the Dutch and English both landed on St. Croix. Later, fighting handed it to Spain, then France, which sold St. Croix to Denmark in 1733. With brief periods of British rule, St. Croix, St. John, and St. Thomas formed the Danish West Indies from the early 1700s to 1917 when Denmark sold them to the U.S. The islanders became U.S. citizens in

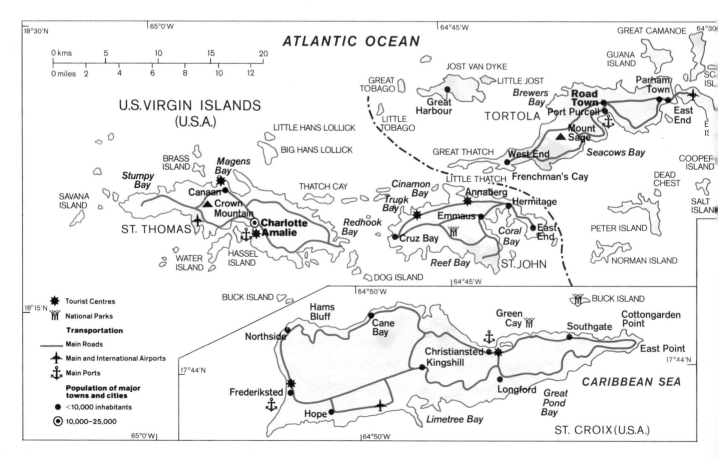

Above: **Flag of the British Virgin Islands**
Blue with the Union flag in the top staff-side corner, and a shield over a scroll toward the outer edge.

SIZE IN RELATION TO U.S. CITY

Same as the Borough of Staten Island, New York City (A)

AREA	**59** square miles (153sq.km.)
POPULATION	**12,000** (1981)
POPULATION DENSITY	**203.4** per square mile (1981)
PRINCIPAL RELIGIONS	**Anglican, Roman Catholic**
OFFICIAL LANGUAGE	**English**
CAPITAL	**Road Town**
CURRENCY	**U.S. dollar** (U.S. $1 = 100 cents)

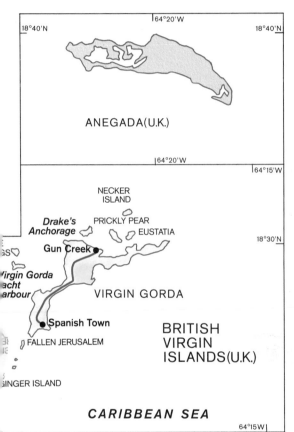

largest three of these are St. Thomas, St. John, and – isolated to the south – St. Croix: easily the biggest of all the Virgin Islands. The roughly 40 islands of the eastern group comprise the British Virgin Islands, of which the three largest are Tortola, Virgin Gorda, and – isolated to the northeast – Anegada.

Typical island landscapes are low rocky peaks, small plains and plateaus, cliffs, lagoons, enticing beaches, and offshore coral reefs. The highest summit is Tortola's Mt. Sage at 1780 feet (541m.). Some of the islands contain springs and rivulets.

Climate These islands arguably have the best weather of the region, with sunshine almost every day, and tropical warmth moderated by trade winds, which also keep humidity comfortably low. Average temperatures range from 82°F. (28°C.) in summer to 77°F. (25°C.) in winter. Annual rainfall averages 45 inches (1143mm.) on the U.S. Virgin Islands, but only 35 inches (889mm.) in the British Virgin Islands. Most rain falls between September and December: the wet season. Hurricanes seldom strike this area.

Vegetation and animals Most islands have a sparse covering of tropical shrubs, trees, and flowers – palms, breadfruit, mangoes, mahogany, orchids and others. Patches of lush rainforest thrive in upland areas of Tortola and St. Croix; while grasses, acacias, and cacti flourish on the lowlands. Apart from deer, large land animals are lacking, although pelicans, bananaquits, and many other birds abound. But the most spectacular wildlife haunts underwater reefs. Buck Island Reef National Monument off St. Croix – the first U.S. underwater national park – has a dazzling array of corals, fishes, and sea fans.

1927, with an elected governor in 1971.

The northeast Virgin Islands effectively became British in 1666 when English planters seized Tortola from the Dutch.

Once noted for pirate haunts, trade in African slaves, and sugar plantations, the islands are now known as vacation centers.

Land Most of the Virgin Islands comprise a string of islands and islets that extend some 50 miles (80km.) east from a point about 40 miles (64km.) east of Puerto Rico. The roughly 60 islands of the western group make up the U.S. Virgin Islands. By far the

St. Ursula, whose martyred maidens gave their name to the islands.
(stamp issued 1867–68)

© DIAGRAM

The Virgin Islands

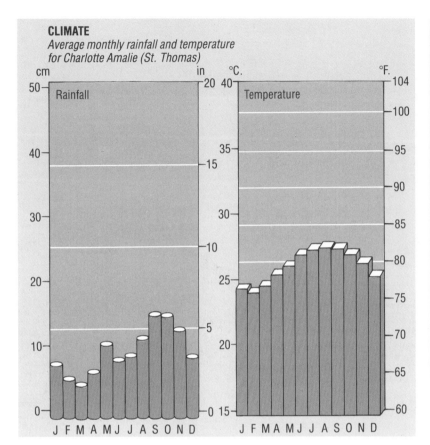

CLIMATE
*Average monthly rainfall and temperature
for Charlotte Amalie (St. Thomas)*

Rainfall

Temperature

J F M A M J J A S O N D

J F M A M J J A S O N D

HISTORICAL REVIEW

1493 Christopher Columbus lands on St. Croix.
1555 Emperor Charles V of Spain claims the territory.
1651 The French possess St. Croix.
1666 St. Thomas is occupied by Denmark.
1672 Annexation of Tortola to the British-administered Leeward Islands.
1754 St. John, St. Thomas and St. Croix come under the Danish crown.
1773 Planters granted civil government in Tortola.
1801–02 Brief occupation of the Danish islands by the British.
1927 U.S.' Act grants U.S. citizenship to the islanders.
1954 A revised Organic Act provides substantial degree of self-government to the U.S. Virgin Islands.
1956 Defederation of the Leeward Islands colony.
1967 Ministerial form of government is established in the British Virgin Islands.
1971 Melvin Herbert Evans is inaugurated as the first elected Governor of the U.S. Virgin Islands.
1980s Racial disturbances in U.S. Islands.

People Most of the inhabitants are descended from African slaves, but Puerto Ricans and mainland Americans have moved into the U.S. Virgin Islands in increasing numbers, and the Chachas of St. Thomas are descended from French Huguenots. Most islanders are Protestants of various denominations, but there are also Roman Catholics and Jews. The official language, English, is largely spoken in a lilting West Indian dialect form, and some islanders speak French or Spanish.

Nearly nine-tenths of the entire population is concentrated in the U.S. Virgin Islands, where half the total lives on St. Thomas. This has the territory's capital, Charlotte Amalie (pop. 12,000 in 1980). The British Virgin Islands' capital is Road Town (pop. 4000) on the island of Tortola.

Social conditions Many islanders farm, fish, or work in tourism, government service, or manufacturing. Thanks to U.S. aid, the U.S. Virgin Islands have one of the highest per capita incomes in the Caribbean. But the black majority has pressed for social change to curb discrimination favoring the white minority. Other social problems stem

from a rapid rise in population and friction between local residents and imported labor.

Education in both island groups is free and compulsory and the literacy rate is high. A college on St. Thomas teaches accountancy and hotel management.

Government The U.S. Virgin Islands is an unincorporated territory of the U.S., subject to the Department of the Interior. There is a Governor elected every four years, and a legislature of 15 elected Senators. Judicial power belongs to a Federal District Court and municipal courts. A nonvoting Delegate represents the U.S. Virgin Islands in the House of Representatives.

The British Virgin Islands is a Crown Colony with a Crown-appointed Governor responsible for security and external affairs; an Executive Council (the Governor, Attorney-General, Chief Minister and three other ministers) which controls finance; and a Legislative council (the Attorney-General, Speakers, and nine elected members).

Communications and transportation The U.S. Virgin Islands have seven radio and four television stations, four daily or almost daily newspapers, and a telephone for almost

VIRGIN ISLANDS (U.S.)

Land Use
Figures expressed as percentage of total land (1982)

A Permanent pasture	26.4%
B Arable	14.7%
C Forest/Woodland	5.9%
D Permanent crops	5.9%
E Other	47.1%

Principal Crops
No significant single crops

Exports
Figures expressed as percentage of total (1978)

A Petroleum products	91%
B Chemicals	4%
C Other	5%

Imports
Figures expressed as percentage of total (1973)

A Crude oil	62%
B Machinery	5%
C Food	4%
D Chemicals	3%
E Motor Vehicles	3%
F Other	23%

Total World Trade
Figures expressed in millions of U.S.$ (1983)

Exports	World	3600
	U.S.	3200
Imports	World	4700
	U.S.	4230

GDP
710 million U.S.$ (1981)

VIRGIN ISLANDS (U.K.)

Land Use
Figures expressed as percentage of total land (1982)

A Permanent pasture	33.3%
B Arable	20.0%
C Forest/Woodland	6.7%
D Permanent crops	6.7%
E Other	33.3%

Principal crops
None significant – mainly food crops

Production
Goods and services expressed as percentage of GDP (1978)

A Wholesale/Retail	26.6%
B Construction	11.2%
C Transport/Communication	9.5%
D Agriculture	9.2%
E Mining/Manufacturing	5.9%
F Government/Other	37.6%

Exports
Figures expressed as percentage of total (1980)

A Fish	42.7%
B Rum	41.9%
C Gravel/Sand	6.5%
D Livestock	4.0%
E Other	4.9%

Imports
Figures expressed as percentage of total (1980)

A Machinery	33.7%
B Fuel	21.8%
C Food/Beverages/Tobacco	13.6%
D Manufactures	6.8%
E Chemicals	3.6%
F Other	20.5%

Total World Trade
Figures expressed in millions of U.S.$ (1981)

Exports	World	2.0
	U.S.	1.8
Imports	World	49.8
	U.S.	34.8

GDP
50 million U.S.$ (1982)

---

every two inhabitants. There are over 1290 miles (800km.) of roads. St. Croix has an international airport and the chief ports are Charlotte Amalie on St. Thomas and Christiansted on St. Croix.

Communications are less well developed on the British Virgin Islands, with its one radio and one television station. There are 62 miles (100km.) of roads. International flights land at Beef Island off Tortola.

Economy Tourism is a major industry, with 1,500,000 mainly cruise-ship visitors to the U.S. islands in 1983 (the British islands received 170,000 in 1980). St. Croix processes imported oil and bauxite and makes clocks, watches, textiles, rum and pharmaceuticals. Rum, paint making, hotel-building and offshore financial services figure in the British islands' economy.

Hilly land and limited rainfall curb agriculture, but the U.S. islands produce vegetables, fruit, sorghum and other crops, while British smallholdings grow bananas, other fruits, vegetables, and sugar cane. Both groups raise livestock.

Islanders catch groupers, lobsters, and tuna, and the British islands export some fish.

The U.S. islands import oil, bauxite, machinery, food, and consumer goods. Food is the British islands' main import. Exports from the U.S. islands include petroleum products, alumina, chemicals, and meat; while the British islands sell farm produce, fish, and sand and gravel.

The British islands mostly sell to the U.S. Virgin Islands, and buy from these and from the U.S. and Puerto Rico. The U.S. Virgin Islands sell mostly to the U.S. and buy from there and from Nigeria, and oil-producing Arab states.

Carib Indians, who inhabited the Virgin Islands before their discovery by Columbus in 1493.

Anguilla and Montserrat

OFFICIAL NAME
Anguilla

Above: **Flag of Anguilla**
White with a turquoise band
along the bottom, and three
circling orange dolphins in the
center of the white sector.

SIZE IN RELATION TO U.S. CITY

A

Smaller than Bronx Borough, New York City (A)

AREA	**34.0** square miles (88sq.km.)
POPULATION	**7,000** (1983 preliminary figure)
POPULATION DENSITY	**205.9** per square mile
PRINCIPAL RELIGIONS	**Protestant, Roman Catholic**
OFFICIAL LANGUAGE	**English**
CAPITAL	**The Valley**
CURRENCY	**East Caribbean dollar** (E. Car. $1 = 100 cents)

The two islands are British Crown colonies in the Leeward Islands, separated by other islands. Each is smaller than Bronx Borough in New York City, and the combined population is only about 20,000. Long, narrow Anguilla (the name is Latin for "eel") lies 150 miles (241km.) east of Puerto Rico. Pear-shaped, mountainous Montserrat lies 106 miles (170km.) south-south-east of Anguilla.

History Christopher Columbus discovered both islands in 1493. Montserrat was colonized by Irish settlers in 1632, and later twice seized by the French (1664 and 1782), but has been continuously British since 1783. Attempts to link it with other West Indian islands ended in 1966.

Anguilla became an English colony in 1650, and was for long administratively linked to St. Kitts. In 1967 Anguilla rejected St. Kitts' domination, withdrew from the new Associated State of Saint Christopher (St. Kitts)-Nevis-Anguilla, and declared independence "under the British flag." Britain reluctantly resumed control but Anguilla gained an improved status, with ministerial government from 1976.

Land Anguilla is a low flat coral island 16 miles (26km.) long and up to 3.5 miles (5.6km.) across. Volcanic Montserrat is 11 miles (18km.) by up to 7 miles (11km.). In its south, sulfur fumes leak from steep fissured cones, and Chance Peak rises to 3002 feet (915m.). Other landmarks are black beaches and a spectacular waterfall.

Climate Both islands have a tropical climate tempered by the Northeast Trade Winds. Temperature averages about 81°F. (27°C.), with a small seasonal variation and occasional extremes from the low 70s F. (low 20sC.) to about 90°F. (35°C.) Anguilla has a low, uncertain rainfall, averaging less than 39 inches (1000mm.); but Montserrat averages 62 inches (1575mm.). Its summits are wetter, and east and south coasts are drier than the national average. Hurricanes can occur on both islands.

Vegetation and animals Low scrub covers Anguilla, whose large wildlife is limited to gamefish offshore. Tropical forest clothes Montserrat's mountainsides, and there is a coastal mangrove swamp where egrets fly in to roost. Most other land is under cultivation or buildings.

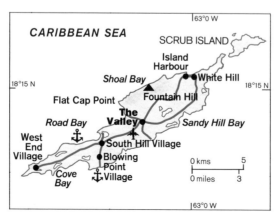

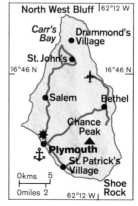

Tourist Centres
Transportation
Main Roads
Main and International Airports
Main Ports

Population of major towns and cities
● <10,000 inhabitants

OFFICIAL NAME
Montserrat

Above: **Flag of Montserrat**
Blue with the Union Flag in the top staff-side corner, and a white disk containing the island's badge toward the outer edge.

SIZE IN RELATION TO U.S. CITY

Same as Bronx Borough, New York City (A)

AREA	**39.5** square miles (102sq.km.)
POPULATION	**13,000** (1983 preliminary figure)
POPULATION DENSITY	**329.1** per square mile
PRINCIPAL RELIGIONS	**Roman Catholic, Anglican**
OFFICIAL LANGUAGE	**English**
CAPITAL	**Plymouth**
CURRENCY	**East Caribbean dollar** (E.Car.$1 = 100 cents)

People These are largely of African and mixed descent, although Montserrat has retired U.S., Canadian, and British citizens. Most people are Roman Catholics, or Protestants of various denominations; and the official language is English.

In the mid 1980s Anguilla's 8000 or so people lived on scattered smallholdings and in several villages, with The Valley as the administrative center. Montserrat's 13,000 or so inhabitants are concentrated in the southwest, in and around the capital Plymouth (pop. 2500).

Social conditions Poor job prospects have caused much emigration from both islands, and in the mid 1980s more than 35 per cent were workless. But Montserrat's better developed economy brought it relative prosperity. Thanks to British aid, even Anguilla saw improvements in roads, water supplies, and other services.

Government Both colonies have Crown-appointed Governors responsible for external affairs and defense. Each has a 7-member Executive Council including the Governor and four elected ministers; and a largely elected 11-member legislative house presided over by a Speaker.

Communications and transportation
Anguilla has a radio station but no television or newspapers, and less than 500 telephones. There are 56 miles (90km.) of road, an airport, and a port at Road Bay. Montserrat has two radio stations including powerful Radio Antilles, cable television, no newspapers, and less than 2000 telephones. There are over 200 miles (322km.) of roads, an airport, and a port at Plymouth.

Economy Anguillans grow subsistence food crops on their 5 per cent of arable land, raise cattle and goats, catch lobsters, and produce sea salt. Tourism, light industry, and offshore banking offer hope of economic improvement, but growth depends heavily on cash aid from outside the island.

Montserrat benefits from fertile soils, tourism, rich retirees, cash aid from expatriates, and light assembly industries. Vegetables, cotton, or tropical fruits grow on much of the land, and there are 3000 cattle. The fish catch supplies local needs and forests yield tropical hardwoods.

On both islands imports (of all kinds) outweigh exports (fish, farm produce, etc.).

A view of the harbor at Plymouth, the capital of Montserrat.
(stamp issued 1932)

ECONOMIC REVIEW (Montserrat)

Land Use	Principal Crops	Production	Exports	Imports	Total World Trade
Figures expressed as percentage of total land (1982)	Only 6000 acres under cultivation	*Goods and services expressed as percentage of GDP (1983)*	*Figures expressed as percentage of total (1982)*	*Figures expressed as percentage of total (1982)*	*Figures expressed in millions of U.S.$ (1982)*
40% Forest/ Woodland		20.0% Government services	49.5% Manufactures	25.5% Food/Beverages/ Tobacco	**Exports** World 2.7
20% Arable		17.1% Commerce	12.9% Machinery/ Transport equipment	22.5% Machinery/Transport equipment	U.S. —
10% Permanent pasture		9.1% Construction	5.7% Raw materials	17.6% Manufactures	**Imports** World 20.2
30% Other		8.2% Manufacturing	5.4% Food/Beverages/ Tobacco	10.8% Fuel	U.S. —
		5.0% Agriculture	26.5% Other	2.5% Raw materials	**GDP**
		Transport/		21.1% Other	32.4 million U.S.$
		4.6% Communication			
		36% Other			

The Netherlands Antilles

OFFICIAL NAME
Nederlandse Antillen

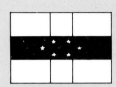

Above: **Flag of the Netherlands Antilles**
A broad blue band bearing six white stars superimposed on a broad vertical red band which divides a white background.

SIZE IN RELATION TO U.S. CITY

Slightly larger than Indianapolis, Indiana (A)

AREA	**383** square miles (993sq.km.)
POPULATION	**256,000** (1983 preliminary figure)
POPULATION DENSITY	**668.4** per square mile (1983)
CURRENCY	**Netherlands Antilles guilder** (1 guilder = 100 cents)
PRINCIPAL RELIGION	**Roman Catholic**
OFFICIAL LANGUAGE	**Dutch**
CAPITAL	**Willemstad** (on Curaçao)

The Netherlands Antilles is a self-governing part of the Netherlands – from 1986 two parts – the Netherlands Antilles and Aruba. It features six small Caribbean islands, in two groups. The main group (Aruba, Bonaire, and Curaçao) lies off northern Venezuela. The other group (St. Eustatius, Saba, and St. Maarten) lies 500 miles (800km.) to the northeast. Oil refining and tourism support the economy.

History Tall Caiquetio Indians were living in the southern islands in 1499 when the Spaniard Alonso de Ojeda reputedly discovered them. (The names of both island groups may be of Indian origin.) Harsh treatment soon killed off most of the Indians. The Spanish held the southern islands until the mid 1630s when a Dutch fleet under Johannes Van Walbeeck seized them for the Dutch West India Company.

Carib Indians inhabited the northern group when Christopher Columbus apparently discovered this in 1493. Lack of local resources discouraged Spanish settlement, but Dutch colonists under Jan Claesz. van Campen colonized St. Maarten in 1630 and St. Eustatius and Saba in 1636.

Northern St. Maarten (St. Martin) became French in 1648, and there were later British and French interventions; otherwise the islands have been Dutch since 1816.

Land The entire Netherlands Antilles is less than one-third the size of Rhode Island, and 93 per cent of its area is accounted for by the southern islands. Aruba, Bonaire, and Curaçao are relatively long, narrow, barren islands with a core of igneous rocks capped by coral limestone. Curaçao, the largest, is 36 miles (58km.) long and up to 8 miles (13km.) across. All three are largely low lying but

Bonaire

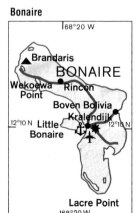

Curaçao

Aruba

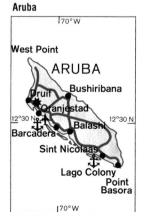

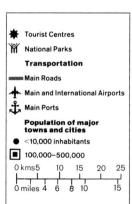

✹	Tourist Centres
⚏	National Parks
	Transportation
▬	Main Roads
✈	Main and International Airports
⚓	Main Ports
	Population of major towns and cities
●	<10,000 inhabitants
▣	100,000–500,000

1499	Curaçao is discovered. Aruba is claimed for Spain.	**1918**	Large oil refinery begins operation in Curaçao.
1527	The Spanish settlement of Curaçao begins.	**1954**	Dutch charter incorporates the Netherlands Antilles into the tripartite Kingdom of the Netherlands.
1634	The Dutch acquire Aruba and also occupy and fortify Curaçao. The native Arawak Indians are not yet exterminated. Until the nineteenth century, European settlement other than garrisons is forbidden.	**1956**	Curaçao is declared as a free trade area.
1825	Discovery of gold in Aruba.	**1970s**	Tourism becomes the economic mainstay of Aruba. An oil refinery also plays an increasingly important role in Aruba's economy.
1863	Abolition of slavery in the Dutch colonies. Period of economic decline begins in Curaçao.	**1986**	Aruba secedes.
1914	The oil industry gains importance in Curaçao.		

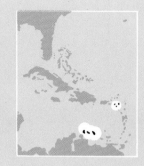

have hilly areas. The highest point is the St. Christoffelberg at 1230 feet (375m.) in northwest Curaçao. Sandy beaches and coral reefs rim much of the land.

The three tiny northern islands consist largely of volcanic rocks. St. Eustatius, the southernmost in the group, resembles a low, lozenge-shaped table with hills and a stumpy volcano, the Quill. Saba is a cliff-rimmed extinct volcano whose summit, Mt. Scenery, reaches 2821 feet (860m.), the highest point in the Netherlands Antilles. St. Maarten, to the north, has hills, lowlands, sandbars and lagoons. It occupies the southern part of the world's smallest island split between two sovereignties.

None of the Dutch Caribbean islands has a permanent river.

Climate This is tropical: warmest in August–September, coolest in January–February, with a range of 83–86°F. (28.5–30°C.) in the south, and 76–81.5°F. (24.5–27.5°C.) in the north. The strong Northeast Trade Winds help to cool both island groups. Rainfall on southern islands averages a low annual 19.7 inches (500mm.) and occurs mostly from October to February; northern islands average 39.4 inches (1000mm.), with August–December as the rainiest time.

Vegetation and animals The dry southern islands mostly support drought-resistant agaves, aloes, cactuses, and shrubs, while mangroves fringe lagoons. On the northern islands, tree-ferns, palms, mahogany, and other tropical trees thrive on the rainiest summits, but savanna covers much of St. Eustatius and St. Maarten.

Native land animals include large iguanas and smaller species of lizard, rattlesnakes (on Aruba), and deer (on Curaçao). Bonaire has flamingos and parrots. In fact there are many

protected tropical birds, but uncontrolled hunting has much reduced the numbers of buzzards and other birds of prey.

People Many are of mixed European/African origin, though most northerners are of Scottish or English descent; Arubans mainly claim Arawak Indian ancestry; and 79 nationalities occur on Curaçao.

The official language is Dutch but English is also used and most southerners speak Papiamento (a local patois) or Spanish. Roman Catholics, Protestants, Jews and Muslims occur in the south; most northern islanders are Protestants.

About 94 per cent of all islanders live in the southern islands, with two-thirds of the entire population on Curaçao and another quarter on Aruba. Willemstad on Curaçao is the capital (pop. 140,000 in 1984).

Social conditions Southerners work in the oil, tourist, manufacturing, and shipbuilding industries; northerners farm, fish and raise livestock. Wages are relatively high, but so is unemployment especially among the unskilled young.

School attendance is over 99 per cent, and education accounts for more than 40 per cent

One of Johannes Van Walbeeck's ships which re-captured the southern islands from the Spanish in the mid 1630s.
(stamp issued 1934)

St. Maarten

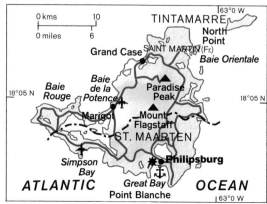

Saba and Sint Eustatius

119

The Netherlands Antilles

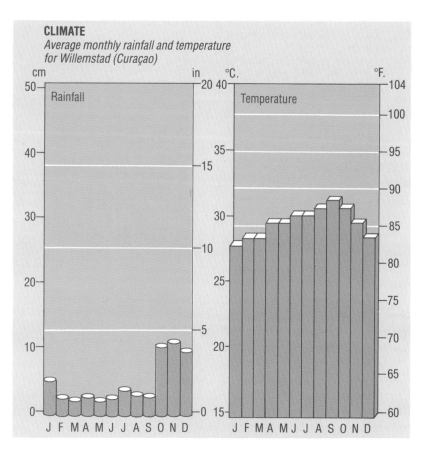

CLIMATE
Average monthly rainfall and temperature for Willemstad (Curaçao)

Rainfall

Temperature

J F M A M J J A S O N D

J F M A M J J A S O N D

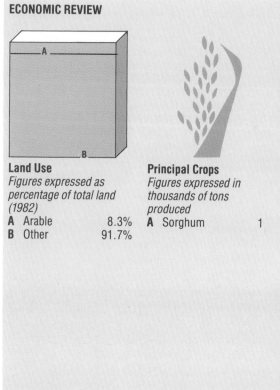

ECONOMIC REVIEW

Land Use
Figures expressed as percentage of total land (1982)
A Arable   8.3%
B Other   91.7%

Principal Crops
Figures expressed in thousands of tons produced
A Sorghum   1

of each island's budget. Centers of higher education include a university teaching law and business administration.

The ratio of hospital beds and doctors per 1000 inhabitants matches that in highly developed countries, and official figures put life expectancy at over 70 years, but there is some malnutrition.

Government The Netherlands Antilles gained internal self government in 1954. A Crown-appointed Governor represents the Dutch monarch. Internal rule is by a Council of Ministers and 22-member Parliament elected every four years. Each island has its own local government.

Aruba's achievement of separate-entity status in 1986 creates the Union of the Netherlands Antilles and Aruba.

Communications and transportation There are three television stations, 15 radio stations, and six daily newspapers.

Road networks give easy access to towns and villages. Each of the six islands has an airport and those on Aruba, Bonaire, Curaçao, and St. Maarten can all handle international flights. Big ships can berth at both groups of islands – and Curaçao's

natural harbor has larger commercial docks than any South American country.

Economy This is based on oil processing, tourism, and service industries. Tax incentives and others are aimed at promoting new industries and tourism to provide employment, which has suffered from oil-refinery automation.

The southern islands collectively form a major center for oil refining, oil transhipment, ship repair, and bunkering. A container terminal opened in 1984.

The country produces consumer goods such as drinks, cigarettes, flour, paint, and soap. But by the 1980s there had been little success in diversifying export-based products. Efforts to develop a petrochemical industry on Aruba, and to assemble electronic equipment on Curaçao had ended with all plants being closed.

Agriculture is also limited. Poor soil and lack of rain explain why only 5 per cent of land is cultivated. Crops grown include sorghum, beans, peanuts, fruit, and vegetables; and the islands support a few thousand each of goats, sheep, and cattle.

Tourism, though, has expanded. By the

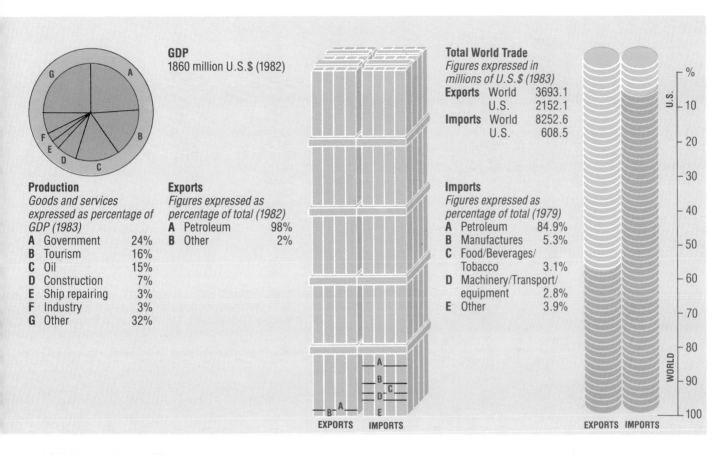

GDP
1860 million U.S.$ (1982)

Total World Trade
Figures expressed in millions of U.S.$ (1983)

Exports	World	3693.1
	U.S.	2152.1
Imports	World	8252.6
	U.S.	608.5

Production
Goods and services expressed as percentage of GDP (1983)

A	Government	24%
B	Tourism	16%
C	Oil	15%
D	Construction	7%
E	Ship repairing	3%
F	Industry	3%
G	Other	32%

Exports
Figures expressed as percentage of total (1982)

A	Petroleum	98%
B	Other	2%

Imports
Figures expressed as percentage of total (1979)

A	Petroleum	84.9%
B	Manufactures	5.3%
C	Food/Beverages/Tobacco	3.1%
D	Machinery/Transport/equipment	2.8%
E	Other	3.9%

EXPORTS IMPORTS

EXPORTS IMPORTS

mid 1980s nearly a million tourists a year came to the islands, especially Curaçao: "shopping center of the Caribbean."

Duty-free storage areas on Aruba and Curaçao have strengthened their role as distribution centers for Latin America. Chief exports are petroleum and petroleum products; chief imports are oil, machinery, transportation equipment, and food.

Imports are largely crude oil from Venezuela, Nigeria, and Saudi Arabia. Exports (chiefly refined oil) go to the U.S., Nigeria, Ecuador, Colombia, Jamaica, etc.

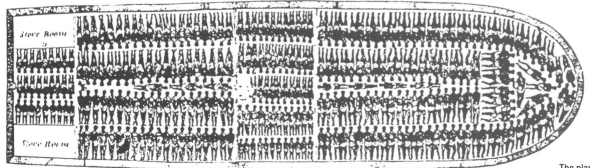

The plan of a ship used to transport African slaves to the New World.

© DIAGRAM

121

The French Antilles

OFFICIAL NAME
Département de la Guadeloupe

Above: **Flag of the French Antilles**
This is the flag of France. a tricolor of three vertical bands: (staff-side) blue, white, and red.

SIZE IN RELATION TO U.S. STATE

Slightly larger than Oklahoma City (A)

AREA	**687** square miles (1,780sq.km.)
POPULATION	**318,000** (1983 preliminary figure)
POPULATION DENSITY	**462.9** per square mile (1983)
PRINCIPAL RELIGION	**Roman Catholic**
OFFICIAL LANGUAGE	**French**
CAPITAL	**Basse-Terre**
CURRENCY	**French franc** (1 franc = 100 centimes)

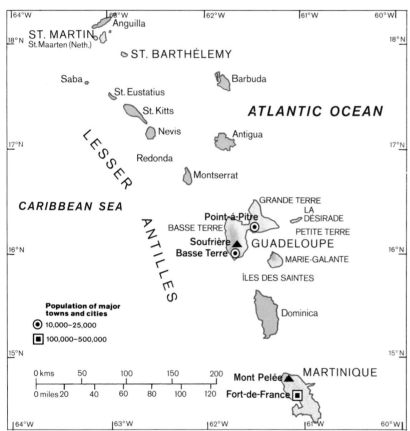

Population of major towns and cities
⊙ 10,000–25,000
▣ 100,000–500,000

The French Antilles comprise two overseas departments of France in the east Caribbean. Martinique island lies half way down the Lesser Antilles arc. Farther north is Guadeloupe with its dependencies: adjacent Marie-Galante, La Désirade, and Îles des Saintes; and St. Martin and St. Barthélemy over 150 miles (240km.) to the northwest. The entire area is less than that of Rhode Island and the population is under a million.

Both main islands have semi-dormant volcanoes; tropical forests, and plantations; calm Caribbean beaches; surf-pounded Atlantic shores; and a Creole culture with carnivals and African dances.

History In 1493 Christopher Columbus sighted all the chief islands. Hostile Carib Indians deterred Spanish settlement, but France colonized the main islands between 1635 and 1648, importing African slaves to work sugar plantations.

The French and Dutch split St. Martin/St. Maarten between them in 1648. There were British takeover attempts between the 1750s and early 1800s, and Sweden held St. Barthélemy from 1784 to 1878.

France's West Indian colonies became

Martinique

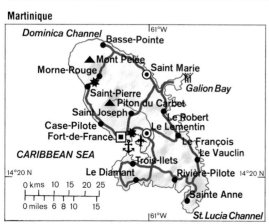

Guadeloupe

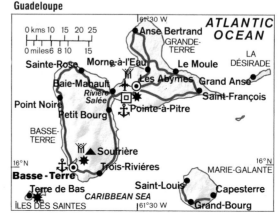

✹ Tourist Centres
⋔ National Parks

Transportation
— Main Roads
✈ Main and International Airports
⚓ Main Ports

Population of major towns and cities
● <10,000 inhabitants
⊙ 10,000–25,000
▣ 25,000–100,000

OFFICIAL NAME
Département de la Martinique

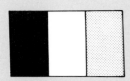

Above: **Flag of the French Antilles**
This is the flag of France. a tricolor of three vertical bands: (staff-side) blue, white, and red.

SIZE IN RELATION TO U.S. STATE

Slightly smaller than Los Angeles (A)

AREA	**425** square miles (1,079sq.km.)
POPULATION	**311,000** (1983 preliminary figure)
POPULATION DENSITY	**745.8** per square mile (1983)
PRINCIPAL RELIGION	**Predominantly Roman Catholic**
OFFICIAL LANGUAGE	**French**
CAPITAL	**Fort-de-France**
CURRENCY	**French franc** (1 franc = 100 centimes)

overseas departments (1946) then regions (1974), and overseas departments with enlarged powers of self government (1982). The 1980s saw a faltering economy, racial tension, and bombings by black nationalists.
Land Martinique, the largest single island, has a core of three mountain masses, reaching 4583 feet (1397m.) with volcanic Mont Pelée in the north. The coast features cliffs, coves, headlands, and coral reefs.

To the north, beyond Dominica, lies butterfly-shaped Guadeloupe – really two islands joined by a bridge over a strait, the Rivière Salée. West of this, mountainous Basse-Terre rises from a rugged coast to 4868 feet (1484m.) at volcanic Soufrière, the highest point in the French Antilles. Grand-Terre is lower, with chalky hills rimmed by beaches. To the south and east lie small offshore islands: from west to east the Les Saintes string of islets; round Marie-Galante; and narrow, arid La Désirade.

Rugged little St. Barthélemy and hilly St. Martin are Guadeloupe's outliers, 150 miles (240km.) to the northwest.
Climate The islands have warm, sunny weather all year. Temperature averages 79°F.

(26°C.) at sea level on Martinique, but only 40°F. (4°C.) on top of Guadeloupe's Soufrière volcano. High peaks get the most rain: over 157 inches (4000mm.) against 39 inches (990mm.) on parts of the main islands' coasts; most rain falls between July and November. Cooling Northeast Trade Winds blow on most days, but humid southern air can bring hurricanes about September.
Vegetation and animals On big islands, surviving natural vegetation includes some coastal mangrove swamps, and tropical lowland forest with mahogany, ferns, and orchids. Higher up grow chestnut trees and bracken; with stunted forest, peat moss, or sedges on the tallest summits. Some of the small islands support dry forest with fan palms and cacti.

Native land animals are few, and mongooses have ravaged wildlife. Martinique has rabbits, a poisonous snake, doves, and ortolans; Basse-Terre is home to raccoons, agoutis (large rodents), and waterfowl.

Hogfish, parrot fish, snapper, and tarpon are among the many fishes swimming in the warm waters off the islands.

St. Martin

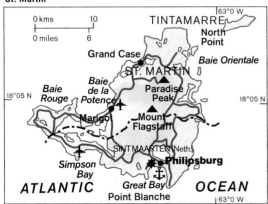

St. Barthélemy

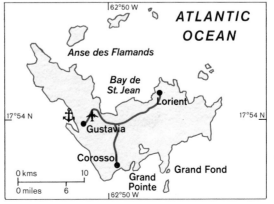

A view of La Soufrière, the highest point in the French Antilles.
(stamp issued 1905–27)

©DIAGRAM

123

The French Antilles

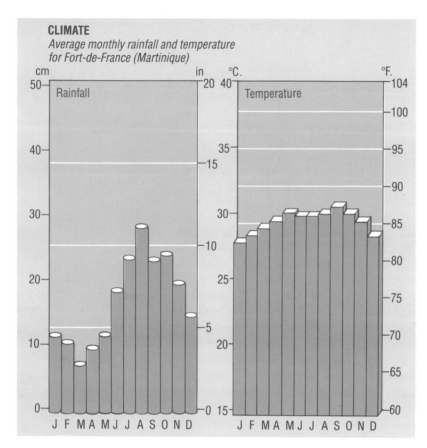

CLIMATE
Average monthly rainfall and temperature for Fort-de-France (Martinique)

Rainfall — cm / in

Temperature — °C. / °F.

J F M A M J J A S O N D

People Most people are Mulattoes or Negroes, except on Les Saintes and St. Barthélemy where the small populations are mainly of French descent.

The official language is French, but a local Creole patois is widely spoken. Roman Catholicism is the chief religion, and there are small Protestant groups.

Some estimates put the mid 1980s' population at over 750,000, almost evenly divided between both departments. Each is densely populated, but many islanders have moved from the countryside into the towns. In the early 1980s nearly one-third of Martinique's population lived in its capital, Fort-de-France (pop. 101,000). Other centers include Pointe-à-Pitre (pop. 24,000) on Grande-Terre, and Guadeloupe's capital Basse-Terre (pop. 16,000) on the island of Basse-Terre. There has been much emigration to France, and some influx of sunseeking French from Europe.

Social conditions Massive French Government aid and a distorted economy partly explain why half the labor force works in administration and services, against 20 per cent in agriculture and 15 per cent in food processing. Average earnings are good for the region but, in the mid 1980s, 20 per cent of the workforce was jobless – hence much Black emigration to France. A tiny minority of Whites and Near Whites more or less run the economy.

French Government help has created effective services. Education is free and compulsory to the age of 16, and health care is exceptionally good for the region. By the mid 1980s average life expectancy stood at 70.5 years.

Government Martinique and Guadeloupe with its dependencies are two overseas departments of France, each administered by a Prefect and (since 1983) an elected General Assembly operating side by side with an indirectly constituted Regional Council. Each department returns two senators to the French Senate, and three Deputies to the National Assembly.

For local government each department is divided into *arrondissements* subdivided into communes. The French system of justice operates.

Communications and transportation The islands have many radio stations, one

GUADELOUPE

Principal Crops	Production	Exports	Imports	Total World Trade
Figures expressed in thousands of tons produced (1982)	*Goods and services expressed as percentage of GDP (1982)*	*Figures expressed as percentage of total (1981)*	*Figures expressed as percentage of total (1981)*	*Figures expressed in millions of U.S.$ (1983)*

Principal Crops
Figures expressed in thousands of tons produced (1982)

A Sugar   864.4
B Bananas   165
C Vegetables   47
D Fruit   3

Production
Goods and services expressed as percentage of GDP (1982)

A Services   80.5%
B Industry   10.0%
C Other   9.5%

Exports
Figures expressed as percentage of total (1981)

A Bananas   35.8%
B Sugar   28.6%
C Rum   7.9%
D Wheat flour   7.8%
E Other   19.9%

Imports
Figures expressed as percentage of total (1981)

A Food   18.4%
B Other   81.6%

Total World Trade
Figures expressed in millions of U.S.$ (1983)

Exports World   78.81
   U.S.   no figures
Imports World   376
   U.S.   19.8
GDP
709 million U.S.$ (1980)

MARTINIQUE

Principal Crops
Figures expressed in thousands of tons produced (1983)

A Sugar cane   199
B Bananas   167.8
C Pineapples   1.3

Production
Goods and services expressed as percentage of GDP (1982)

A Industry   10%
B Other   90%

Exports
Figures expressed as percentage of total (1983)

A Agricultural produce   88.4%
B Other   11.6%

Imports
Figures expressed as percentage of total (1983)

A Energy   18.4%
B Food   17.2%
C Other   64.4%

Total World Trade
Figures expressed in millions of U.S.$ (1983)

Exports World   173.44
   U.S.   no figures
Imports World   645.38
   U.S.   no figures
GDP
758.4 million U.S.$ (1980)

television channel, a local daily newspaper, and more than 140,000 telephones. Guadeloupe and Martinique have well-developed road networks, and nearly one-fifth of Guadeloupe's 1240 road miles (2000km.) are highways. There are international airports near Pointe-à-Pitre and Fort-de-France, and flights to the smaller islands. The chief ports are those of Fort-de-France and Pointe-à-Pitre.

Economy Both departments consume more than they produce and depend on French Government aid. This is why services (largely public services) account for four-fifths of Guadeloupe's gross national product. Other economic activity is chiefly farming, food processing, and tourism.

About a quarter of the French Antilles is arable land, and one-fifth pasture. Half of Guadeloupe's cropland is under sugar cane – but Martinique's cane acreage was savagely cut to protect European Economic Community sugar-beet growers. Martinique's farmers largely switched to bananas, pineapples, and eggplants – all also grown on Guadeloupe. The islands have some 135,000 cattle, 80,000 pigs, 55,000 goats, and 50,000 sheep.

Fisheries produce fish, lobsters, crayfish, clams, and octopus. Minerals and forests contribute little to the economy.

There is fruit canning, sugar refining, and rum distilling, with oil refining and cement production on Martinique.

By the mid 1980s about 300,000 tourists a year reportedly visited each of the two departments – drawn by Caribbean beaches and climate and a colorful lifestyle.

More than half the total value of exports from each department comes from bananas. Other main exports include Guadeloupe's sugar and rum, and Martinique's petroleum products, rum, sugar, and pineapples.

Both departments import food, machinery and transportation equipment, oil, and consumer goods.

Mainland France is the dominant trading partner. Others include Venezuela and the U.S.

A pineapple, one of the fruits grown on both Martinique and Guadeloupe.

Antigua and Barbuda; St. Kitts-Nevis

OFFICIAL NAME
Antigua and Barbuda

Above: **Flag of Antigua and Barbuda**
A red background flanks a
broad V of horizontal bands:
black (at top), blue, and
white, with a rising gold sun in
the black band.

SIZE IN RELATION TO U.S. CITY

A

Slightly smaller than Colombus, Ohio (A)

AREA	**171** square miles (442sq.km.)
POPULATION	**78,000** (1983 preliminary figure)
POPULATION DENSITY	**456.1** per square mile (1983)
PRINCIPAL RELIGION	**Anglican**
OFFICIAL LANGUAGE	**English**
CAPITAL	**St. John's**
CURRENCY	**East Caribbean dollar** (E.Car.$1 = 100 cents)

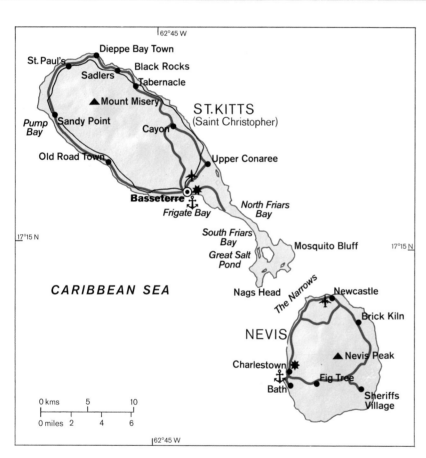

Between them these two young nations in
the East Caribbean's Leeward Islands group
match the area of Memphis, Tennessee and
hold about 130,000 people. Each country
consists mainly of two islands, and ranks
among the less developed Caribbean
members of the Commonwealth.

History Christopher Columbus discovered
both groups of islands in 1493. English
colonization started with St. Kitts in 1625,
followed by Nevis in 1628 and Antigua in
1632. France disputed ownership of St. Kitts
until 1713 and seized St. Kitts and Nevis in
1782, but the British had regained complete
control by the end of the Napoleonic Wars.
Britain granted both future nations internal
self-government in 1967, and full
independence came in the 1980s: to Antigua
and Barbuda in 1981, and to St. Kitts-Nevis in
1983.

Land Club-shaped St. Kitts is about 23
miles (37km.) by 5 miles (8km.). Nearby
Nevis is smaller and circular. Both have
volcanic peaks over 3000 feet (914m.). Forty
miles (64km.) east of Nevis, Antigua, 13 miles
(21km.) across, lies south of slightly smaller
Barbuda.

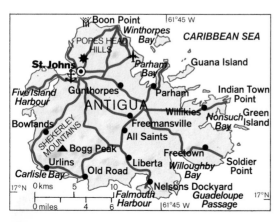

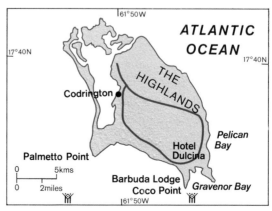

✹	Tourist Centres
♛	National Parks
	Transportation
▬	Main Roads
—	Railways
✈	Main and International Airports
⚓	Main Ports
	Population of major towns and cities
●	<10,000 inhabitants
◉	10,000–25,000

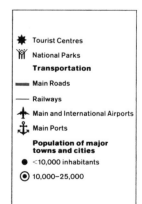

OFFICIAL NAME
Saint Christopher and Nevis

Above: **Flag of St. Kitts-Nevis**
Green (top staff-side) and red (bottom outer) segments flank two narrow yellow bands edging a broad diagonal black band with stars.

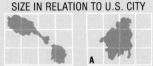

SIZE IN RELATION TO U.S. CITY

Slightly smaller than Austin, Texas (A)

AREA	**104** square miles (269sq.km.)
POPULATION	**53,000** (1983 preliminary figure)
POPULATION DENSITY	**509.6** per square mile (1983)
PRINCIPAL RELIGIONS	**Protestant, Roman Catholic**
OFFICIAL LANGUAGE	**English**
CAPITAL	**Basseterre**
CURRENCY	**East Caribbean dollar** (E.Car.$1 = 100 cents)

Climate The Northeast Trade Winds temper the tropical heat, temperatures averaging 80°F. (27°C.). Antigua and Barbuda are drier than mountainous St. Kitts and Nevis, where annual rainfall can exceed 80 inches (2032mm.) in the highlands. There are occasional hurricanes.

Vegetation and animals Scrub covers much of Barbuda, but tropical forest sprawls on the mountains of St. Kitts and Nevis. Wildlife-rich Barbuda has ducks, plovers, frigate birds, and wild pigs.

People Most are of African or mixed origin. There are Protestants and Catholics, and all speak English. In the mid 1980s most of St. Kitts' 36,000 people lived near the coast, 16,000 in the capital Basseterre; many of Nevis's 13,000 lived in or near Charlestown in the west. About one-third of the 78,000 Antiguans lived in the capital, St. John's, and Barbuda had about 1500 inhabitants.

Social conditions On St. Kitts-Nevis agriculture is a major area of employment, while on Antigua and Barbuda tourism occupies up to two-thirds of the workforce. Unemployment is respectively 15 and 20 per cent. Both countries offer free, compulsory education, and some health care is free.

Government In both nations the head of state is the British monarch represented by a Governor-General. Antigua and Barbuda have a 17-member Senate and a House of Representatives. St. Kitts-Nevis has a Cabinet government headed by a Prime Minister, and there is a National Assembly. Nevis Island also has its own Premier and Assembly.

Communications and transportation Each country has its own radio and television services and automatic telephone system. St. Kitts-Nevis has about 124 miles (200km.) of roads, an international airport, and a main port at Charlestown on Nevis. Antigua and Barbuda have about 621 miles (1000km.) of roads, an international airport, and a main port at St. John's on Antigua.

Economy Sugar cane dominates St. Kitts' economy, but U.S. tariff concessions are attracting foreign investment in light industry. Antigua and Barbuda depend heavily on tourism. They grow no cash crops, but have a big fishing industry and some small-scale manufacturing.

ECONOMIC REVIEW
(below)

A: ANTIGUA AND BARBUDA
B: ST. KITTS NEVIS

Land Use
Figures expressed as percentage of total land
A (1982) **B** (1982)
Principal Crops
Figures expressed in thousands of tons produced
A (1982) **B** (1984)
Production
Goods and services expressed as percentage of GDP
A (1982) **B** (1978)
Exports / Imports
Figures expressed as percentage of total
A (1981) **B** (1982)
Total World Trade
Figures expressed in millions of U.S.$
A (1982) **B** (1981)
GDP
A (1982) **B** (1982)

	Land Use	Principal Crops	Production	Exports	Imports	Total World Trade
A	18.2% Arable	84 Molasses	18.8% Transport/ Communication	59.0% Manufactures Food/Beverages/	32.6% Food/Beverages/ Tobacco	**Exports** World 124.2
	Forest/	17 Sugar				U.S. 40.3
	15.9% Woodland	15 Cotton	14.3% Government	20.4% Tobacco	24.6% Manufactures	**Imports** World 34.2
	65.9% Other	5 Cocoa	8.1% Manufacturing	20.6% Other	42.8% Other	U.S. 26.2
		2.8 Bananas	58.8% Other			**GDP** 137 million U.S.$
B	22.2% Arable	31.7 Sugar	15.4% Agriculture	58.8% Sugar/Molasses	22.1% Food/Beverages/ Tobacco	**Exports** World 24.26
	Forest/		12.7% Industry	13.7% Garments	Transport	U.S. 10.24
	16.7% Woodland		9.6% Trade	7.4% Electrical goods	20.5% equipment	**Imports** World 47.71
	61.1% Other		6.2% Construction	5.8% Shoes	57.4% Other	U.S. 14.4
			56.1% Other	14.3% Other		**GDP** 14.4 million U.S.$

©DIAGRAM

Dominica and St. Lucia

OFFICIAL NAME
Dominica

Above: **Flag of Dominica**
Ten green stars encircle a
green parrot on a red disk
imposed on a cross of yellow,
white, and black bands
(yellow at top and staff-side).
The background is green.

SIZE IN RELATION TO U.S. CITY

Slightly smaller than New York City (A)

AREA	**290** square miles (750sq.km.)
POPULATION	**81,000** (1983 preliminary figure)
POPULATION DENSITY	**279.3** per square mile (1983)
PRINCIPAL RELIGION	**Roman Catholic**
OFFICIAL LANGUAGE	**English**
CAPITAL	**Roseau**
CURRENCY	**East Caribbean dollar** (E.Car.$1 = 100 cents)

Abrupt volcanic mountains and lush tropical vegetation make these among the loveliest of all East Caribbean nations. Both lie in the Windward Islands group: Dominica 25 miles (40km.) north of the French island Martinique; St. Lucia 22 miles (35km.) to its south. French customs coexist with British in both Commonwealth countries. Their combined population of 210,000 occupies an area half the size of Rhode Island.

History Warlike Carib Indians inhabited both islands when Christopher Columbus discovered Dominica in 1493 and an unknown sailor found St. Lucia about 1500. French colonists settled the islands in the 1600s, but next century these kept changing hands in a Franco-British tug of war. Britain finally gained Dominica in 1805, and St. Lucia in 1814, but granted each island internal self-government in 1967. Full independence came for Dominica in 1978, and for St. Lucia in 1979.

Land Oblong Dominica and pear-shaped St. Lucia are both aligned from north to south and about 28 miles (45km.) long by up to 15 miles (24km.) across. Each has rugged volcanic mountains, boiling sulfur springs,

The volcanic Pitons, a
spectacular landmark on St.
Lucia.
(stamp issued 1902)

fertile valleys, and scores of streams tumbling to the sea; but only St. Lucia boasts sandy beaches. Outstanding landmarks are Dominica's mist-capped Morne Diablotin, at 4747 feet (1447m.) the highest summit in the Lesser Antilles, and St. Lucia's cone-shaped volcanic Pitons which rise spectacularly from the sea.

Climate This is tropical, moderated by the Northeast Trade Winds. Sea-level temperatures of 78–90°F. (26–32°C.) contrast with 55°F. (13°C.) on mountain peaks. Both islands have high rainfall, especially Dominica with 70 inches (1800mm.) a year on coasts and more than 236 inches (6000mm.) on high mountains. Each island is sometimes liable to severe hurricane damage.

Vegetation and animals Dominica is the most heavily forested West Indian island, with luxuriant tropical rain forest, and deciduous forest and scrub on dry lowlands; forest and woodland also cover upland St. Lucia. Wildlife includes the St. Lucia parrot, iguanas, boas, and the poisonous *fer-de-lance* snake. On Dominica opossums have nearly wiped out a rare dove.

People Most are Negro or of mixed Black and White origin. Dominicans include Syrians and Caribs – last of the Indians who gave the Caribbean its name. Some St. Lucians are Asian Indians.

On both islands most people are Roman Catholics, and many speak a French patois as well as the official language, English.

In the mid 1980s Dominica held about 80,000 people, St. Lucia 130,000. Most Dominicans live near coasts, especially in and around the capital Roseau (1983 pop. about 18,000). Forty per cent of St. Lucians live in towns, including the capital Castries (1982 pop. about 50,000).

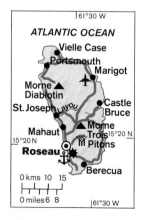

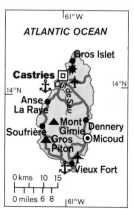

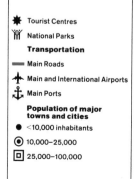

OFFICIAL NAME
St. Lucia

Above: **Flag of St. Lucia**
Blue with a central emblem: a white-edged black pyramid containing a yellow pyramid. Shown left is the St. Lucian coat of arms.

SIZE IN RELATION TO U.S. CITY

A

Size of El Paso, Texas (A)

AREA	**238** square miles (616sq.km.)
POPULATION	**125,000** (1983 preliminary figure)
POPULATION DENSITY	**525.2** per square mile (1983)
PRINCIPAL RELIGION	**Roman Catholic**
OFFICIAL LANGUAGE	**English**
CAPITAL	**Castries**
CURRENCY	**East Caribbean dollar** (E.Car.$1 = 100 cents)

Social conditions In both countries the main field of employment is farming, followed by services, then industry and commerce. Average incomes are very low, but in the mid 1980s so was inflation. Education programs produced literacy rates of around 80 per cent. A mid 1980s estimate put average life expectancy in both countries in the mid to high 60s, but gave St. Lucia's infant mortality rate as more than twice Dominica's low 12.6 per 1000.

Government In each country a Prime Minister is head of government. Head of state in the republic of Dominica is a President elected by the House of Assembly which has 21 elected and 9 appointed members. In the parliamentary state of St. Lucia, head of state is a Governor-General representing the British monarch, and there is an 11-member appointed Senate and a 17-member elected House of Assembly. For local government Dominica has 25 village councils and two town councils; and St. Lucia is divided into 16 parishes and Castries.

Communications and transportation
Dominica has a radio service, cable

television, and a weekly newspaper, and by 1980 had 4600 telephones. There are 466 miles (750km.) of roads, two airports, and one main port: Roseau. St. Lucia has two radio services, a television service, a twice weekly newspaper, and by 1982 had 9500 telephones. There are 500 miles (800km.) of roads, two airports, and main ports at Castries and Vieux Fort.

Economy After recession, both nations' economies improved by the mid 1980s. Each island's earnings depend largely on growing bananas for export, and processing coconuts and other tropical crops. Other exported products include soap and bottled water from Dominica, and clothes made in St. Lucia. Forestry is developing on Dominica, and fish provide much of its protein. Both islands profit from tourism; St. Lucia gets up to 100,000 visitors a year. The islands' main trading partners include the United Kingdom, U.S., and Caribbean countries.

ECONOMIC REVIEW
(below)
A: DOMINICA
B: ST. LUCIA

Land Use
Figures expressed as percentage of total land
A *(1982)* **B** *(1982)*
Principal Crops
Figures expressed in thousands of tons produced
A *(1983)* **B** *(1983)*
Production
Goods and services expressed as percentage of GDP
A *(1978)* **B** *(1983)*
Exports / Imports
Figures expressed as percentage of total
A *(1982)* **B** *(1982)*
Total World Trade
Figures expressed in millions of U.S.$
A *(1983)* **B** *(1982)*
GDP
A *(1982)* **B** *(1983)*

	Land Use	Principal Crops	Production	Exports	Imports	Total World Trade		
A	41.3% Forest/ Woodland	28.7 Bananas	41.2% Agriculture	36.7% Bananas	31.4% Food/Beverages/	**Exports** World	27.4
	13.3% Permanent crops		10.0% Trade	34.8% Soap	24.0% Tobacco		U.S.	—
	45.4% Other		7.3% Construction/Gas/ Electricity/Water	3.0% Coconut oil	Manufactures	**Imports** World	45.3
			41.5% Other	25.5% Other	44.6% Other		U.S.	—
						GDP 72 million U.S.$		
B	19.6% Permanent crops	54.4 Bananas	17.1% Construction	37.6% Bananas	34.3% Manufactures	**Total World Trade**		
	13.1% Forest/ Woodland		16.8% Agriculture	12.6% Cardboard	25.0% Food/Beverages/	**Exports** World	37.66
	67.3% Other		14.8% Trade	9.9% Clothing	Tobacco		U.S.	2.89
			9.2% Industry	6.3% Coconut oil	40.7% Other	**Imports** World	118.4
			42.1% Other	33.6% Other			U.S.	43.3
						GDP 139.8 million U.S.$		

St. Vincent and the Grenadines; Grenada

Above: Flag of St. Vincent & Grenadines
Vertical bands of blue (staff-side), yellow and green, separated by narrow white bands; the yellow bears a coat of arms.

OFFICIAL NAME
St. Vincent and the Grenadines

SIZE IN RELATION TO U.S. CITY

Slightly larger than Seattle, Washington (A)

AREA	**150** square miles (389sq.km.)
POPULATION	**102,000** (1983 estimate)
POPULATION DENSITY	**680.0** per square mile (1983)
PRINCIPAL RELIGIONS	**Methodist, Anglican, Roman Catholic**
OFFICIAL LANGUAGE	**English**
CAPITAL	**Kingstown**
CURRENCY	**East Caribbean dollar** (E.Car.$1 = 100 cents)

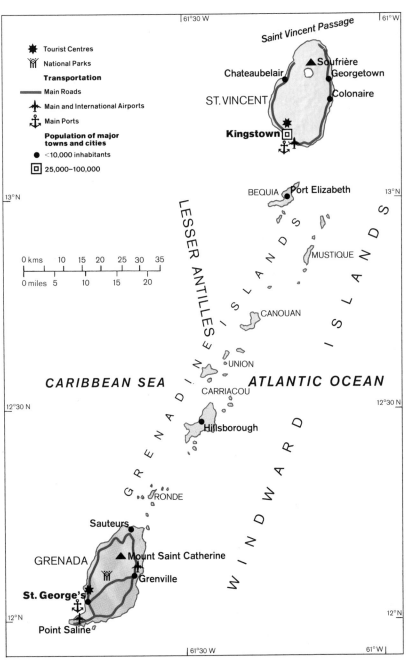

These southeast Caribbean nations are the southernmost of the Windward Islands group. Each is twice the size of Washington D.C.; volcanic; mountainous; covered in lush vegetation; and thickly populated. Spice-rich Grenada is the smallest independent country in the Western Hemisphere. St. Vincent has one of the Caribbean's two active volcanoes, and grows nine-tenths of the world's arrowroot, a food thickener.

History Christopher Columbus reputedly discovered both islands in 1498. By the early 1600s France was claiming Grenada, and England, St. Vincent. French and English crushed local Caribs and fought one another. Britain finally secured St. Vincent in 1783 and Grenada in 1796, but granted full independence to Grenada in 1974, and to St. Vincent in 1979. In 1983 Grenada suffered a bloody coup, but its Marxist leaders were overthrown in an ensuing U.S.-led invasion.

Land Each main island is roughly oval, aligned north-south, about 20 miles (32km.) long, and up to 11 miles (18km.) across. A ridge of volcanic mountains forms each island's spine, and there are fairly frequent eruptions from St. Vincent's Soufrière, the islands' highest point at 4048 feet (1234m.). A chain of tiny islands – the Grenadines – links the two major islands. Northern Grenadines belong to St. Vincent; southern ones are Grenada's.

Climate This is sunny and hot from December through May, with a rainy season from June to November. The temperature averages 82°F. (28°C.). Grenada's annual rainfall ranges from 40 inches (1016mm.) in the southwest to 160 inches (4064mm.) in the mountains, and most of St. Vincent gets more than 80 inches (2032mm.).

Vegetation and animals Tropical crops

OFFICIAL NAME
State of Grenada

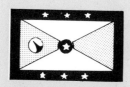

Above: **Flag of Grenada**
A red border with six yellow stars surrounds a rectangle with yellow top and bottom segments and green side segments, and a yellow star in a central red disk.

SIZE IN RELATION TO U.S. CITY

A

Same as Detroit (A)

AREA	**133** square miles (344sq.km.)
POPULATION	**114,000** (1983 preliminary figure)
POPULATION DENSITY	**857.1** per square mile (1983)
PRINCIPAL RELIGIONS	**Roman Catholic, Anglican**
OFFICIAL LANGUAGE	**English**
CAPITAL	**St. George's**
CURRENCY	**East Caribbean dollar** (E.Car.$1 = 100 cents)

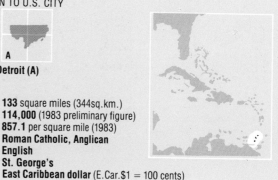

cover lowlands and terraced hillsides, but tropical forest with ferns and flowering shrubs sprawls up mountains. Birds abound and there are land crabs, iguanas, turtles, and American opossums, African monkeys, and Indian mongooses.

People These are chiefly of African or mixed origin, with some Asian Indians and Europeans. Most Grenadians are Roman Catholics, but Anglicans predominate on St. Vincent. All islanders speak English, and Grenadians use a French-African patois. Both islands are heavily populated. Some mid 1980s estimates gave Grenada 114,000 people (8000 in the capital St. George's) and St. Vincent 134,000 (34,000 in the capital Kingstown).

Social conditions Overdependence on inadequate, poorly paid agricultural work has kept incomes low and unemployment high, but both countries offer free education and claim more than 90 per cent literacy. One 1985 estimate gave life expectancy as 71 in Grenada and 65 in St. Vincent, but ranked St. Vincent's infant mortality rate the second highest in the Caribbean.

Government Each Commonwealth country has a Governor-General representing the British monarch as head of state, and a Prime Minister as head of government. St. Vincent's House of Assembly has elected and appointed members. Grenada has an appointed Senate and an elected House of Parliament.

Communications and transportation Grenada has radio and television services, a daily newspaper, 6000 telephones, 500 miles (800km.) of roads, an international airport, and one main port: St. George's. St. Vincent has its own radio, two weekly newspapers, 6000 telephones, 620 miles (1000km.) of roads, landing strips for small planes, and one main port: Kingstown.

Economy Agriculture and tourism are the mainstay of each nation. Each farms at least 40 per cent of its land. Crops include cacao, mace, and 30 per cent of the world's nutmegs on Grenada; bananas, arrowroot, and coconuts on St. Vincent. Each processes agricultural produce and makes some consumer goods. Trading partners include Britain, Trinidad and Tobago, and the U.S.

ECONOMIC REVIEW
(below)
A: ST. VINCENT AND THE GRENADINES
B: GRENADA

Land Use
Figures expressed as percentage of total land
A *(1982)* **B** *(1982)*
Principal Crops
Figures expressed in thousands of tons produced
A *(1983)* **B** *(1983)*
Production
Goods and services expressed as percentage of GDP
A *(1983)* **B** *(1980)*
Exports / Imports
Figures expressed as percentage of total
A *(1981)* **B** *(1982)*
Total World Trade
Figures expressed in millions of U.S.$
A *(1983)* **B** *(1983)*
GDP
A *(1983)* **B** *(1982)*

	Land Use	Principal Crops	Production	Exports	Imports	Total World Trade
A	41.2% Forest/ Woodland	27.6 Bananas	17.7% Agriculture	41.1% Bananas	31.8% Food/Beverages/ Tobacco	**Exports** World 37.98 U.S. —
	38.2% Arable	2.8 Sugar	15.4% Industry	24.6% Flour	28.5% Manufactures	**Imports** World 23.5 U.S. —
	20.6% Other		66.9% Other	13.9% Mill feed	14.5% Machinery	**GDP**
				4.3% Arrowroot	25.2% Other	95.6 million U.S.$
				16.1% Other		
B	26.5% Permanent crops	12 Bananas	26.2% Agriculture	24.9% Cocoa	31.1% Food/Beverages/ Tobacco	**Total World Trade**
	14.7% Arable	2 Nutmeg	16.3% Trade	18.3% Bananas	22.9% Manufactures	**Exports** World 18.92 U.S. —
	58.8% Other	2 Cocoa	57.5% Other	16.3% Nutmeg	46.0% Other	**Imports** World 55.63 U.S. —
				13.1% Clothing		**GDP**
				27.4% Other		107.6 million U.S.$

Barbados

Above: **Flag of Barbados**
Vertical stripes of blue, gold,
blue with a central black
trident. Shown left is the
Barbadian coat of arms.

OFFICIAL NAME
Barbados

SIZE IN RELATION TO U.S. CITY

Slightly larger than San Jose, California (A)

AREA	**166** square miles (430sq.km.)
POPULATION	**260,000** (1983 preliminary figure)
POPULATION DENSITY	**1,566.2** per square mile (1983)
CURRENCY	**East Caribbean dollar** (E.Car.$1 = 100 cents)
PRINCIPAL RELIGION	**Anglican**
OFFICIAL LANGUAGE	**English**
CAPITAL	**Bridgetown**

The easternmost West Indian island, pear-shaped Barbados is isolated by 100 miles (160km.) of Atlantic from St. Vincent in the main Windward Islands group to the west of it. This small, crowded, Commonwealth nation has a record of stable, civilized life, and a higher standard of living than most Caribbean islands.

History Indians reputedly inhabited the island in 1536 when Portugal's Pedro a Campos named it *los Barbudos* ("the bearded ones") after its bearded fig trees. English colonists landed in 1627, and by 1800 settlers had grown rich from sugar cane produced by African slaves. Britain clung to Barbados through wars with France, Spain, and the U.S., but finally granted full independence in 1966. Since then, tourism and manufacturing have helped offset declining sugar production.

Land This is 21 miles (34km.) long and up to 14 miles (22.5km.) across. Most of it is low with gently rolling hills, reaching 1115 feet (340m.) at (north-central) Mt. Hillaby. Below the thin topsoil coral rock overlies sandstone and clay, and there are underground rivers. Rugged east coast cliffs contrast with the low, white, sandy beaches of the west coast.

Climate Temperatures seldom vary from the range 72–86°F. (22–30°C.). Annual rainfall averages 60 inches (1524mm.) with more on the inland hills, less on the northeast and south coasts. The wet season is June to November, but droughts can occur. The Northeast Trade Winds have a cooling effect and there are occasional hurricanes.

Vegetation and animals A small patch of bearded figs and other trees recalls the old forests, now replaced by sugar cane and plants such as frangipani, mahogany, and poinciana. Egrets and hummingbirds are among the scores of bird species. There are monkeys and mongooses, tree frogs, and dolphins and barracudas offshore.

People The inhabitants are over 70 per cent Negroes and 8 per cent Europeans; the rest are of mixed or other origin. Most are Anglican Protestants. All speak English, many with a creolized variation. The roughly 300,000 inhabitants make this one of the world's most densely peopled nations. Two-fifths of the people live in towns, notably the

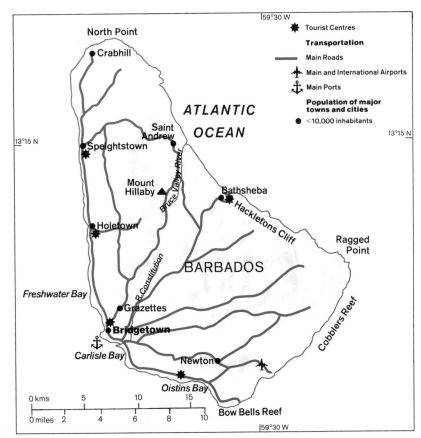

HISTORICAL REVIEW

1518	Spanish landed in search of slaves.	**1958**	First prime minister of the Federation of West Indies elected.
1536	Portuguese landed.	**1965**	Barbados left the Federation.
1627	English colonists settled unopposed. Brought slaves and began cultivation of sugar cane.	**1966**	Independence. Remained member of Commonwealth.
1834	Abolition of slavery.	**1981**	Tom Adams (Barbados Labor Party) re-elected.
1937	Moyne Commission recommended enfranchisement of women and adult suffrage. Development of trade unionism and political parties.	**1982**	Visit by Ronald Reagan. Decline in sugar production forced deflationary government policies.
1952	Adult suffrage granted.	**1983**	Barbados "launching pad" for U.S. invasion of Grenada.
1942– 58	Barbados housed Development and Welfare Organization for West Indies.	**1984**	By-election won by David Simmons (BLP).

capital Bridgetown (pop. over 100,000).

Social conditions Income averaged U.S.$4300 per head in 1983. About 66 per cent of the labor force work in services and government, 25 per cent in commerce and industry, and 10 per cent in agriculture; but unemployment reached 18 per cent in 1985. There is free education and a 97 per cent literacy rate. By the mid 1980s life expectancy was high, and both infant mortality and population increase were low.

Government A Governor-General represents the British monarch as head of state. The Prime Minister is head of government. There is a Senate of 21 appointed members, and a 27-member House of Assembly elected every five years by popular vote. For local government Barbados is divided into 11 parishes and Bridgetown. A Supreme Court administers justice.

Communications and transportation There are several radio services, a television channel, and more than 50,000 telephones. Sales of two daily newspapers total over 40 per 100 inhabitants. There are 1019 miles (1640km.) of roads, mostly surfaced, an international airport, and a deepwater port at Bridgetown Harbor.

Economy Tourism and manufacturing have replaced sugar as the chief earners of foreign exchange, and offshore banking is expanding. Sugar cane still takes up most of the island's 60 per cent of cultivated land and accounts for much of its exports, but diversification favors vegetables, root crops, fruits, and livestock. Fishing is a growing industry and the country has some oil and gas. Its manufactured goods include clothes, electronic goods, and handicrafts.

Slave labor on a sugar plantation.

ECONOMIC REVIEW

Land Use Figures expressed as percentage of total land (1982)	Principal Crops Figures expressed in thousands of tons produced (1983)	Production Goods and services expressed as percentage of GDP (1983)	Exports Figures expressed as percentage of total (1984)	Imports Figures expressed as percentage of total (1984)	Total World Trade Figures expressed in millions of U.S.$ (1983)
76.5% Arable	100.5 Sugar	26.6% Wholesale/Retail (inc. hotels)	53.4% Electrical components	35.8% Machinery/Transport/ equipment	**Exports** World 356.7
9.4% Permanent pasture	0.8 Onions	12.0% Manufacturing Transport/	11.1% Clothing	14.1% Food/Beverages Manufactured	U.S. 186.73
14.1% Other		7.3% Communication	9.8% Sugar	13.6% goods	**Imports** World 620.9
		6.3% Construction	2.5% Rum/Molasses	12.6% Fuel	U.S. 214.5
		47.8% Other	23.2% Other	Miscellaneous	**GDP**
				9.0% manufactures	1062 million U.S.$
				7.0% Chemicals	
				7.9% Other	

©DIAGRAM

Trinidad and Tobago

Above: **Flag of Trinidad and Tobago**
Red with a white-edged broad black band that runs diagonally from top staff-side edge to bottom outer edge.

OFFICIAL NAME
Trinidad and Tobago

SIZE IN RELATION TO U.S. STATE

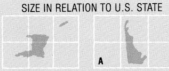

Slightly smaller than Delaware (A)

AREA	**1980** square miles (5128sq.km.)
POPULATION	**1,140,000** (1983 preliminary figure)
POPULATION DENSITY	**575.6** per square mile (1983)
CURRENCY	**Trinidad and Tobago dollar** (T.T.$1 = 100 cents)
PRINCIPAL RELIGIONS	**Roman Catholic, Anglican, Hindu**
OFFICIAL LANGUAGE	**English**
CAPITAL	**Port-of-Spain**
ADMINISTRATIVE DIVISIONS	**Eight counties, Tobago and four cities**

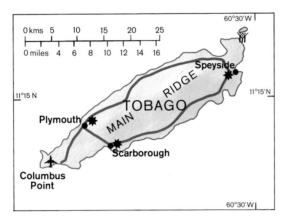

Trinidad and Tobago are best known as lush tropical islands with a colorful Caribbean culture. They form the Caribbean's seventh largest country, ranking sixth in size for population. Oil, gas, and asphalt help to give this the region's highest per capita income. Trinidad is the southernmost West Indian island, at one point only 7 miles (11km.) off northeast Venezuela.

History Indians already inhabited Trinidad when Christopher Columbus discovered both islands in 1498. He reputedly named Trinidad for three prominent hilltops.

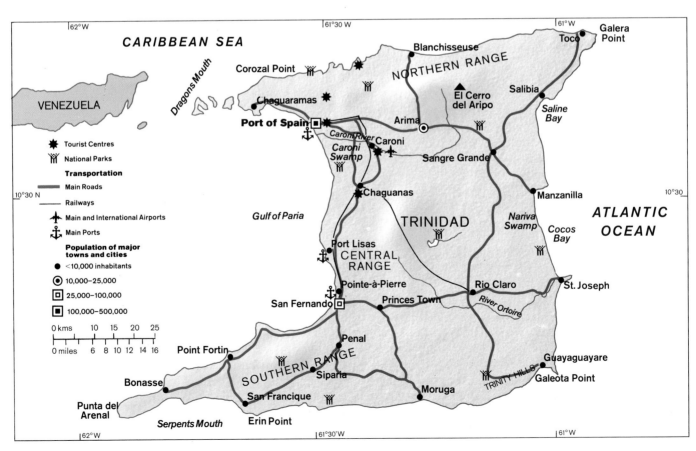

HISTORICAL REVIEW

1498	Columbus sights Trinidad.		Commission).
1777	Trinidad is placed under the jurisdiction of the Captain-General and Intendant of Venezuela.	**1940**	Colonial Development and Welfare Act.
		1947–48	Constitutional Reform Committee.
1802	Trinidad is ceded to Britain by Treaty of Amiens.	**1951**	Commonwealth Sugar Agreement.
		1956	Formation of Eric Williams' Peoples' National Movement (PNM).
1885–91	Governor William Robinson attempts to diversify the economy.	**1958**	Inauguration of the West Indies Federation.
1889	Tobago linked to Trinidad in a federal union.	**1961**	Constitutional change grants full internal self governments.
1898	Tobago becomes a ward of the united colony of Trinidad and Tobago.	**1962**	Disollution of Federation. Independence granted 31st August.
1925	First elections to the Legislative Council. Cipriani is elected.	**1976**	Became a republic.
1938–39	West India Royal Commission (Moyne	**1980**	Tobago granted a degree of self-government.

Spanish settlement of Trinidad started in 1532, but in the 1600s English, Dutch, and French all raided the island, and a British force seized it in 1797. Meanwhile, England, France, Holland and Spain disputed Tobago's ownership. Both islands formally became British in 1802, under the Treaty of Amiens.

Under British colonial rule the islands were politically joined in 1889. They gained independence in 1962 and became a republic inside the Commonwealth in 1976.

Oil and industry have brought relative prosperity to a cosmopolitan population descended from African slaves, Asian laborers, and European colonists.

Land Trinidad and Tobago are isolated extensions of mainland South America. Trinidad is basically a rectangle with three projecting corners. Without these peninsulas it extends 50 miles (80km.) from north to south, and 31 miles (50km.) from west to east. Three hilly areas – the Northern, Central, and Southern ranges – cross Trinidad from west to east. The Northern Range is tallest and its highest point is Mt. Aripo at 3085 feet (940m.). But most of Trinidad is low, level land with fertile soil.

Tobago is a cigar-shaped island about 26 miles (42km.) long and 7½ miles (12km.) wide. The Main Ridge, its mountain spine, reaches 1899 feet (579m.) but slopes down to a coral plain in the southwest.

Climate This is hot and humid. Average temperatures on Trinidad range from 77°F. (25°C.) in January to 81°F. (27°C.) in May. Seasonal temperature differences are less than those between day and night. Most rain falls between May and December. On both islands the mountainous northeast gets over 108 inches (2750m.) of rain a year, but the southwest has less than half that much. The Northeast Trades are the prevailing winds; hurricanes are rare.

Vegetation and animals Woods and forests cover much of the land. Primeval forest ranges from mountain woodland to tropical-evergreen-forest, deciduous-tropical-forest in drier areas, and mangrove swamp on coasts. Some savanna survives on dry land.

Trinidad's South American mammals include agoutis (rabbit-like rodents), armadillos, and peccaries (wild swine). There are also colorful egrets, flamingos, scarlet ibises, and hummingbirds; alligator-like caimans; and many snakes, lizards, and frogs.

People Trinidadians are a zestful people, famous for carnivals, steel bands, and cricket. Theirs is the region's most mixed population. Descendants of African slaves make up about 41 per cent of the total as do those of Asian Indians, brought in as cheap labor when slavery ended; others claim British, French, Portuguese, Spanish, or Chinese ancestry. Tobago's population is chiefly black.

Most people are Roman Catholic, Hindu, Anglican, or Muslim, in that order. The official language is English, but Hindi, French, and Spanish are spoken.

Most of the population is concentrated in northwest Trinidad, at the capital Port-of-Spain (pop. about 350,000 with suburbs in 1984) or near the southwest-central industrial center of San Fernando (pop. 37,000).

Social conditions By the 1980s, islanders averaged half the U.S. per capita income, much more than in most Caribbean countries. About two-thirds of the labor force works in construction, mining, or commerce, and about one-tenth on the

Columbus discovers Trinidad in 1498, reputedly named for its three prominent hilltops. *(stamp issued 1898)*

©DIAGRAM

135

Trinidad and Tobago

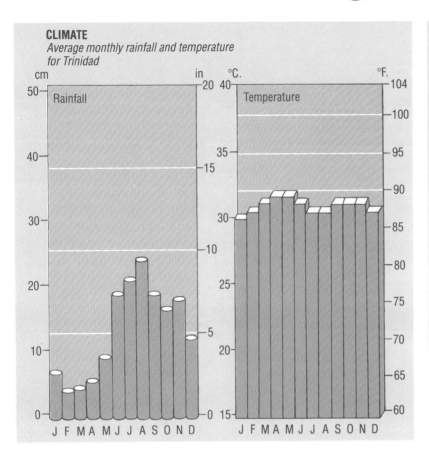

CLIMATE
Average monthly rainfall and temperature for Trinidad

Rainfall

Temperature

J F M A M J J A S O N D

J F M A M J J A S O N D

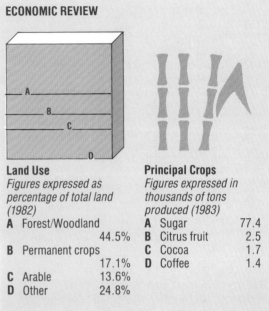

ECONOMIC REVIEW

Land Use
Figures expressed as percentage of total land (1982)
A Forest/Woodland
            44.5%
B Permanent crops
            17.1%
C Arable   13.6%
D Other   24.8%

Principal Crops
Figures expressed in thousands of tons produced (1983)
A Sugar   77.4
B Citrus fruit 2.5
C Cocoa   1.7
D Coffee   1.4

land; but an unofficial estimate put unemployment as high as 21 per cent in the mid 1980s.

Education is free and the literacy rate is over 90 per cent. Higher education centers include technical institutes and a branch of the University of the West Indies.

In the early 1980s there was only one doctor per 2000 people compared with one per 460 in the U.S. but life expectancy averaged 70 years by the mid 1980s.

Government The republic is a parliamentary democracy in the Commonwealth. Its head of state is the President, elected by an appointed Senate and a popularly elected House of Representatives. The head of government is the Prime Minister. For local government the country is divided into eight counties, Tobago, and four cities.

Communications and transportation
Besides the single television station there are two radio stations, several daily newspapers, and over 80,000 telephones.

The islands have about 4000 miles (6440km.) of all-weather roads, no railroads, but several airports; Piarco International Airport stands near the capital. The main

ports are Port-of-Spain, Pointe à Pierre, and Port Lisas.

Economy Trinidad and Tobago have one of the highest economic outputs in the West Indies. This depends heavily on offshore and onshore supplies of oil and gas, and on refining local and imported oil. In 1983 the petroleum industry accounted for nearly one-quarter of the total value of the gross domestic product, but Trinidad's oil could run dry by the mid 1990s. Another source of mineral wealth is asphalt from Trinidad's famous Pitch Lake.

Attempts at industrial diversification have produced – with varying success – an iron and steel mill, alumina smelter, and urea and methanol plants.

Agriculture makes only a small contribution to the value of economic output, although the soil is rich and up to one-quarter of Trinidad is cultivated. Crops include sugar, cane, coffee, coconuts, beans, and fruit; there is also some livestock. However, the islands import most of their food.

Forestry produces timber including cedar and mahogany, and a replanting program has

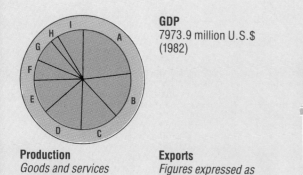

GDP
7973.9 million U.S.$
(1982)

Production
*Goods and services
expressed as percentage of
GDP (1983)*

A	Petroleum	22.9%
B	Construction	15.0%
C	Transport/ Communication	13.6%
D	Government	13.0%
E	Commerce	10.8%
F	Finance	7.6%
G	Manufacturing	7.0%
H	Agriculture/Forestry/ Fishing	2.5%
I	Other	7.6%

Exports
*Figures expressed as
percentage of total (1982)*

A	Minerals/Fuel	88.3%
B	Chemicals	4.8%
C	Machinery/Transport equipment	2.6%
D	Other	4.3%

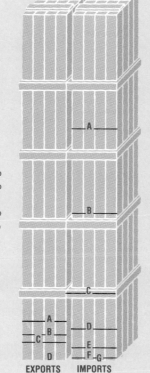

EXPORTS IMPORTS

Total World Trade
*Figures expressed in
millions of U.S.$ (1983)*

Exports	World	2343.5
	U.S.	1406.5
Imports	World	2502.8
	U.S.	1063.8

Imports
*Figures expressed as
percentage of total (1982)*

A	Machinery/Transport equipment	32.4%
B	Minerals/Fuels	25.2%
C	Manufactures	22.8%
D	Food/Beverages/ Tobacco	11.3%
E	Chemicals	4.9%
F	Crude materials	2.9%
G	Other	0.5%

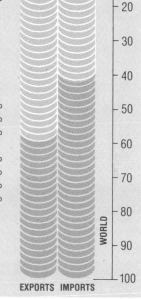

EXPORTS IMPORTS

stressed pitch pine and teak. Fish provide an important source of protein.

The republic mainly exports oil and oil products, asphalt, chemicals, and foodstuff. Tourist income came from nearly 200,000 visitors a year by the 1980s.

Imports include crude oil, machinery, manufactured goods, chemicals, and food.

Trading partners include the U.S., Saudia Arabia, the United Kingdom, Canada, and various Caribbean countries.

A woodcut taken from the Journal of Christopher Columbus, 1502.

Further Reading List

REGIONAL PROFILE

An excellent general history of the colonization of the area by the Spanish, British, and Dutch is *The Funnel of Gold*, by Mendel Peterson (Little, Brown & Co., 1975). It has many early illustrations of the history of the area. *The Early Spanish Main* by Carl O. Sauer (University of California Press, 1966) deals exclusively with the first thirty years after Columbus when Spain dominated the area. This historical geography explains many of the economic and political directions taken by Spain.

A highly enjoyable biography of buccaneer Sir Henry Morgan is *The Buccaneer King*, by Dudley Pope (Dodd, Mead & Co., 1977). It describes the area in the seventeenth century through the buccaneer's eyes. One of the greatest buccaneer adventures is described in exciting detail in *The Sack of Panamá* (Viking, 1981) by Peter Earle. Another book by Peter Earle, *The Treasure of the Concepción* (Viking, 1979) describes the search for the flagship of Spain's Mexican silver fleet that sank in a storm on a coral reef north of Hispaniola (Dominican Republic) in 1641 with a cargo of silver coin, bullion, and jewels.

The Spanish Empire in America by C. H. Haring (Harcourt, Brace & World, 1963) is a concise history of Spain's attempt to transfer the Spanish style of government and society from the Old World to the New, and the changes brought about in a remote and very different environment. This book also mentions Spanish South America. An excellent sociological study of the multicultural origins of Caribbean society is *Main Currents in Caribbean Thought* by Gordon Lewis (Johns Hopkins University Press, 1983). This book defines and traces the evolution of the area's ideology from its unique historical mixture of peoples and beliefs. *Rift and Revolution* (American Enterprises Institute for Public Policy Research, 1983) is a series of articles divided into two sections. The first concerns the domestic dimensions of the crisis in Central America, and the second has articles on Soviet strategy and policies, European socialism, other Latin American countries' policies, and the concerns of the U.S.

CENTRAL AMERICA

An excellent archeological study of Central America is Doris Stone's *Pre-Columbian Man Finds Central America* (Peabody Museum Press, 1972). It also gives a good description of the geography and terrain of the area as well as the ethnography. Many excellent pictures of artifacts are included.

Spanish Central America by Murdo J. MacLeod (University of California Press, 1973) describes the discovery and conquest of colonial Central America and the eventual decline of Spain's control from 1520–1720. For an understanding of twentieth-century Central American economy, read *The Central American Common Market* (Praeger, 1972) by Donald H. McClelland. It provides some insight into the relative success of the area's economic development and integration.

For an understanding of the various governments in Central America, read *Revolution in Central America*, edited by the Stanford Central American Network (Westview Press, 1983). This book discusses each country's revolution, use of land, population, the church's role, and government violation of human rights. Another book on current politics is Wolf Grabendorf's *Political Change in Central America* (Westview Press, 1984). It is an excellent reader with short articles written by experts in each area. The book is divided into two sections; one deals with internal policies and the other with external interests and strategies. The scope of Adrian J. English's *Armed Forces of Latin America* (Jane's, 1985) goes beyond Central America to include the other South American countries, providing the best information available on the military establishments of each country. There is a historical sketch of each country's armed and paramilitary forces including data on military expenditures, force size, and type of weaponry used. For a thorough analysis of recent history in Central America, Philip Berryman's *Inside Central America* (Pantheon, 1985) is an excellent work.

Three books that describe the U.S. involvement in Central America are: *Endless War* by James Chace (Vintage, 1984); *The Morass* by Richard A. White (Harper & Row, 1984), and *Central America* by Lester D. Langley (Crown, 1985). Each book describes the history of the U.S. involvement, the current situation, and future concerns.

Guatemala *Guatemala* by Nathan L. Whetten (Yale University Press, 1961) is a study of the land and the people. It deals with both economic and social issues. *Guatemala in Rebellion* by Jonathan L. Fried (Grove Press, 1983) concentrates on recent developments, but it also provides a good basic history of the early years. *Indian Crafts of Guatemala and El Salvador* by Lilly de Jongh Osborne (University of Oklahoma Press, 1965) gives a well-illustrated history of local costumes, material used for the manufacture of textiles, looms used, and weaving techniques. Other crafts mentioned are: mats, hats, basketry, ceramics, gourds, and engraving.

A good study of the economic development of Guatemala is *Machine Age Maya* by Manning Nash (University of Chicago Press, 1967). It compares both factory and farm to economic and social development

and changes. For a personal view of day-to-day life over the past few years, see *Campesino*, edited and translated by James D. Sexton (University of Arizona Press, 1985). It tells of the economic and social problems encountered when starting a business in Guatemala. An interesting book on recent U.S. involvement in Guatemala is *Bitter Fruit* by Stephen Schlesinger (Doubleday, 1982). It discusses the CIA, the United Fruit Company, and the overthrow of the Guatemalan presidency.

Belize An interesting book with emphasis on the early colonial history is *British Honduras* by Stephen L. Craiger (Allen & Unwin, 1951). This enjoyable book describes the early English buccaneers on the Spanish Main. Another excellent history is *Formerly British Honduras* by William D. Setzekorn (Ohio University Press, 1981). It provides good descriptions of the geography, people, culture, and the economic promise of this small country. D. A. G. Waddell's *British Honduras* (Oxford University Press, 1961) is a short overview concentrating on the land and people. It contains a discussion of the climate, flora and fauna, race, language, and educational and cultural activities. *Colonialism and Underdevelopment* by Norman Ashcroft (Teachers College Press, 1973) is a short economic history. It describes the rural patterns of life, small-scale farming, the urban consumer, and the politics of underdevelopment.

Honduras *The Conquest and Colonization of Honduras* by Robert S. Chamberlain (Carnegie Institution of Washington, 1953) is an interesting study of the Spanish conquest in the first half of the sixteenth century. A compact and objective history of contemporary Honduran society is James D. Rudolph's *Honduras* (American University Press, 1983). An excellent and comprehensive study is *Honduras* by James A. Morris (Westview Press, 1984). It deals mostly with the political and military development of the country, with sections on the land, people, economy, and national development.

Scarcity and Survival in Central America by William H. Durham (Stanford University Press, 1979) is a rather technical study of the origins of the 1969 Soccer War between El Salvador and Honduras. It is primarily a case study in human ecology, dealing with overpopulation and adaptation to environment. *Mosquito Coast* by Peter Keenagh (Houghton Mifflin, 1938) is an older but still interesting personal narrative of a journey through the jungles of Honduras. William V. Davidson's *Historical Geography of the Bay Islands, Honduras* (Southern University Press, 1974) is an interesting study of a culturally diverse area, an English-speaking settlement under Honduran rule. These islands have been occupied by at least nine distinct groups from aboriginal times to the present.

El Salvador An excellent, if somewhat technical, archeological history of El Salvador is *Archeology and Volcanism in Central America* (University of Texas Press, 1983). It is profusely illustrated with photographs and line drawings of artifacts. *Indian Crafts of Guatemala and El Salvador* by Lilly de Jongh Osborne (University of Oklahoma Press, 1965) is an excellent history of local costumes and the native textile industry. It also describes weaving, basketry, ceramics, gourds, and engraving.

El Salvador in Transition by Enrique A. Baloyra (University of North Carolina Press, 1982) contains a brief description of the early history of El Salvador, while concentrating on the last forty years. A book that provides an accurate and critical introduction to the current situation and its historical background is *El Salvador* (Central American Information Office, 1982). It also includes sections on: land and poverty, urbanization and industrialization, state terrorism and human rights, and U.S. economic and military aid.

Salvador by Joan Didion (Simon & Schuster, 1983) is a very short but excellent description of her visit and impressions of the country. *Salvador Witness* by Ana Carrigan (Simon & Schuster, 1984) explores the meaning of Jean Donovan's death in relation to the political situation in El Salvador. *Witness to War* by Charles Clements (Bantam, 1984) is the autobiography of an American volunteer doctor with the guerrillas. His exploits expose "the animal horror wrought by the Salvador right." *Weakness and Deceit* by Raymond Bonner (Times Books, 1984) explores the U.S. foreign policy in El Salvador. It also describes the Cuban and Nicaraguan influence over the past few years.

Nicaragua

Nicaragua An excellent, if somewhat technical, introduction to earliest Nicaragua is *Archaeology of the Rivas Region, Nicaragua* (Wilfrid Laurier University Press, 1980) by Paul F. Healy. It describes the local geology, climate, flora and fauna, and the cultural remains of the Rivas region with many line drawings and illustrations. Eduardo Crawley's *Nicaragua in Perspective* (St. Martin's Press, 1984) is an excellent basic history from early Spanish control to the twentieth century, with emphasis on the U.S. involvement from the 1920s to current times. For an excellent collection of articles on the current political situation, see *Nicaragua under Siege* (Synthesis Publications, 1984). Although this book is sympathetic to the Sandinista regime, it presents an excellent analysis of current affairs.

An interesting biography is *Somoza* by Bernard Diederich (Dutton, 1981). It presents a picture of governmental mismanagement and greed by the three presidents of the Somoza family, the last being Anastasio Somoza Debayle, assassinated while in exile in Paraguay in 1980. Two books specifically on the current revolution are: *Fire from the Mountain* (Crown, 1984), which describes the making of a Sandinista; and *The Nicaragua Reader* (Grove, 1984), a collection of short pieces on the revolution, the U.S. and Central America. For an excellent analysis of the U.S. involvement in Nicaragua, see Karl Grossman's *Nicaragua: America's New Vietnam?* (Permanent Press, 1984).

Costa Rica A beautifully illustrated (mostly in color) book on the early art of Costa Rica is *Between Continents/Between Seas: Pre-Columbian Art of Costa Rica* (Abrams, 1981). This book describes the three different cultural areas that produced artifacts of distinctly different styles. Another excellent book on archeology is Doris Stone's *Pre-Columbian Man in Costa Rica* (Peabody Museum Press, 1977). This book presents a more popular view of archeology.

Richard Biesanz's *The Costa Ricans* (Prentice-Hall, 1982) gives a short description of early Costa Rican history, but the main emphasis of the book is on cultural aspects of current life in Costa Rica. *Democracy in Costa Rica* by Charles D. Ameringer (Praeger, 1982) deals with the nature and development of democracy in Costa Rica, a country with a history of democratic stability in an unstable part of the world. Also by Charles D. Ameringer is *Don Pepe* (University of New Mexico Press, 1978), a biography of José Figueres, the victor of the forty-five-day civil war and twice elected president in recent history. Stacy May's *Costa Rica* (Twentieth Century Fund, 1952) is a good study in economic development of a mostly agricultural country. The age of the study makes its information somewhat dated, but as a history it is still valid.

Panama A good general history of Panama is David Howarth's *The Golden Isthmus* (Collins, 1966). *Before the Five Frontiers* by Alex Perez-Venero (AMS Press, 1978) is a carefully documented history offering some insight into the Panamanian leaders.

A Panama Forest and Shore by Burton L. Gordon (Boxwood Press, 1982) is an interesting discussion of the natural history of the Bocas del Toro Province in western Panama and the effects of the European presence on the rain forest. Joanne M. Kelly's *Cuna* (A. S. Barnes & Co., 1966) is a personal description of daily village life of the Cuna Indians of Panama.

An excellent biography of General Omar Torrijos is Graham Greene's *Getting to Know the General* (Simon & Schuster, 1984). It also discusses some of the critical changes in the region's politics from 1976 to 1981.

The classic book on the building of the Panama Canal is David McCullough's *The Path Between the Seas* (Simon & Schuster, 1977). Not only is it filled with vivid detail describing the building of the Canal, but it tells the story of many of the people who built it. *Panama Odyssey* by William J. Jorden (University of Texas Press, 1984) describes the recent diplomatic history surrounding the Panama Canal Treaty which returned control of the Canal to Panama. For a more personal view of the Canal Zone read *Red, White, and Blue Paradise* by Herbert and Mary Knapp (Harcourt, Brace, Jovanovich, 1984). It describes life in the Canal Zone during its seventy-five years of existence as a worker's paradise.

An interesting history from pre-Columbian inhabitants to the settlement of the islands by the Europeans is Virgina Radcliffe's *Caribbean Heritage* (Walker & Co., 1976). *Peoples and Cultures of the Caribbean* (Natural History Press, 1971) is an anthropological study offering a series of articles on land use, economy, and the religion and folklore of the area. Philip Sherlock's *West Indian Nations* (St. Martin's Press, 1973) is a short history that includes chapters on Spain's island colonies, pirates' nests and plantations, the Atlantic slave trade, and various independence movements. As a history of the British in the Caribbean, Carl Bridenbaugh's *No Peace Beyond the Line* (Oxford University Press, 1972) is an interesting narrative with a good grasp of the social and economic conditions of the times. Louise L. Cripps's *The Spanish Caribbean from Columbus to Castro* (G. K. Hall & Co., 1979) is an interesting comparison of three Spanish islands: Cuba, Dominican Republic, and Puerto Rico. Presenting the similarities in geography, pre-Columbian Indians, heritage, and people, it questions the vast differences in their recent political development.

Troy S. Floyd's *The Columbus Dynasty in the Caribbean 1492–1526* (University of New Mexico Press, 1973) describes some of the civil and religious institutions established by Spain and Christopher Columbus and his son, Diego Colon. The *Development of the British West Indies 1700–1763* by Frank W. Pitman (Archon Books, 1967) investigates the industrial and social conditions in the British West Indies. It also describes the social history of the British settlers on various islands.

Helmut Blume's *The Caribbean Islands* (Longman, 1974) is an excellent study of the region. It deals with the topography, climate, flora and fauna, as well as the agriculture and economy of the area. For a description of the political relationships of the islands, see Anthony Payne's *The Politics of the Caribbean Community 1961–1979* (St. Martin's Press, 1980). This book also deals with the economic integration, functional cooperation, and foreign policy coordination of the area.

An excellent economic history of the British West Indies from 1623 to 1775 is Richard B. Sheridan's *Sugar and Slavery* (Johns Hopkins University Press, 1973). This book describes the role of slavery in the making of sugar. Jay R. Mandle's *Patterns of Caribbean Development* (Gordon & Breach Science Pub., 1982) is an appraisal of the current efforts to overcome the region's legacy of underdevelopment.

Bermuda A series of excellent books on the history of Bermuda were written by Henry C. Wilkinson: *Adventures of Bermuda* (Oxford University Press, 1933) on the discovery and colonization of Bermuda; *Bermuda in the Old Empire* (Oxford University Press, 1950) on the early history of the area; and *Bermuda from Sail to Steam* (Oxford University Press, 1950, 2 volumes), the definitive history of Bermuda from 1784 to 1901. An excellent short history is W. S. Zuill's *The Story of Bermuda and Her People* (Macmillan, 1973). It describes the educational, cultural, social, and political changes that have occurred since 1900. Gilbert Butland's *Bermuda: A New Study* (Vantage

Further Reading List

Press, 1980) describes the island's physical setting, natural history, and economic, social, and political character.

Bahamas *Homeward Bound* by Sandra Riley (Island Research, 1983) is a readable history of colonial times to 1850. A good general history of the area is Michael Craton's *A History of the Bahamas* (Collins, 1962). It provides a good summary of events leading up to modern-day Bahamas. Colin A. Hughes's *Race and Politics in the Bahamas* (St. Martin's Press, 1981) includes a short history of the development of Bahamian society to 1953. The rest of the book is a study of the developing political awareness of the black community. An excellent book on contemporary life is *The Quiet Revolution in the Bahamas* by Doris L. Johnson (Family Islands Press, 1972). It highlights the problems faced by the first black government.

Turks and Caicos Islands, Cayman Islands *Caymanian Politics* by Ulf Hannerz (University of Stockholm Press, 1974) is an interesting social and political history of contemporary life on the Cayman Islands. Archie Carr's *The Windward Road* (University Presses of Florida, 1979) describes a naturalist's study of the habitat of the Green Turtle. The study also describes many other animals indigenous to the area.

Cuba An excellent general history is *Cuba from Columbus to Castro* by Jaime Suchlicki (Scribner's, 1974). It shows the development of Cuba from a Spanish colony with a sugarcane-based economy through the many rebellions and dictatorships to Castro. One of the most interesting episodes in Cuban history is described in *The Spanish American War* by G. J. A. O'Toole (Norton, 1984). New material relating to American espionage and the sinking of the *Maine* is presented in a highly readable narrative.

John Dorschner's *The Winds of December* (Coward, McCann & Geoghegan, 1980) describes the revolution in detail. Also included are short profiles of the Cuban leaders during the late 1950s. An interesting book on contemporary Cuban society is Lorrin Philipson's *Freedom Flights* (Random House, 1980). It is a collection of twenty narratives of ordinary people. The *Bay of Pigs* by Peter Wyden (Simon & Schuster, 1979) is a compelling story of the planning and failure of the landings. Included is an interview with Fidel Castro.

Theodore Draper's *Castroism: Theory and Practice* (Praeger, 1965) is an excellent study of early Castroism, both social and economic plans. *The Economy of Socialist Cuba* by Carmelo Mesa-Lago (University of New Mexico Press, 1981) provides an interesting analysis of the economy of Cuba today.

José Martí, Cuban Patriot by Richard B. Gray (University of Florida Press, 1962) is an excellent biography. It describes the development of his philosophy and his growth as a national hero. Donald C. Hodges's *The Legacy of Ché Guevara* (Thames & Hudson, 1977) is a series of articles and speeches by Ché Guevara. It shows the influence of Ché throughout Latin America and other revolutionary groups in the world. *Fidel Castro Speaks* (Grove Press, 1969) is a collection of his ideas on politics, economics, socialism, and communism as he presented them to the Cuban people.

Jamaica A good readable history of Jamaica from Columbus to present times is George Hunt's *Jamaica* (B. T. Batsford Ltd., 1976). Following the chapters on the different regions is a "Travellers' Digest" listing hints for future vacationers. Barry Floyd's *Jamaica* (St. Martin's Press, 1979) presents a concise geological survey of the island. It also describes the economic, social, and cultural development from colonial times to the present. For an in-depth study of the separation between the European planters and their former slaves from 1830 to 1865, see *Two Jamaicas* by Philip Curtin (Harvard University Press, 1955).

Port Royal, Jamaica by Michael Pawson (Clarendon Press, 1975) describes the everyday life in Port Royal prior to the devastating earthquake of 1692. Included are sections on geography, topography, and economic development during the seventeenth century. For a look at contemporary Jamaica, see Aggrey Brown's *Color, Class, and Politics in Jamaica* (Transaction Books, 1979). *Jamaica Talk* by Frederic Cassidy (Macmillan, 1982) shows the development and evolution of the English language over 300 years. It illustrates the etymology of the words for animals, plants, fish, etc., and the differences between domestic and social life.

Haiti Thomas Ott's *The Haitian Revolution, 1789–1804* (University of Tennessee Press, 1973) is an interesting history of the events and ideas that shaped the times. Voodoo and its influence on culture and politics is the subject of an interesting, but scholarly book by Harold Courlander and Remy Bastien, *Religion and Politics in Haiti* (Institute for Cross-Cultural Research, 1966). Robert I. Rotberg's *Haiti: The Politics of Squalor* (Houghton Mifflin, 1971) presents an excellent study of the problems of contemporary Haiti. Emphasis is on human resources, structure of the economy, and future economic development.

For a biography of the central figure in the Haitian revolution, see *Toussaint L'Ouverture* (Prentice-Hall, 1973). It describes his life as a slave and his development as a military and political genius. He died shortly before France granted independence to Haiti in 1803. David Nicholls's *From Dessalines to Duvalier* (Cambridge University Press, 1979) presents a social history from 1804 to 1971 as well as short biographical sketches of the leaders of that time. *Papa Doc* by Bernard Diederich (McGraw-Hill, 1969) is an excellent popular biography of Dr. François Duvalier and his role in the development of contemporary Haiti.

Dominican Republic Howard J. Wiarda's *The Dominican Republic: A Caribbean Crucible* (Westview Press, 1982) is a good general history. Culture, social structure, economy, and political development are all discussed. *Arms and Politics in the Dominican Republic* by G. Pope Atkins (Westview Press, 1981) presents a study of recent military and political events. Joaquín Balaguer's tenure as president (1966–1978) and the first years of Antonio Guzmán are emphasized. Two interesting books on Trujillo are German E. Ornes's *Trujillo: Little Caesar of the Caribbean* (Thomas Nelson & Sons, 1958), which deals more with the regime than the man; and Bernard Diederich's *Trujillo: The Death of the Goat* (Little, Brown & Co., 1978), a riveting account of the plot to assassinate the ruthless dictator. Read together, these books give an interesting insight into the recent history of the Dominican Republic.

Area Handbook for the Dominican Republic by Thomas E. Weil (USGPO, 1973) is a comprehensive description of the social, political, economic, and general safety conditions in this area. A brief discussion of the geography, population, living conditions, religion, and education is also included. For a systems analysis of the use of land and resources, see Gustavo A. Antonini's *Population and Energy* (University Presses of Florida, 1975). It includes a study of the agricultural economy and of the ecological factors involved in developing land for other uses.

Puerto Rico An excellent study of the pre-1898 social, political, and cultural history that shaped Puerto Rico is Arturo Morales Carrión's *Puerto Rico* (Norton, 1983). It provides a balanced perspective of what constitutes Puerto Rico as a people, a cultural nationality, and a distinctive Caribbean community. *Geography of Puerto Rico* by Rafael Picó (Aldine Publishing Co., 1974) describes the physical, economic, social, and geographic factors that influence life on the island. *Puerto Rico and Puerto Ricans* (John Wiley & Sons, 1974) is a collection of articles dealing mostly with social, cultural, and political aspects of life in Puerto Rico. One of the articles, "Colonial Policies of the U.S.," was written by Theodore Roosevelt. Philip Sterling's *The Quiet Rebels* (Zenith Books, 1968) is a collection of four biographies of early political leaders of Puerto Rico: José Celso Barbosa, Luis Muñoz Rivera, José de Diego, and Luis Muñoz Marín.

Stan Steiner's *The Islands* (Harper & Row, 1974) is a comparative study of life in Puerto Rico with the life of a Puerto Rican in New York or Chicago. It highlights many of the problems in Puerto Rico and in the U.S. Eduardo Seda's *Social Change and Personality* (Northwestern University Press, 1973) illustrates the sociocultural and psychological consequences of economic development in one community. It also delves into sorcery, witchcraft, spiritualism, and psychodrama as practiced in this community.

Puerto Rico: The Case for Independence by Louise L. Cripps (Schenkman Publishing Co., 1974) is a brief history of American domination and presents the arguments of statehood and independence for Puerto Rico. Gordon K. Lewis's *Notes on the Puerto Rican Revolution* (Monthly Review Press, 1974) is a general discussion of society in the 1960s and 1970s. It describes the changes that have occurred and the importance of nationalist feelings for an independent Puerto Rico.

An interesting economic history is Ralph Hancock's *Puerto Rico: A Success Story* (Van Nostrand Co., 1960). It describes the early one-crop economy and conditions as they existed in 1940. In the twenty years from 1940 to 1960 Puerto Rico created a favorable climate for business so that the economy is stable and diversified. For a slightly different view of the economy, see Sakari Sariola's *Puerto Rican Dilemma* (National University Publishers, 1979). It is an appraisal of economic developments on the future of the commonwealth status of Puerto Rico and economic dependence on the U.S.

Virgin Islands William W. Boyer's *America's Virgin Islands* (Carolina Academic Press, 1983) is an excellent history from the time of discovery in 1493 by Columbus to the present. It emphasizes the American period from 1917 and deals with the current problem of tourism. Darwin D. Creque's *The U.S. Virgins and the Eastern Caribbean* (Whitmore Publishing Co., 1968) is a good political history concentrating on the twentieth century. A study of contemporary life is Ellis Gladwin's *Living in the Changing Caribbean* (Macmillan, 1970). Norwell Harrigan's *The Inter-Virgin Islands Conference* (University Presses of Florida, 1980) is an interesting study of two political entities (U.S. Virgin Islands and British Virgin Islands) with similar economic problems. It presents the possibilities for economic cooperation.

Netherlands Antilles *A Short History of the Netherlands Antilles and Surinam* by Cornelis C. H. Goslinga (Martinus Nijhoff, 1979) is an interesting account of the discovery, colonization, and economic development of the area. *Historical Dictionary of the French and Netherlands Antilles* by Albert Gastmann (Scarecrow Press, 1978) provides historical information important to both the French and Netherlands Antilles. It is divided into three sections: general information, French Antilles, and Netherlands Antilles. John Y. and Dorothy L. Keur's *Windward Children* (Royal Van Gorcum, Ltd., 1960) is an interesting study of human ecology of St. Maarten, Saba, and St. Eustatius. It discusses the role of natural environment (climate, physiography, soil, and vegetation) on the character of the islands' populations. Fuat M. Andic's *Government Finance and Planned Development* (Institute of Caribbean Studies, 1968) is an analysis of the economies of the Netherlands Antilles and Surinam. While this report is somewhat dated, it provides a good study of the economics of developing nations.

French Antilles An interesting study of early French settlement is Nellis M. Crouse's *French Pioneers in the West Indies 1624–1664* (Columbia University Press, 1940). It also provides a short geologic history of the formation of the islands. Arvin Murch's *Black Frenchmen* (Schenkman Publishing Co., 1971) is a contemporary history of the area, dealing with the decision to remain an integral part of France rather than voting for independence. *The Tragedy of Pelee* by George Kennen (Negro University Press, 1969) is the interesting first-person account of the U.S. attempt to aid victims of the volcanic eruption of Mont Pelee

on Martinique on May 8, 1902. Albert Gastmann's *Historical Dictionary of the French and Netherlands Antilles* (Scarecrow Press, 1978) provides historical information about both the French and Netherlands Antilles.

Leeward Islands Elsa V. Goveia's *Slave Society in the British Leeward Islands at the End of the Eighteenth Century* (Yale University Press, 1965) is an excellent study of the political, economic, and social organization of a slave society and their interrelationships. *Under an English Heaven* by Donald E. Westlake (Simon & Schuster, 1972) is an interesting contemporary history of Anguilla and St. Kitts. Both islands chose colonialism rather than independence from Great Britain. *Five of the Leeward Islands* by Douglas Hall (Caribbean Universities Press, 1971) is a comparative study of the economic and social differences and similarities of the islands. Ellis Gladwin's *Living in the Changing Caribbean* (Macmillan, 1970) is a study of contemporary life on the Virgin Islands, Leeward Islands, and Windward Islands. It also discusses the economic development and tourist trade of these islands.

Windward Islands *Maurice Bishop Speaks* (Pathfinder Press, 1983) provides a short history of Bishop's government, its achievements and its overthrow as well as many of his speeches and interviews. Hugh O'Shaughnessy's *Grenada* (Dodd, 1985) provides an eyewitness account of the U.S. invasion. It also analyzes the events leading up to the 1979 coup of Maurice Bishop over President Eric Gairy. *Windward Road* (University of Massachusetts, 1973) is a collection of short anthropological studies of the economic, social, linguistic, and educational patterns on St. Vincent Island. Ellis Gladwin's *Living in the Changing Caribbean* (Macmillan, 1970) is a study of the contemporary way of life on the Virgin Islands, Leeward Islands, and Windward Islands.

Barbados An excellent short history is Ronald Tree's *A History of Barbados* (Granada, 1981). It also includes a three-day tour of the island. F. A. Hoyos's *Barbados* (Macmillan, 1978) is another good history from the Amerindians of long ago to independence. An interesting study of the commerce between the colonies of North America and the colonies of the West Indies is *Barbados* by David H. Makinson (Mouton, 1964). It presents the economic interdependence of the colonies during the eighteenth century. *The Economic Geography of Barbados* by Otis P. Starkey (Columbia University Press, 1939) describes the development of the sugar economy during 1625–1748 and the evolution of a planter aristocracy from 1748 to 1833.

Trinidad and Tobago A good history of Trinidad and Tobago is Gertrude Carmichael's *The History of the West Indian Islands of Trinidad and Tobago 1498–1900* (Alvin Redman, 1961). It describes the discovery and colonization of the islands through each governor's tenure to 1900. *A History of Modern Trinidad 1783–1962* by Bridget Brereton (Heinemann, 1981) describes

the slave economy and British rule to independence in 1962. David L. Niddrie's *Tobago* (Litho Press Co., 1980) describes the geophysical features, plants, and animals of the island. Also included is a short history of Tobago and the future hopes of the islanders. Michael Lieber's *Street Life* (G. K. Hall & Co., 1981) is an interesting ethnographic study of everyday life in urban Trinidad.

Linda Vertrees, Head of Acquisitions Division, Chicago Public Library

Index

143

Index